The Editor

KATHERINE LINEHAN is Professor Emerita of English at Oberlin College. She is the author of articles on Robert Louis Stevenson, George Gissing, and George Eliot.

W. W. NORTON & COMPANY, INC.
Also Publishes

ENGLISH RENAISSANCE DRAMA: A NORTON ANTHOLOGY
edited by David Bevington et al.

THE NORTON ANTHOLOGY OF AFRICAN AMERICAN LITERATURE
edited by Henry Louis Gates Jr. and Nellie Y. McKay et al.

THE NORTON ANTHOLOGY OF AMERICAN LITERATURE
edited by Nina Baym et al.

THE NORTON ANTHOLOGY OF CHILDREN'S LITERATURE
edited by Jack Zipes et al.

THE NORTON ANTHOLOGY OF DRAMA
edited by J. Ellen Gainor, Stanton B. Garner Jr., and Martin Puchner

THE NORTON ANTHOLOGY OF ENGLISH LITERATURE
edited by M. H. Abrams and Stephen Greenblatt et al.

THE NORTON ANTHOLOGY OF LITERATURE BY WOMEN
edited by Sandra M. Gilbert and Susan Gubar

THE NORTON ANTHOLOGY OF MODERN AND CONTEMPORARY POETRY
edited by Jahan Ramazani, Richard Ellmann, and Robert O'Clair

THE NORTON ANTHOLOGY OF POETRY
edited by Margaret Ferguson, Mary Jo Salter, and Jon Stallworthy

THE NORTON ANTHOLOGY OF SHORT FICTION
edited by R. V. Cassill and Richard Bausch

THE NORTON ANTHOLOGY OF THEORY AND CRITICISM
edited by Vincent B. Leitch et al.

THE NORTON ANTHOLOGY OF WORLD LITERATURE
edited by Sarah Lawall et al.

THE NORTON FACSIMILE OF THE FIRST FOLIO OF SHAKESPEARE
prepared by Charlton Hinman

THE NORTON INTRODUCTION TO LITERATURE
edited by Alison Booth and Kelly J. Mays

THE NORTON READER
edited by Linda H. Peterson and John C. Brereton

THE NORTON SAMPLER
edited by Thomas Cooley

THE NORTON SHAKESPEARE, BASED ON THE OXFORD EDITION
edited by Stephen Greenblatt et al.

For a complete list of Norton Critical Editions, visit
www.wwnorton.com/college/English/nce_home.htm

A NORTON CRITICAL EDITION

Robert Louis Stevenson
STRANGE CASE OF DR. JEKYLL AND MR. HYDE

AN AUTHORITATIVE TEXT
BACKGROUNDS AND CONTEXTS
PERFORMANCE ADAPTATIONS
CRITICISM

Edited by

KATHERINE LINEHAN
OBERLIN COLLEGE

W • W • NORTON & COMPANY • *New York* • *London*

ABOUT THE COVER IMAGE: *Portrait of Robert Louis Stevenson and His Wife Fanny* (detail), the second of three Stevenson portraits Sargent produced in the 1880s, was painted in Stevenson's home in Bournemouth two months before Stevenson began writing *Strange Case of Dr. Jekyll and Mr. Hyde.* Stevenson gave the following account of the picture in an October 1885 letter to a friend: "Sargent was down again and painted a portrait of me walking about in my own dining room, in my own velveteen jacket and twisting, as I go my own moustache: at one corner a glimpse of my wife in an Indian dress and seated in a chair that was once my grandfather's, but since some months goes by the name of Henry James's for it was there the novelist loved to sit—adds a touch of poesy and comicality. It is, I think, excellent but is too eccentric to be exhibited. I am at one extreme corner; my wife, in this wild dress and looking like a ghost is at the extreme other end, between us an open door exhibits my palatial entrance hall and a part of my respected staircase. All this is touched in lovely with that witty touch of Sargent's; but of course it looks dam queer as a whole" (*Letters,* ed. Booth and Mehew, 5:137).

Library of Congress Cataloging-in-Publication Data

Stevenson, Robert Louis, 1850–1894.
    Strange case of Dr. Jekyll and Mr. Hyde: an authoritative text, backgrounds and contexts, performance adaptations, criticism / Robert Louis Stevenson; edition by Katherine Linchan.
        p. cm.—(A Norton critical edition)
    Includes bibliographical references.
                    ISBN 0-393-97465-0 (pbk.)
    1. Physicians—Fiction.   2. London (England)—Fiction.   3. Multiple personality—Fiction.   4. Stevenson, Robert Louis, 1850–1894. Strange case of Dr. Jekyll and Mr. Hyde. I. Linchan, Katherine. II. Title.

PR5485.A2 L56 2002
823'.8—dc21   2002026541
                                                                                                    Rev.

W. W. Norton & Company, Inc.
500 Fifth Avenue, New York, N.Y. 10110
www.wwnorton.com

W. W. Norton & Company Ltd.
15 Carlisle Street, London W1D 3BS

Contents

CONTENTS

Illustrations

Preface

In anything fit to be called by the name of reading, the process itself should be absorbing and voluptuous; we should gloat over a book, be rapt clean out of ourselves, and rise from the perusal, our mind filled with the busiest, kaleidoscopic dance of images, incapable of sleep or of continuous thought.
—Robert Louis Stevenson, "A Gossip on Romance," 1882

The Jekyll and Hyde legend as we know it from popular culture—movie versions, cartoon spin-offs, psychological tag phrase and all—began with the January 1886 publication of a low-cost little book that took Britain and America by storm. Its author had increasingly been identified by critics as a man to watch. His previous work ranged from essays and travel literature to a wide variety of fiction for adults and several successful books for children. The ten-chapter tale that now appeared under the title *Strange Case of Dr. Jekyll and Mr. Hyde* struck many reviewers as marking a new level of achievement in its power to provide spellbinding entertainment while intimating a valuable moral. A few dissenters, however, irritated by a suspense plot resolved by the unlikely device of transforming powders, questioned whether Mr. Stevenson might not on this occasion have crossed a line into the opportunistic sensationalism of the crowd-pleasing railway fiction and shilling shockers that his publishing format brought to mind.

The verdict of time suggests that *Strange Case of Dr. Jekyll and Mr. Hyde* combines enduring breadth of appeal with outstanding literary worth. From Stevenson's day until our own, the tale has never been out of print, and its popularity has been worldwide. More than eighty translations have appeared, in at least thirty different languages. Since its publication, the tale has also generated an ongoing stream of critical commentary and garnered tributes from writers as various as Henry James, Gerard Manley Hopkins, Vladimir Nabokov, John Fowles, Jorge Luis Borges, Stephen King, Joyce Carol Oates, and Italo Calvino. Several of those writers point out an aspect of the story which helps explain its liability to be dismissed as shallowly sensationalistic: the unobtrusiveness with which the tale's stylistic virtuosity and thoughtfulness of conception blend into the dramatic intensity of the narrative. Stevenson's interest in letting thought and artistry melt inconspicuously into the flow of page-turning excitement in his sensation fiction certainly owes something to market motives, as he himself was always ready to acknowledge. However, the deeper motive is surely the one suggested by my epigraph from "A Gossip on Romance" and borne out by wider acquaintance with Stevenson's writing: his commitment to ensuring his readers just the sort of "absorbing and voluptuous" engagement with a text he deemed necessary to make a work "fit to be called by the name of reading."

The result in *Strange Case of Dr. Jekyll and Mr. Hyde* is a story of simple-seeming surfaces and uncertain depths, a narrative whose layered complexity makes it at once the most brilliantly accessible and brilliantly recondite of texts. As a horror thriller, the tale sweeps us forcefully along in a build-up of suspense which reaches a partial climax in Utterson's discovery of a dead body and then draws us into a still more gripping spiral of dread through the documents of two dead men. Moreover, as a horror thriller about human duality which shows the relentless supplanting of the most presentable side of self by the most unpresentable one, the tale exhibits a remarkable ability to hit a nerve and produce a shock of recognition for generation after generation of readers. Yet as an allegory, the tale proves confoundingly difficult to pin down. Is Jekyll's fate a moral warning against abandoning accountability for the appetites of the body? A dire prophecy about the advancing powers of science? A trenchant criticism of Victorian society's repressive standards of virtue and respectability? A symbolic enactment of the loss of self-control that can come with regression, addiction, madness, or sleep? A philosophical provocation to recognize the multiplicity of what passes socially as a unified self? Might Hyde's evil be inflected by Stevenson's unconscious? Is indeterminacy itself the point? Looking closely, we start to see how craftily the text has engineered the tricky depths that lie below its fast-moving surface. Words carry shifting possibilities. Jekyll's narrative reliability in the final chapter is questionable. In what comes as a surprise to readers familiar with sex-filled movie versions of the story, the text turns out always to hover around, never to reveal, the specific pleasures that Jekyll is eager to pursue through the guilt-free anonymity of Hyde.

Stevenson provided only limited commentary about the authorial conception underlying the tale. Explaining the story's origin in his 1888 essay "A Chapter on Dreams," he reports that several scenes in a nightmare gave him the idea of a voluntary change becoming involuntary. He seized upon the idea, he says, as answering both to his immediate need for a marketable plot and his longstanding interest in "that strong sense of man's double being, which must at times come in upon and overwhelm the mind of every thinking creature." This account can reinforce our appreciation of the tale's hallucinatory vividness of scene and sensation, and can deepen our interest in its treatment of the interchanges of identity linked with sleep and dreaming. However, it hardly interprets the Jekyll-Hyde duality nor the significance of Jekyll's nemesis. Stevenson's references to the tale in letters to friends offer only a few further glimpses of his thinking, most notably about the tale's engagement with the evils of hypocrisy and the perpetual human conflict between the desires of the flesh and those of the spirit.

Those references tend to come as fleeting, often cryptic remarks. In general, Stevenson's attitude seemed to be that, as he put it to one correspondent who asked him to supply a "key" to his allegory: "I conceive I could not make my allegory better, nay, that I could not fail to weaken it if I tried. I have said my say as I was best able; others must look for what was meant." At one level this statement speaks for the wisdom of recognizing that such meaning as the tale may hold speaks for itself best in its textually embodied state, bristling with possibility and charged with the imaginative response generated by the reading experience. At another level, the statement acknowledges that allegory inevitably calls for interpretation; it simply insists that the burden of that interpretation falls on the reader. Stevenson goes on to say: "the allegorist is one, the commentator is another; I conceive they are two parts."

Commentators have indeed taken up the challenge to interpret *Strange Case of Dr. Jekyll and Mr. Hyde* with an energy and breadth of speculation that I have been hard pressed to represent adequately in this Norton Critical Edition. The "Criticism" section in this volume offers five interpretive commentaries, three of them oriented toward the tale's allegorical dimension (Chesterton, Brantlinger, Linehan), two toward its handling of style and narrative technique (Nabokov, Garrett). In the "Backgrounds and Contexts" section, a series of excerpts grouped under the headings of "Literary, Scientific, and Sociohistorical Contexts" aims to stimulate readers' thinking about resonances to be found between the tale and various aspects of Victorian culture. These excerpts, while different in kind from applied criticism, are selected with an eye to demonstrating interpretive possibilities that critics have urged as relevant to understanding the Jekyll-Hyde duality. The "Reception" section gives ample evidence of the immediate religious and moral relevance the tale had for Victorian readers.

A section on "Performance Adaptations" shows, on the other hand, the versatility with which the central plot premise of the tale has been reworked over the ensuing century and more as a vehicle for modern social and psychological concerns. That section offers an historical overview of stage and film dramatizations of the tale, as well as a closer look at the influential stage version produced by T. R. Sullivan and Richard Mansfield in 1887 and the 1931 film version directed by Rouben Mamoulian, starring Frederic March.

A section on Victorian sensation fiction includes the full text of "Markheim," a Christmas "crawler" that Stevenson wrote a year before composing *Strange Case of Dr. Jekyll and Mr. Hyde*. The two tales bear comparison for, among other things, their interest in drawing readers into the haunted consciousness of a murderer who appears an unlikely candidate for the act of brutality he commits.

The "Composition and Production" section includes, besides Stevenson's comments about the tale in letters and "A Chapter on Dreams," his first biographer's summary of the now well-known composition story told by Stevenson's widow and stepson: Stevenson producing a first draft in an amazing three days, burning it in agreement with his wife's suggestion that the allegory needed development, and in another three days producing essentially the tale we know today. Biographer Graham Balfour (Stevenson's cousin) presents the story with the useful reminder that Stevenson in fact put in a good deal of further work on the manuscript over the ensuing weeks.

The "Textual Appendix" in this book allows a glimpse of that further work, drawing on extant manuscript fragments of the tale to illustrate the painstaking care Stevenson took in revising and polishing his writing.

The annotations to the text found in this edition fit the picture of an intensely literary author who carries his knowledge lightly, partly through an affinity for the abstract simplicity of the fable. Topical allusions are virtually nonexistent and only a few actual London place names are mentioned. However, the text frequently features unusual word usages that subtly evoke older meanings or give a fresh twist to a familiar word or phrase. It also contains an abundance of muffled literary echoes, particularly biblical ones, that operate almost subliminally within the narrative. A number of such allusions are newly noted in this edition.

The text of *Strange Case of Dr. Jekyll and Mr. Hyde* used for this Norton Critical Edition is the first British edition, published by Longmans, Green, and Co. on January 9, 1886. This is the only edition which was set directly from Stevenson's manuscript and for which he read page proofs. (The American edition, released in a coordinated arrangement by Charles Scribner's Sons four days earlier, had been set from printed pages sent in advance from Longmans.) A few errors and inconsistencies in spelling and punctuation have been silently corrected and quotation punctuation has been Americanized. Title punctuation has been brought into conformity with standard practice. (In the first edition, the abbreviations "Dr."

and "Mr." are followed by periods everywhere except on the title page and cover. This edition uses the periods throughout, except when citing works whose titles reproduce the tale's own first-edition title form.) British spellings and section heading formats have been preserved untouched.

Throughout this book, *Letters* refers to the 1994–95 eight-volume *The Letters of Robert Louis Stevenson*, edited by Bradford A. Booth and Ernest Mehew (Yale University Press). The abbreviation OED refers to the Oxford English Dictionary. Footnote citations of the Bible are from the King James Version.

Many people helped with this book, and I am glad to be able to offer thanks where thanks are due. An Oberlin faculty research group, consisting of Sandra Zagarell, Paula Richman, Laurie McMillin, and Wendy Kozol, patiently and thoughtfully reviewed draft materials. My textual annotations owe a debt both to past editors of the text on whose work I build (Jenni Calder, Emma Letley, Richard Dury, Barry Qualls and Susan Wolfson, Leonard Wolf, and Martin Danahay), and to Oberlin colleagues Robert Longsworth and Tom Van Nortwick, who helped me track down several previously unrecognized literary allusions. Former students Rumaan Alam and Alex Bernstein provided useful research assistance. Numerous friends and relatives served in their time-honored way as sustainers; numerous librarians and curators in theirs as wizardly information retrievers. Several people in the latter category went well beyond the call of duty, most notably Chris Quist of the Monterey Stevenson House, Mike Delahant of the Saranac Lake Robert Louis Stevenson Memorial Cottage, David Shayt of the Smithsonian Museum of American History, and Judy Throm of the Archives of American Art, Smithsonian Institution. Norton editor Carol Bemis gave prompt, shrewd advice from beginning to end. I have a particularly deep debt of gratitude, finally, to Stevenson scholars Barry Menikoff, Richard Dury, and above all, Roger Swearingen and Ernest Mehew. In response to all of my questions, they gave generously and invaluably of their expertise—not least out of an enthusiasm, which I share, for enhancing modern readers' appreciation of the pleasures of an acquaintance with Robert Louis Stevenson.

The Text of
STRANGE CASE OF DR. JEKYLL AND MR. HYDE

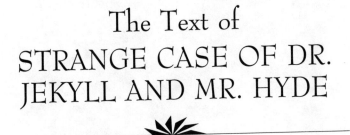

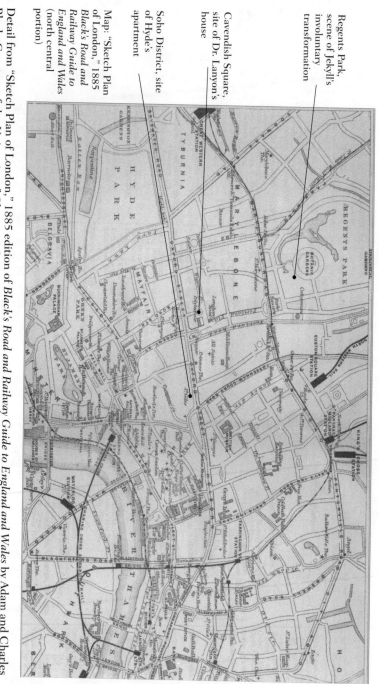

Regents Park, scene of Jekyll's involuntary transformation

Cavendish Square, site of Dr. Lanyon's house

Soho District, site of Hyde's apartment

Map: "Sketch Plan of London," 1885 Black's Road and Railway Guide to England and Wales (north central portion)

Detail from "Sketch Plan of London," 1885 edition of Black's Road and Railway Guide to England and Wales by Adam and Charles Black. Courtesy of the University of Chicago Library.

Strange Case

OF

DR JEKYLL

AND

MR HYDE

BY

R. L. STEVENSON

LONDON
LONGMANS, GREEN, AND CO.
1886

Price One Shilling

Cover, first British paper-covered edition, January, 1886. (Note the publisher's pen-and-ink alteration of the date, from 1885 to 1886.) Though subsequent editions have often inserted the word "The" before "Strange" in titling this work, Stevenson in fact wrote the title out for his publisher exactly as it appears here, presumably wanting its abruptness to heighten the sense of strangeness surrounding his "strange case." Courtesy of the Harry Elkins Widener Collection, Houghton Library of the Harvard College Library. HEW 10.10.21.

TO

KATHARINE DE MATTOS.[1]

———————

It's ill to loose the bands that God decreed to bind;[2]
Still will we be the children of the heather and the wind.
Far away from home, O it's still for you and me
That the broom is blowing bonnie[3] in the north countrie.

1. A favorite cousin of Stevenson's. The poem here appearing under her name was adapted by Stevenson from a longer poem he had written her several months earlier celebrating their shared Scottish background.
2. Stevenson's original version of this line read, "We cannae break the bonds that God decreed to bind." As revised here, the line may be intended to echo the verses in Job in which God, rebuking Job's presumption in questioning Him, asks "Canst thou . . . loose the bands of Orion?" and "who hath loosed the bands of the wild ass?" (Job 38:31 and 39:5).
3. I.e., that the Scotch broom (a flowering bush) is blooming handsomely.

CONTENTS

————◇————

Strange Case
of
Dr. Jekyll and Mr. Hyde.

STORY OF THE DOOR.

Mr. Utterson the lawyer was a man of a rugged countenance, that was never lighted by a smile; cold, scanty and embarrassed in discourse; backward in sentiment; lean, long, dusty, dreary and yet somehow lovable. At friendly meetings, and when the wine was to his taste, something eminently human beaconed from his eye; something indeed which never found its way into his talk, but which spoke not only in these silent symbols of the after-dinner face, but more often and loudly in the acts of his life. He was austere with himself; drank gin when he was alone, to mortify a taste for vintages; and though he enjoyed the theatre, had not crossed the doors of one for twenty years. But he had an approved[1] tolerance for others; sometimes wondering, almost with envy, at the high pressure of spirits involved in their misdeeds; and in any extremity inclined to help rather than to reprove. "I incline to Cain's heresy," he used to say quaintly: "I let my brother go to the devil in his own way."[2] In this character, it was frequently his fortune to be the last reputable acquaintance and the last good influence in the lives of down-going men. And to such as these, so long as they came about his chambers, he never marked a shade of change in his demeanour.

No doubt the feat was easy to Mr. Utterson; for he was undemonstrative at the best, and even his friendships seemed to be founded in a similar catholicity[3] of good-nature. It is the mark of a modest man to accept his friendly circle ready-made from the hands of opportunity; and that was the lawyer's way. His friends were those of his own blood or those whom he had known the longest; his affections, like ivy, were the growth of time, they implied no aptness in

1. Proven.
2. Adam and Eve's firstborn son Cain murdered his brother Abel and afterwards asked, "Am I my brother's keeper?" (Genesis 4:5).
3. Breadth.

the object. Hence, no doubt, the bond that united him to Mr. Rich-ard Enfield, his distant kinsman, the well-known man about town. It was a nut to crack for many, what these two could see in each other or what subject they could find in common. It was reported by those who encountered them in their Sunday walks, that they said nothing, looked singularly dull, and would hail with obvious relief the appearance of a friend. For all that, the two men put the greatest store by these excursions, counted them the chief jewel of each week, and not only set aside occasions of pleasure, but even resisted the calls of business, that they might enjoy them uninterrupted.

It chanced on one of these rambles that their way led them down a by-street in a busy quarter of London. The street was small and what is called quiet, but it drove a thriving trade on the week-days. The inhabitants were all doing well, it seemed, and all emulously hoping to do better still, and laying out the surplus of their gains in coquetry;[4] so that the shop fronts stood along that thoroughfare with an air of invitation, like rows of smiling saleswomen. Even on Sun-day, when it veiled its more florid charms and lay comparatively empty of passage, the street shone out in contrast to its dingy neigh-bourhood, like a fire in a forest; and with its freshly painted shutters, well-polished brasses, and general cleanliness and gaiety of note, instantly caught and pleased the eye of the passenger.[5]

Two doors from one corner, on the left hand going east, the line was broken by the entry of a court; and just at that point, a certain sinister block of building thrust forward its gable on the street. It was two storeys high; showed no window, nothing but a door on the lower storey and a blind forehead of discoloured wall on the upper; and bore in every feature, the marks of prolonged and sordid negli-gence. The door, which was equipped with neither bell nor knocker, was blistered and distained.[6] Tramps slouched into the recess and struck matches on the panels; children kept shop upon the steps; the schoolboy had tried his knife on the mouldings; and for close on a generation, no one had appeared to drive away these random vis-itors or to repair their ravages.

Mr. Enfield and the lawyer were on the other side of the by-street; but when they came abreast of the entry, the former lifted up his cane and pointed.

"Did you ever remark that door?" he asked; and when his com-panion had replied in the affirmative, "It is connected in my mind," added he, "with a very odd story."

<hr>

4. I.e., the shopkeeper-inhabitants were spending recent profits on new visual attractions to lure customers.
5. Passer-by.
6. Discolored.

"Indeed?" said Mr. Utterson, with a slight change of voice, "and what was that?"

"Well, it was this way," returned Mr. Enfield: "I was coming home from some place at the end of the world, about three o'clock of a black winter morning, and my way lay through a part of town where there was literally nothing to be seen but lamps. Street after street, and all the folks asleep—street after street, all lighted up as if for a procession and all as empty as a church—till at last I got into that state of mind when a man listens and listens and begins to long for the sight of a policeman. All at once, I saw two figures: one a little man who was stumping along eastward at a good walk, and the other a girl of maybe eight or ten who was running as hard as she was able down a cross street. Well, sir, the two ran into one another naturally enough at the corner; and then came the horrible part of the thing; for the man trampled calmly over the child's body and left her screaming on the ground. It sounds nothing to hear, but it was hellish to see. It wasn't like a man; it was like some damned Juggernaut.[7] I gave a view halloa,[8] took to my heels, collared my gentleman, and brought him back to where there was already quite a group about the screaming child. He was perfectly cool and made no resistance, but gave me one look, so ugly that it brought out the sweat on me like running. The people who had turned out were the girl's own family; and pretty soon, the doctor, for whom she had been sent, put in his appearance. Well, the child was not much the worse, more frightened, according to the Sawbones;[9] and there you might have supposed would be an end to it. But there was one curious circumstance. I had taken a loathing to my gentleman at first sight. So had the child's family, which was only natural. But the doctor's case was what struck me. He was the usual cut and dry apothecary,[1] of no particular age and colour, with a strong Edinburgh accent, and about as emotional as a bagpipe. Well, sir, he was like the rest of us; every time he looked at my prisoner, I saw that Sawbones turn sick and white with the desire to kill him. I knew what was in his mind, just as he knew what was in mine; and killing being out of the question, we did the next best. We told the man we could and would make such a scandal out of this, as should make his name stink from one end of London to the other. If he had any friends or any credit, we undertook that he should lose them. And all the time, as we were

7. An inexorable destructive force; the term derives from accounts given by early European travelers to India of religious worshippers being crushed to death beneath the wheels of the huge processional chariot of the Hindu deity Jagganath.
8. The shout given by a huntsman on seeing a fox break cover. This usage by Stevenson is quoted in the OED.
9. Slang for a doctor, especially a surgeon.
1. A dispenser of drugs; here an archaic and hence semi-facetious term for a doctor.

pitching it in red hot, we were keeping the women off him as best we could, for they were as wild as harpies. I never saw a circle of such hateful faces; and there was the man in the middle, with a kind of black, sneering coolness—frightened too, I could see that—but carrying it off, sir, really like Satan. 'If you choose to make capital out of this accident,' said he, 'I am naturally helpless. No gentleman but wishes to avoid a scene,' says he. 'Name your figure.' Well, we screwed him up to a hundred pounds[2] for the child's family; he would have clearly liked to stick out; but there was something about the lot of us that meant mischief, and at last he struck.[3] The next thing was to get the money; and where do you think he carried us but to that place with the door?—whipped out a key, went in, and presently came back with the matter of ten pounds in gold and a cheque for the balance on Coutts's,[4] drawn payable to bearer and signed with a name that I can't mention, though it's one of the points of my story, but it was a name at least very well known and often printed.[5] The figure was stiff; but the signature was good for more than that, if it was only genuine. I took the liberty of pointing out to my gentleman that the whole business looked apocryphal, and that a man does not, in real life, walk into a cellar door at four in the morning and come out of it with another man's cheque for close upon a hundred pounds. But he was quite easy and sneering. 'Set your mind at rest,' says he, 'I will stay with you till the banks open and cash the cheque myself.' So we all set off, the doctor, and the child's father, and our friend and myself, and passed the rest of the night in my chambers; and next day, when we had breakfasted, went in a body to the bank. I gave in the cheque myself, and said I had every reason to believe it was a forgery. Not a bit of it. The cheque was genuine."

"Tut-tut," said Mr. Utterson.

"I see you feel as I do," said Mr. Enfield. "Yes, it's a bad story. For my man was a fellow that nobody could have to do with, a really damnable man; and the person that drew the cheque is the very pink of the proprieties,[6] celebrated too, and (what makes it worse) one of your fellows who do what they call good. Black mail, I suppose; an honest man paying through the nose for some of the capers of his youth. Black Mail House is what I call that place with the door, in

2. A large sum at the time; as a rough point of comparison, consider the figure mentioned in George Gissing's novel *The Odd Women* (1893) as the salary of a character working as a mathematical lecturer at a London college in 1888, namely, one hundred and fifty pounds a year.

3. Surrendered; from the nautical term "strike," meaning to lower the topsails or haul down the flag as a sign of surrender or salute. This figurative usage by Stevenson is quoted in the OED.

4. The most elite bank in Great Britain, catering to a wealthy, respectable clientele which at its upper end included the British Royal Family.

5. Presumably in the London papers, which regularly featured news and gossip about the town's most eminent citizens.

6. The height of proper conduct or respectability.

consequence. Though even that, you know, is far from explaining all," he added, and with the words fell into a vein of musing.

From this he was recalled by Mr. Utterson asking rather suddenly: "And you don't know if the drawer of the cheque lives there?"

"A likely place, isn't it?" returned Mr. Enfield. "But I happen to have noticed his address; he lives in some square or other."

"And you never asked about—the place with the door?" said Mr. Utterson.

"No, sir: I had a delicacy," was the reply. "I feel very strongly about putting questions; it partakes too much of the style of the day of judgment. You start a question, and it's like starting a stone. You sit quietly on the top of a hill; and away the stone goes, starting others; and presently some bland old bird (the last you would have thought of) is knocked on the head in his own back garden and the family have to change their name. No, sir, I make it a rule of mine: the more it looks like Queer Street,[7] the less I ask."

"A very good rule, too," said the lawyer.

"But I have studied the place for myself," continued Mr. Enfield. "It seems scarcely a house. There is no other door, and nobody goes in or out of that one but, once in a great while, the gentleman of my adventure. There are three windows looking on the court on the first floor;[8] none below; the windows are always shut but they're clean. And then there is a chimney which is generally smoking; so somebody must live there. And yet it's not so sure; for the buildings are so packed together about that court; that it's hard to say where one ends and another begins."

The pair walked on again for a while in silence; and then "Enfield," said Mr. Utterson, "that's a good rule of yours."

"Yes, I think it is," returned Enfield.

"But for all that," continued the lawyer, "there's one point I want to ask: I want to ask the name of that man who walked over the child."

"Well," said Mr. Enfield, "I can't see what harm it would do. It was a man of the name of Hyde."

"Hm," said Mr. Utterson. "What sort of a man is he to see?"

"He is not easy to describe. There is something wrong with his appearance; something displeasing, something downright detestable. I never saw a man I so disliked, and yet I scarce know why. He must be deformed somewhere; he gives a strong feeling of deformity, although I couldn't specify the point.[9] He's an extraordinary looking

---

7. In London slang, a figurative allusion to living in troubled circumstances, especially debt.
8. I.e., the first floor above the ground floor, or what North Americans would call the second floor.
9. This obscure aura of deformity might for Stevenson's original readers have raised any of several associations current at the time: Christian lore about the Devil, said to be cunning in his concealment of his bestialized horns, tail, or cleft foot when he appeared in human

man, and yet I really can name nothing out of the way. No, sir; I can make no hand of it; I can't describe him. And it's not want of memory; for I declare I can see him this moment."

Mr. Utterson again walked some way in silence and obviously under a weight of consideration. "You are sure he used a key?" he inquired at last.

"My dear sir . . ." began Enfield, surprised out of himself.

"Yes, I know," said Utterson; "I know it must seem strange. The fact is, if I do not ask you the name of the other party, it is because I know it already. You see, Richard, your tale has gone home. If you have been inexact in any point, you had better correct it."

"I think you might have warned me," returned the other with a touch of sullenness. "But I have been pedantically exact, as you call it. The fellow had a key; and what's more, he has it still. I saw him use it, not a week ago."

Mr. Utterson sighed deeply but said never a word; and the young man presently resumed. "Here is another lesson to say nothing," said he. "I am ashamed of my long tongue. Let us make a bargain never to refer to this again."

"With all my heart," said the lawyer. "I shake hands on that, Richard."

SEARCH FOR MR. HYDE.

That evening, Mr. Utterson came home to his bachelor house in sombre spirits and sat down to dinner without relish. It was his custom of a Sunday, when this meal was over, to sit close by the fire, a volume of some dry divinity[1] on his reading desk, until the clock of the neighbouring church rang out the hour of twelve, when he would go soberly and gratefully to bed. On this night, however, as soon as the cloth was taken away, he took up a candle and went into his business room. There he opened his safe, took from the most private part of it a document endorsed on the envelope as Dr. Jekyll's Will, and sat down with a clouded brow to study its contents. The will was holograph,[2] for Mr. Utterson, though he took charge of it now that it was made, had refused to lend the least assistance in the making of it; it provided not only that, in case of the decease of Henry Jekyll,

---

form; Gothic fiction's tales of villains or monster-men whose depravity is only hinted at by surface appearances; and neo-Darwinist theories interpreting animal-like features in humans as signs of a grotesque criminality or under-evolution.

1. Theology. Utterson's austere Sunday evening routine, along with his earlier-mentioned abstinence from theater-going and "mortification" of a taste for wine, reflect the puritanical ethos which the Evangelical movement helped to spark in nineteenth-century British Christianity.

2. Wholly written by the person in whose name it appears.

M.D., D.C.L., LL.D., F.R.S.,[3] &c., all his possessions were to pass into the hands of his "friend and benefactor Edward Hyde," but that in case of Dr. Jekyll's "disappearance or unexplained absence for any period exceeding three calendar months," the said Edward Hyde should step into the said Henry Jekyll's shoes without further delay and free from any burthen or obligation, beyond the payment of a few small sums to the members of the doctor's household. This document had long been the lawyer's eyesore. It offended him both as a lawyer and as a lover of the sane and customary sides of life, to whom the fanciful was the immodest. And hitherto it was his ignorance of Mr. Hyde that had swelled his indignation; now, by a sudden turn, it was his knowledge. It was already bad enough when the name was but a name of which he could learn no more. It was worse when it began to be clothed upon with detestable attributes; and out of the shifting, insubstantial mists that had so long baffled his eye, there leaped up the sudden, definite presentment[4] of a fiend.

"I thought it was madness," he said, as he replaced the obnoxious paper in the safe, "and now I begin to fear it is disgrace."

With that he blew out his candle, put on a great coat and set forth in the direction of Cavendish Square, that citadel of medicine,[5] where his friend, the great Dr. Lanyon, had his house and received his crowding patients. "If anyone knows, it will be Lanyon," he had thought.

The solemn butler knew and welcomed him; he was subjected to no stage of delay, but ushered direct from the door to the dining-room where Dr. Lanyon sat alone over his wine. This was a hearty, healthy, dapper, red-faced gentleman, with a shock of hair prematurely white, and a boisterous and decided manner. At sight of Mr. Utterson, he sprang up from his chair and welcomed him with both hands. The geniality, as was the way of the man, was somewhat theatrical to the eye; but it reposed on genuine feeling. For these two were old friends, old mates both at school[6] and college, both thorough respecters of themselves and of each other, and, what does

---

3. Doctor of Medicine, Doctor of Civil Law, Doctor of Laws, and Fellow of the Royal Society. The first two credentials reflect Jekyll's professional training in medicine and law. The second two reflect his subsequent professional achievement: Doctor of Laws was commonly an honorary degree; and fellowship in the venerable Royal Society (members since its founding in the seventeenth century included Sir Isaac Newton, Sir William Herschel, and Michael Faraday) was by invitation only, with just fifteen new fellows being chosen each year on the basis of distinguished contributions to natural science.
4. Image.
5. Fashionable physicians, surgeons, and dentists had by late Victorian times become the chief tenants of the once-aristocratic homes in this square at the foot of Harley Street in west central London.
6. One of the select, all-male boarding schools where sons of the well-to-do were educated from the age of about eleven to eighteen. "Old boy" ties could readily carry over through university years and into later adult life.

not always follow, men who thoroughly enjoyed each other's company.

After a little rambling talk, the lawyer led up to the subject which so disagreeably preoccupied his mind.

"I suppose, Lanyon," said he, "you and I must be the two oldest friends that Henry Jekyll has?"

"I wish the friends were younger," chuckled Dr. Lanyon. "But I suppose we are. And what of that? I see little of him now."

"Indeed?" said Utterson. "I thought you had a bond of common interest."

"We had," was the reply. "But it is more than ten years since Henry Jekyll became too fanciful for me. He began to go wrong, wrong in mind; and though of course I continue to take an interest in him for old sake's sake as they say, I see and I have seen devilish little of the man. Such unscientific balderdash," added the doctor, flushing suddenly purple, "would have estranged Damon and Pythias."[7]

This little spirt[8] of temper was somewhat of a relief to Mr. Utterson. "They have only differed on some point of science," he thought; and being a man of no scientific passions (except in the matter of conveyancing)[9] he even added: "It is nothing worse than that!" He gave his friend a few seconds to recover his composure, and then approached the question he had come to put. "Did you ever come across a protégé of his—one Hyde?" he asked.

"Hyde?" repeated Lanyon. "No. Never heard of him. Since my time."

That was the amount of information that the lawyer carried back with him to the great, dark bed on which he tossed to and fro, until the small hours of the morning began to grow large. It was a night of little ease to his toiling mind, toiling in mere[1] darkness and besieged by questions.

Six o'clock struck on the bells of the church that was so conveniently near to Mr. Utterson's dwelling, and still he was digging at the problem. Hitherto it had touched him on the intellectual side alone; but now his imagination also was engaged or rather enslaved; and as he lay and tossed in the gross darkness of the night and the curtained room, Mr. Enfield's tale went by before his mind in a scroll of lighted pictures. He would be aware of the great field of lamps of a nocturnal city; then of the figure of a man walking swiftly; then of a child running from the doctor's; and then these met, and that human Juggernaut trod the child down and passed on regardless of her screams.

7. Damon and Phintias, usually called Pythias, were two philosophers of ancient Greece whose friendship was proverbial: when Pythias was condemned to death, Damon temporarily took his friend's place in captivity at the risk of his own life.
8. Spurt.
9. The drawing of deeds for transfer of property.
1. Absolute, pure (an obsolete usage which occurs again later in the tale).

Or else he would see a room in a rich house, where his friend lay asleep, dreaming and smiling at his dreams; and then the door of that room would be opened, the curtains of the bed plucked apart, the sleeper recalled, and lo! there would stand by his side a figure to whom power was given,[2] and even at that dead hour, he must rise and do its bidding.[3] The figure in these two phases haunted the lawyer all night; and if at any time he dozed over, it was but to see it glide more stealthily through sleeping houses, or move the more swiftly and still the more swiftly, even to dizziness, through wider labyrinths of lamplighted city, and at every street corner crush a child and leave her screaming. And still the figure had no face by which he might know it; even in his dreams, it had no face, or one that baffled him and melted before his eyes; and thus it was that there sprang up and grew apace in the lawyer's mind a singularly strong, almost an inordinate, curiosity to behold the features of the real Mr. Hyde. If he could but once set eyes on him, he thought the mystery would lighten and perhaps roll altogether away, as was the habit of mysterious things when well examined. He might see a reason for his friend's strange preference or bondage (call it which you please) and even for the startling clauses of the will. And at least it would be a face worth seeing: the face of a man who was without bowels of mercy:[4] a face which had but to show itself to raise up, in the mind of the unimpressionable Enfield, a spirit of enduring hatred.

From that time forward, Mr. Utterson began to haunt the door in the by-street of shops. In the morning before office hours, at noon when business was plenty and time scarce, at night under the face of the fogged city moon, by all lights and at all hours of solitude or concourse, the lawyer was to be found on his chosen post.

"If he be Mr. Hyde," he had thought, "I shall be Mr. Seek."

And at last his patience was rewarded. It was a fine dry night; frost in the air; the streets as clean as a ballroom floor; the lamps, unshaken by any wind, drawing a regular pattern of light and shadow. By ten o'clock, when the shops were closed, the by-street was very solitary and, in spite of the low growl of London from all round, very silent. Small sounds carried far; domestic sounds out of the houses were clearly audible on either side of the roadway; and the rumour[5] of the approach of any passenger preceded him by a long time. Mr. Utterson had been some minutes at his post, when he was aware of

2. An echo of Revelation 13:5 and 13:7, where it is said of the demonic beast who blasphemes against God that "power was given" him by the dragon (i.e., the devil).
3. This dream is reminiscent, accidentally or not, of the scene in Mary Shelley's *Frankenstein* (1818) in which Victor Frankenstein wakes from a tormented sleep to see the monster he has just created forcing his way into Frankenstein's bedroom and opening the curtains of his bed.
4. Compassion (from an old notion of bowels as the body's center of sympathetic emotions); cf. Colossians 3:12, "bowels of mercy."
5. Noise.

an odd, light footstep drawing near. In the course of his nightly patrols, he had long grown accustomed to the quaint effect with which the footfalls of a single person, while he is still a great way off, suddenly spring out distinct from the vast hum and clatter of the city. Yet his attention had never before been so sharply and decisively arrested; and it was with a strong, superstitious prevision of success that he withdrew into the entry of the court.

The steps drew swiftly nearer, and swelled out suddenly louder as they turned the end of the street. The lawyer, looking forth from the entry, could soon see what manner of man he had to deal with. He was small and very plainly dressed, and the look of him, even at that distance, went somehow strongly against the watcher's inclination. But he made straight for the door, crossing the roadway to save time; and as he came, he drew a key from his pocket like one approaching home.

Mr. Utterson stepped out and touched him on the shoulder as he passed. "Mr. Hyde, I think?"

Mr. Hyde shrank back with a hissing intake of the breath. But his fear was only momentary; and though he did not look the lawyer in the face, he answered coolly enough: "That is my name. What do you want?"

"I see you are going in," returned the lawyer. "I am an old friend of Dr. Jekyll's—Mr. Utterson of Gaunt Street—you must have heard my name; and meeting you so conveniently, I thought you might admit me."

"You will not find Dr. Jekyll; he is from home," replied Mr. Hyde, blowing in the key.[6] And then suddenly, but still without looking up, "How did you know me?" he asked.

"On your side," said Mr. Utterson, "will you do me a favour?"

"With pleasure," replied the other. "What shall it be?"

"Will you let me see your face?" asked the lawyer.

Mr. Hyde appeared to hesitate, and then, as if upon some sudden reflection, fronted about with an air of defiance; and the pair stared at each other pretty fixedly for a few seconds. "Now I shall know you again," said Mr. Utterson. "It may be useful."

"Yes," returned Mr. Hyde, "it is as well we have met; and *à propos*, you should have my address." And he gave a number of a street in Soho.[7]

"Good God!" thought Mr. Utterson, "can he too have been think-

---

6. This puzzling phrase may refer to blowing the bit or shank of the key clean of dust; in any case, the action is best understood as an idling gesture undertaken to avoid having to look Utterson in the face.
7. A district in central London known in Victorian times for its crowded immigrant populations and squalid entertainments, including taverns, music halls, and brothels. It is roughly a mile east of fashionable Cavendish Square where Dr. Lanyon lives.

ing of the will?" But he kept his feelings to himself and only grunted in acknowledgement of the address.

"And now," said the other, "how did you know me?"

"By description," was the reply.

"Whose description?"

"We have common friends," said Mr. Utterson.

"Common friends?" echoed Mr. Hyde, a little hoarsely. "Who are they?"

"Jekyll, for instance," said the lawyer.

"He never told you," cried Mr. Hyde, with a flush of anger. "I did not think you would have lied."

"Come," said Mr. Utterson, "that is not fitting language."

The other snarled aloud into a savage laugh; and the next moment, with extraordinary quickness, he had unlocked the door and disappeared into the house.

The lawyer stood awhile when Mr. Hyde had left him, the picture of disquietude. Then he began slowly to mount the street, pausing every step or two and putting his hand to his brow like a man in mental perplexity. The problem he was thus debating as he walked, was one of a class that is rarely solved. Mr. Hyde was pale and dwarfish, he gave an impression of deformity without any nameable malformation, he had a displeasing smile, he had borne himself to the lawyer with a sort of murderous mixture of timidity and boldness, and he spoke with a husky, whispering and somewhat broken voice; all these were points against him, but not all of these together could explain the hitherto unknown disgust, loathing and fear with which Mr. Utterson regarded him. "There must be something else," said the perplexed gentleman. "There *is* something more, if I could find a name for it. God bless me, the man seems hardly human! Something troglodytic,[8] shall we say? or can it be the old story of Dr. Fell?[9] or is it the mere radiance of a foul soul that thus transpires through, and transfigures, its clay continent?[1] The last, I think; for O my poor old Harry Jekyll, if ever I read Satan's signature upon a face, it is on that of your new friend."

Round the corner from the by-street, there was a square of ancient, handsome houses, now for the most part decayed from their high estate and let in flats and chambers to all sorts and conditions

---

8. Characteristic of a troglodyte, or cave-dweller.

9. A man who inspires an unspeakable or unfathomable repugnance. The allusion derives from a verse written by a seventeenth-century Oxford student, Thomas Brown, who retaliated against a disciplinarian dean, Dr. John Fell, by loosely translating a Latin epigram by Martial to read: "I do not love thee, Dr. Fell, / The reason why I cannot tell; / But this I know, and know full well, / I do not love thee, Dr. Fell."

1. Its earthly container, i.e., the body. This usage of "continent" by Stevenson is quoted in the OED.

of men: map-engravers, architects, shady lawyers and the agents of obscure enterprises. One house, however, second from the corner, was still occupied entire; and at the door of this, which wore a great air of wealth and comfort, though it was now plunged in darkness except for the fan-light, Mr. Utterson stopped and knocked. A well-dressed, elderly servant opened the door.

"Is Dr. Jekyll at home, Poole?" asked the lawyer.

"I will see, Mr. Utterson," said Poole, admitting the visitor, as he spoke, into a large, low-roofed, comfortable hall, paved with flags,[2] warmed (after the fashion of a country house) by a bright, open fire, and furnished with costly cabinets of oak. "Will you wait here by the fire, sir? or shall I give you a light in the dining-room?"

"Here, thank you," said the lawyer, and he drew near and leaned on the tall fender.[3] This hall, in which he was now left alone, was a pet fancy of his friend the doctor's; and Utterson himself was wont to speak of it as the pleasantest room in London. But to-night there was a shudder in his blood; the face of Hyde sat heavy on his memory; he felt (what was rare with him) a nausea and distaste of life; and in the gloom of his spirits, he seemed to read a menace in the flickering of the firelight on the polished cabinets and the uneasy starting of the shadow on the roof. He was ashamed of his relief, when Poole presently returned to announce that Dr. Jekyll was gone out.

"I saw Mr. Hyde go in by the old dissecting room door, Poole," he said. "Is that right, when Dr. Jekyll is from home?"

"Quite right, Mr. Utterson, sir," replied the servant. "Mr. Hyde has a key."

"Your master seems to repose a great deal of trust in that young man, Poole," resumed the other musingly.

"Yes, sir, he do indeed," said Poole. "We have all orders to obey him."

"I do not think I ever met Mr. Hyde?" asked Utterson.

"O, dear no, sir. He never *dines* here," replied the butler. "Indeed we see very little of him on this side of the house; he mostly comes and goes by the laboratory."

"Well, good night, Poole."

"Good night, Mr. Utterson."

And the lawyer set out homeward with a very heavy heart. "Poor Harry Jekyll," he thought, "my mind misgives me he is in deep waters! He was wild when he was young; a long while ago to be sure; but in the law of God, there is no statute of limitations. Ay, it must be that; the ghost of some old sin, the cancer of some concealed disgrace:

2. I.e., flagstones.
3. A metal frame put in front of a fireplace to keep embers from rolling out onto the floor.

punishment coming, *pede claudo*,[4] years after memory has forgotten and self-love condoned the fault." And the lawyer, scared by the thought, brooded awhile on his own past, groping in all the corners of memory, lest by chance some Jack-in-the-Box of an old iniquity should leap to light there. His past was fairly blameless; few men could read the rolls of their life with less apprehension; yet he was humbled to the dust by the many ill things he had done, and raised up again into a sober and fearful gratitude by the many that he had come so near to doing, yet avoided. And then by a return on his former subject, he conceived a spark of hope. "This Master Hyde, if he were studied," thought he, "must have secrets of his own: black secrets, by the look of him; secrets compared to which poor Jekyll's worst would be like sunshine. Things cannot continue as they are. It turns me cold to think of this creature stealing like a thief to Harry's bedside; poor Harry, what a wakening! And the danger of it; for if this Hyde suspects the existence of the will, he may grow impatient to inherit. Ay, I must put my shoulder to the wheel—if Jekyll will but let me," he added, "if Jekyll will only let me." For once more he saw before his mind's eye, as clear as a transparency, the strange clauses of the will.

DR. JEKYLL WAS QUITE AT EASE.

A fortnight later, by excellent good fortune, the doctor gave one of his pleasant dinners to some five or six old cronies, all intelligent, reputable men and all judges of good wine; and Mr. Utterson so contrived that he remained behind after the others had departed. This was no new arrangement, but a thing that had befallen many scores of times. Where Utterson was liked, he was liked well. Hosts loved to detain the dry lawyer, when the light-hearted and the loose-tongued had already their foot on the threshold; they liked to sit awhile in his unobtrusive company, practicing for solitude; sobering their minds in the man's rich silence after the expense[1] and strain of gaiety. To this rule, Dr. Jekyll was no exception; and as he now sat on the opposite side of the fire—a large, well-made, smooth-faced[2] man of fifty, with something of a slyish cast perhaps, but every mark of capacity and kindness—you could see by his looks that he cherished for Mr. Utterson a sincere and warm affection.

---

4. Latin, "on limping foot." Utterson is recalling the closing line of an ode on male virtue by the Roman poet Horace (65–8 B.C.), "*raro antecedentem scelestum/deseruit pede Poena claudo*": "seldom has Vengeance abandoned a wicked man through lameness of foot though he has got a start on her" (Horace, *Odes*, 3.2.32).
1. Expenditure of energy.
2. Literally, having a face free from hair, wrinkles, etc.; used figuratively, the term means having or assuming a bland, ingratiating, or insinuating manner.

"I have been wanting to speak to you, Jekyll," began the latter. "You know that will of yours?"

A close observer might have gathered that the topic was distasteful; but the doctor carried it off gaily. "My poor Utterson," said he, "you are unfortunate in such a client. I never saw a man so distressed as you were by my will; unless it were that hide-bound pedant, Lanyon, at what he called my scientific heresies. O, I know he's a good fellow—you needn't frown—an excellent fellow, and I always mean to see more of him; but a hide-bound pedant for all that; an ignorant, blatant pedant. I was never more disappointed in any man than Lanyon."

"You know I never approved of it," pursued Utterson, ruthlessly disregarding the fresh topic.

"My will? Yes, certainly, I know that," said the doctor, a trifle sharply. "You have told me so."

"Well, I tell you so again," continued the lawyer. "I have been learning something of young Hyde."

The large handsome face of Dr. Jekyll grew pale to the very lips, and there came a blackness about his eyes. "I do not care to hear more," said he. "This is a matter I thought we had agreed to drop."

"What I heard was abominable," said Utterson.

"It can make no change. You do not understand my position," returned the doctor, with a certain incoherency of manner. "I am painfully situated, Utterson; my position is a very strange—a very strange one. It is one of those affairs that cannot be mended by talking."

"Jekyll," said Utterson, "you know me: I am a man to be trusted. Make a clean breast of this in confidence; and I make no doubt I can get you out of it."

"My good Utterson," said the doctor, "this is very good of you, this is downright good of you, and I cannot find words to thank you in. I believe you fully; I would trust you before any man alive, ay, before myself, if I could make the choice; but indeed it isn't what you fancy; it is not so bad as that; and just to put your good heart at rest, I will tell you one thing: the moment I choose, I can be rid of Mr. Hyde. I give you my hand upon that; and I thank you again and again; and I will just add one little word, Utterson, that I'm sure you'll take in good part: this is a private matter, and I beg of you to let it sleep."

Utterson reflected a little looking in the fire.

"I have no doubt you are perfectly right," he said at last, getting to his feet.

"Well, but since we have touched upon this business, and for the last time I hope," continued the doctor, "there is one point I should like you to understand. I have really a very great interest in poor Hyde. I know you have seen him; he told me so; and I fear he was rude. But I do sincerely take a great, a very great interest in that young man; and if I am taken away, Utterson, I wish you to promise me that you will bear with him and get his rights for him. I think you would, if you knew all; and it would be a weight off my mind if you would promise."

"I can't pretend that I shall ever like him," said the lawyer.

"I don't ask that," pleaded Jekyll, laying his hand upon the other's arm; "I only ask for justice; I only ask you to help him for my sake, when I am no longer here."

Utterson heaved an irrepressible sigh. "Well," said he. "I promise."

THE CAREW MURDER CASE.

Nearly a year later, in the month of October 18—,[1] London was startled by a crime of singular ferocity and rendered all the more notable by the high position of the victim. The details were few and startling. A maid servant living alone in a house not far from the river, had gone upstairs to bed about eleven. Although a fog rolled over the city in the small hours, the early part of the night was cloudless, and the lane, which the maid's window overlooked, was brilliantly lit by the full moon. It seems she was romantically given, for she sat down upon her box, which stood immediately under the window, and fell into a dream of musing. Never (she used to say, with streaming tears, when she narrated that experience) never had she felt more at peace with all men or thought more kindly of the world. And as she so sat she became aware of an aged and beautiful gentleman with white hair, drawing near along the lane; and advancing to meet him, another and very small gentleman, to whom at first she paid less attention. When they had come within speech (which was just under the maid's eyes) the older man bowed and accosted the other with a very pretty manner of politeness. It did not seem as if the subject of his address were of great importance; indeed, from his pointing, it sometimes appeared as if he were only inquiring his way; but the moon shone on his face as he spoke, and the girl was pleased to watch it, it seemed to breathe such an innocent and old-world kindness of disposition, yet with something high too, as of a well-founded self-content. Presently her eye wandered to the other, and she was surprised to recognise in him a certain Mr. Hyde, who had once visited her master and for whom she had conceived a dislike. He had in his hand a heavy cane, with which he was trifling; but he answered never a word, and seemed to listen with an ill-contained

---

1. Stevenson followed a then-familiar literary convention in using a dash for the final two digits of a date so as to leave the exact year unspecified. Draft fragments of the tale show that at an earlier stage of composition he included several fully specified dates that set the action of the story in the years 1883–85.

impatience. And then all of a sudden he broke out in a great flame of anger, stamping with his foot, brandishing the cane, and carrying on (as the maid described it) like a madman. The old gentleman took a step back, with the air of one very much surprised and a trifle hurt; and at that Mr. Hyde broke out of all bounds and clubbed him to the earth. And next moment, with ape-like fury, he was trampling his victim under foot, and hailing down a storm of blows, under which the bones were audibly shattered and the body jumped upon the roadway. At the horror of these sights and sounds, the maid fainted.

It was two o'clock when she came to herself and called for the police. The murderer was gone long ago; but there lay his victim in the middle of the lane, incredibly mangled. The stick with which the deed had been done, although it was of some rare and very tough and heavy wood, had broken in the middle under the stress of this insensate cruelty; and one splintered half had rolled in the neighbouring gutter—the other, without doubt, had been carried away by the murderer. A purse and a gold watch were found upon the victim; but no cards or papers, except a sealed and stamped envelope, which he had been probably carrying to the post, and which bore the name and address of Mr. Utterson.

This was brought to the lawyer the next morning, before he was out of bed; and he had no sooner seen it, and been told the circumstances, than he shot out a solemn lip. "I shall say nothing till I have seen the body," said he; "this may be very serious. Have the kindness to wait while I dress." And with the same grave countenance he hurried through his breakfast and drove to the police station, whither the body had been carried. As soon as he came into the cell, he nodded.

"Yes," said he, "I recognise him. I am sorry to say that this is Sir Danvers Carew."[2]

"Good God, sir," exclaimed the officer, "is it possible?" And the next moment his eye lighted up with professional ambition. "This will make a deal of noise," he said. "And perhaps you can help us to the man." And he briefly narrated what the maid had seen, and showed the broken stick.

Mr. Utterson had already quailed at the name of Hyde; but when the stick was laid before him, he could doubt no longer: broken and battered as it was, he recognised it for one that he had himself presented many years before to Henry Jekyll.

"Is this Mr. Hyde a person of small stature?" he inquired.

"Particularly small and particularly wicked-looking, is what the maid calls him," said the officer.

2. "Sir" is either the formal title conferred for his lifetime on a man who is given a knighthood or the title borne by a hereditary baronet.

Mr. Utterson reflected; and then, raising his head, "If you will come with me in my cab," he said, "I think I can take you to his house."

It was by this time about nine in the morning, and the first fog of the season.[3] A great chocolate-coloured pall lowered[4] over heaven, but the wind was continually charging and routing these embattled vapours; so that as the cab crawled from street to street, Mr. Utterson beheld a marvellous number of degrees and hues of twilight; for here it would be dark like the back-end of evening; and there would be a glow of a rich, lurid brown, like the light of some strange conflagration; and here, for a moment, the fog would be quite broken up, and a haggard shaft of daylight would glance in between the swirling wreaths. The dismal quarter of Soho seen under these changing glimpses, with its muddy ways, and slatternly passengers, and its lamps, which had never been extinguished or had been kindled afresh to combat this mournful reinvasion of darkness, seemed, in the lawyer's eyes, like a district of some city in a nightmare. The thoughts of his mind, besides, were of the gloomiest dye; and when he glanced at the companion of his drive, he was conscious of some touch of that terror of the law and the law's officers, which may at times assail the most honest.

As the cab drew up before the address indicated, the fog lifted a little and showed him a dingy street, a gin palace,[5] a low French eating house, a shop for the retail of penny numbers[6] and twopenny salads, many ragged children huddled in the doorways, and many women of many different nationalities passing out, key in hand, to have a morning glass; and the next moment the fog settled down again upon that part, as brown as umber, and cut him off from his blackguardly surroundings. This was the home of Henry Jekyll's favourite; of a man who was heir to quarter of a million sterling.[7]

An ivory-faced and silvery-haired old woman opened the door. She had an evil face, smoothed by hypocrisy; but her manners were excellent. Yes, she said, this was Mr. Hyde's, but he was not at home; he had been in that night very late, but had gone away again in less than an hour; there was nothing strange in that; his habits were very irregular, and he was often absent; for instance, it was nearly two months since she had seen him till yesterday.

"Very well then, we wish to see his rooms," said the lawyer; and

3. In modern terms, smog; by the late nineteenth century, smoke pollution in industrialized London had become so thick that when mixed with fog, especially during the winter months, it produced famously sky-darkening, choking hazes that could last for days or weeks on end.
4. I.e., loured; looked dark and threatening.
5. The phrase was used contemptuously of the cheapest type of drinking establishment.
6. Cheap serial installments of popular sensation fiction, also known as "penny dreadfuls."
7. I.e., pounds sterling.

when the woman began to declare it was impossible, "I had better tell you who this person is," he added. "This is Inspector Newcomen of Scotland Yard."

A flash of odious joy appeared upon the woman's face. "Ah!" said she, "he is in trouble! What has he done?"

Mr. Utterson and the inspector exchanged glances. "He don't seem a very popular character," observed the latter. "And now, my good woman, just let me and this gentleman have a look about us."

In the whole extent of the house, which but for the old woman remained otherwise empty, Mr. Hyde had only used a couple of rooms; but these were furnished with luxury and good taste. A closet was filled with wine; the plate was of silver, the napery[8] elegant; a good picture hung upon the walls, a gift (as Utterson supposed) from Henry Jekyll, who was much of a connoisseur; and the carpets were of many plies and agreeable in colour. At this moment, however, the rooms bore every mark of having been recently and hurriedly ransacked; clothes lay about the floor, with their pockets inside out; lockfast[9] drawers stood open; and on the hearth there lay a pile of gray ashes, as though many papers had been burned. From these embers the inspector disinterred the butt end of a green cheque book, which had resisted the action of the fire; the other half of the stick was found behind the door; and as this clinched his suspicions, the officer declared himself delighted. A visit to the bank, where several thousand pounds were found to be lying to the murderer's credit, completed his gratification.

"You may depend upon it, sir," he told Mr. Utterson: "I have him in my hand. He must have lost his head, or he never would have left the stick or, above all, burned the cheque book. Why, money's life to the man. We have nothing to do but wait for him at the bank, and get out the handbills."[1]

This last, however, was not so easy of accomplishment; for Mr. Hyde had numbered few familiars—even the master of the servant maid had only seen him twice; his family could nowhere be traced; he had never been photographed; and the few who could describe him differed widely, as common observers will. Only on one point, were they agreed; and that was the haunting sense of unexpressed deformity with which the fugitive impressed his beholders.

INCIDENT OF THE LETTER.

It was late in the afternoon, when Mr. Utterson found his way to Dr. Jekyll's door, where he was at once admitted by Poole, and carried

---

8. Domestic linens, especially table linens.
9. Fastened or secured by a lock (Scottish usage).
1. Printed sheets circulated locally by hand describing known or suspected criminals and seeking information from the public to aid in their identification and arrest.

down by the kitchen offices[1] and across a yard which had once been a garden, to the building which was indifferently[2] known as the laboratory or the dissecting rooms. The doctor had bought the house from the heirs of a celebrated surgeon; and his own tastes being rather chemical than anatomical, had changed the destination of the block[3] at the bottom of the garden. It was the first time that the lawyer had been received in that part of his friend's quarters; and he eyed the dingy windowless structure with curiosity, and gazed round with a distasteful sense of strangeness as he crossed the theatre,[4] once crowded with eager students and now lying gaunt and silent, the tables laden with chemical apparatus, the floor strewn with crates and littered with packing straw, and the light falling dimly through the foggy cupola. At the further end, a flight of stairs mounted to a door covered with red baize; and through this, Mr. Utterson was at last received into the doctor's cabinet.[5] It was a large room, fitted round with glass presses,[6] furnished, among other things, with a cheval-glass[7] and a business table, and looking out upon the court by three dusty windows barred with iron. The fire burned in the grate; a lamp was set lighted on the chimney shelf, for even in the houses the fog began to lie thickly; and there, close up to the warmth, sat Dr. Jekyll, looking deadly sick. He did not rise to meet his visitor, but held out a cold hand and bade him welcome in a changed voice.

"And now," said Mr. Utterson, as soon as Poole had left them, "you have heard the news?"

The doctor shuddered. "They were crying it in the square," he said. "I heard them in my dining room."

"One word," said the lawyer. "Carew was my client, but so are you, and I want to know what I am doing. You have not been mad enough to hide this fellow?"

"Utterson, I swear to God," cried the doctor, "I swear to God I will never set eyes on him again. I bind my honour to you that I am done with him in this world. It is all at an end. And indeed he does not want my help; you do not know him as I do; he is safe, he is quite safe; mark my words, he will never more be heard of."

The lawyer listened gloomily; he did not like his friend's feverish manner. "You seem pretty sure of him," said he; "and for your sake,

---

1. Rooms devoted to kitchen functions.
2. Without difference or distinction.
3. I.e., had changed the purpose of the building.
4. A surgical or anatomical theater, with seats for students arranged around a central lecturing or demonstration platform.
5. A private chamber; etymologically connected with the tale's earlier use of "cabinet" as a furniture piece ("costly cabinets of oak") around the idea of a little cabin, room, or repository.
6. Shelved cupboards with glass doors.
7. A full-length mirror pivotally attached to a stationary frame in which it may be tilted.

I hope you may be right. If it came to a trial, your name might appear."

"I am quite sure of him," replied Jekyll; "I have grounds for certainty that I cannot share with anyone. But there is one thing on which you may advise me. I have—I have received a letter; and I am at a loss whether I should show it to the police. I should like to leave it in your hands, Utterson; you would judge wisely I am sure; I have so great a trust in you."

"You fear, I suppose, that it might lead to his detection?" asked the lawyer.

"No," said the other. "I cannot say that I care what becomes of Hyde; I am quite done with him. I was thinking of my own character, which this hateful business has rather exposed."

Utterson ruminated awhile; he was surprised at his friend's selfishness, and yet relieved by it. "Well," said he, at last, "let me see the letter."

The letter was written in an odd, upright hand and signed "Edward Hyde": and it signified, briefly enough, that the writer's benefactor, Dr. Jekyll, whom he had long so unworthily repaid for a thousand generosities, need labour under no alarm for his safety as he had means of escape on which he placed a sure dependence. The lawyer liked this letter well enough; it put a better colour on the intimacy than he had looked for; and he blamed himself for some of his past suspicions.

"Have you the envelope?" he asked.

"I burned it," replied Jekyll, "before I thought what I was about. But it bore no postmark. The note was handed in."

"Shall I keep this and sleep upon it?" asked Utterson.

"I wish you to judge for me entirely," was the reply. "I have lost confidence in myself."

"Well, I shall consider," returned the lawyer. "And now one word more: it was Hyde who dictated the terms in your will about that disappearance?"

The doctor seemed seized with a qualm of faintness; he shut his mouth tight and nodded.

"I knew it," said Utterson. "He meant to murder you. You have had a fine escape."

"I have had what is far more to the purpose," returned the doctor solemnly: "I have had a lesson—O God, Utterson, what a lesson I have had!" And he covered his face for a moment with his hands.

On his way out, the lawyer stopped and had a word or two with Poole. "By the by," said he "there was a letter handed in to-day: what was the messenger like?" But Poole was positive nothing had come except by post; "and only circulars by that," he added.

This news sent off the visitor with his fears renewed. Plainly the letter had come by the laboratory door; possibly, indeed, it had been written in the cabinet; and if that were so, it must be differently judged, and handled with the more caution. The newsboys, as he went, were crying themselves hoarse along the footways: "Special edition. Shocking murder of an M.P."[8] That was the funeral oration of one friend and client; and he could not help a certain apprehension lest the good name of another should be sucked down in the eddy of the scandal. It was, at least, a ticklish decision that he had to make; and self-reliant as he was by habit, he began to cherish a longing for advice. It was not to be had directly; but perhaps, he thought, it might be fished for.

Presently after, he sat on one side of his own hearth, with Mr. Guest, his head clerk, upon the other, and midway between, at a nicely calculated distance from the fire, a bottle of a particular old wine that had long dwelt unsunned in the foundations of his house. The fog still slept on the wing above the drowned city, where the lamps glimmered like carbuncles;[9] and through the muffle and smother of these fallen clouds, the procession of the town's life was still rolling in through the great arteries with a sound as of a mighty wind. But the room was gay with firelight. In the bottle the acids were long ago resolved; the imperial dye[1] had softened with time, as the colour grows richer in stained windows; and the glow of hot autumn afternoons on hillside vineyards, was ready to be set free and to disperse the fogs of London. Insensibly the lawyer melted. There was no man from whom he kept fewer secrets than Mr. Guest; and he was not always sure that he kept as many as he meant. Guest had often been on business to the doctor's; he knew Poole; he could scarce have failed to hear of Mr. Hyde's familiarity about the house; he might draw conclusions: was it not as well, then, that he should see a letter which put that mystery to rights? and above all since Guest, being a great student and critic of handwriting, would consider the step natural and obliging? The clerk, besides, was a man of counsel; he would scarce read so strange a document without dropping a remark; and by that remark Mr. Utterson might shape his future course.

"This is a sad business about Sir Danvers," he said.

"Yes, sir, indeed. It has elicited a great deal of public feeling," returned Guest. "The man, of course, was mad."

"I should like to hear your views on that," replied Utterson. "I have a document here in his handwriting; it is between ourselves, for I scarce know what to do about it; it is an ugly business at the best.

8. Member of Parliament.
9. Precious stones of a red or fiery color.
1. A shade of crimson or purple recalling the dye used to color imperial robes worn in ancient Rome.

But there it is; quite in your way:[2] a murderer's autograph."

Guest's eyes brightened, and he sat down at once and studied it with passion. "No, sir," he said; "not mad; but it is an odd hand."

"And by all accounts a very odd writer," added the lawyer.

Just then the servant entered with a note.

"Is that from Dr. Jekyll, sir?" inquired the clerk. "I thought I knew the writing. Anything private, Mr. Utterson?"

"Only an invitation to dinner. Why? do you want to see it?"

"One moment. I thank you, sir;" and the clerk laid the two sheets of paper alongside and sedulously compared their contents. "Thank you, sir," he said at last, returning both; "it's a very interesting autograph."

There was a pause, during which Mr. Utterson struggled with himself. "Why did you compare them, Guest?" he inquired suddenly.

"Well, sir," returned the clerk, "there's a rather singular resemblance; the two hands are in many points identical: only differently sloped."

"Rather quaint," said Utterson.

"It is, as you say, rather quaint," returned Guest.

"I wouldn't speak of this note, you know," said the master.

"No, sir," said the clerk. "I understand."

But no sooner was Mr. Utterson alone that night, than he locked the note into his safe where it reposed from that time forward. "What!" he thought. "Henry Jekyll forge for a murderer!" And his blood ran cold in his veins.

REMARKABLE INCIDENT OF DR. LANYON.

Time ran on; thousands of pounds were offered in reward, for the death of Sir Danvers was resented as a public injury; but Mr. Hyde had disappeared out of the ken[1] of the police as though he had never existed. Much of his past was unearthed, indeed, and all disreputable: tales came out of the man's cruelty, at once so callous and violent, of his vile life, of his strange associates, of the hatred that seemed to have surrounded his career; but of his present whereabouts, not a whisper. From the time he had left the house in Soho on the morning of the murder, he was simply blotted out; and gradually, as time drew on, Mr. Utterson began to recover from the hotness of his alarm, and to grow more at quiet with himself. The death of Sir Danvers was, to his way of thinking, more than paid for by the disappearance of Mr. Hyde. Now that that evil influence had been withdrawn, a new life began for Dr. Jekyll. He came out of his seclusion, renewed relations with his friends, became once more

2. In your area of expertise or interest.
1. Sight; knowledge.

their familiar guest and entertainer; and whilst he had always been known for charities, he was now no less distinguished for religion. He was busy, he was much in the open air, he did good; his face seemed to open and brighten, as if with an inward consciousness of service; and for more than two months, the doctor was at peace.

On the 8th of January Utterson had dined at the doctor's with a small party; Lanyon had been there; and the face of the host had looked from one to the other as in the old days when the trio were inseparable friends. On the 12th, and again on the 14th, the door was shut against the lawyer. "The doctor was confined to the house," Poole said, "and saw no one." On the 15th, he tried again, and was again refused; and having now been used for the last two months to see his friend almost daily, he found this return of solitude to weigh upon his spirits. The fifth night, he had in Guest to dine with him; and the sixth he betook himself to Dr. Lanyon's.

There at least he was not denied admittance; but when he came in, he was shocked at the change which had taken place in the doctor's appearance. He had his death-warrant written legibly upon his face. The rosy man had grown pale; his flesh had fallen away; he was visibly balder and older; and yet it was not so much these tokens of a swift physical decay that arrested the lawyer's notice, as a look in the eye and quality of manner that seemed to testify to some deep-seated terror of the mind. It was unlikely that the doctor should fear death; and yet that was what Utterson was tempted to suspect. "Yes," he thought, "he is a doctor, he must know his own state and that his days are counted; and the knowledge is more than he can bear." And yet when Utterson remarked on his ill-looks, it was with an air of great firmness that Lanyon declared himself a doomed man.

"I have had a shock," he said, "and I shall never recover. It is a question of weeks. Well, life has been pleasant; I liked it; yes, sir, I used to like it. I sometimes think if we knew all, we should be more glad to get away."

"Jekyll is ill, too," observed Utterson. "Have you seen him?"

But Lanyon's face changed, and he held up a trembling hand. "I wish to see or hear no more of Dr. Jekyll," he said in a loud, unsteady voice. "I am quite done with that person; and I beg that you will spare me any allusion to one whom I regard as dead."

"Tut-tut," said Mr. Utterson; and then after a considerable pause, "Can't I do anything?" he inquired. "We are three very old friends, Lanyon; we shall not live to make others."

"Nothing can be done," returned Lanyon; "ask himself."

"He will not see me," said the lawyer.

"I am not surprised at that," was the reply.

"Some day, Utterson, after I am dead, you may perhaps come to learn the right and wrong of this. I cannot tell you. And in the meantime, if you can sit and talk with me of other things, for God's sake, stay and do so; but if you cannot keep clear of this accursed topic, then, in God's name, go, for I cannot bear it."

As soon as he got home, Utterson sat down and wrote to Jekyll, complaining of his exclusion from the house, and asking the cause of this unhappy break with Lanyon; and the next day brought him a long answer, often very pathetically worded, and sometimes darkly mysterious in drift. The quarrel with Lanyon was incurable. "I do not blame our old friend," Jekyll wrote, "but I share his view that we must never meet. I mean from henceforth to lead a life of extreme seclusion; you must not be surprised, nor must you doubt my friendship, if my door is often shut even to you. You must suffer me to go my own dark way. I have brought on myself a punishment and a danger that I cannot name. If I am the chief of sinners,[2] I am the chief of sufferers also. I could not think that this earth contained a place for sufferings and terrors so unmanning; and you can do but one thing, Utterson, to lighten this destiny, and that is to respect my silence." Utterson was amazed; the dark influence of Hyde had been withdrawn, the doctor had returned to his old tasks and amities; a week ago, the prospect had smiled with every promise of a cheerful and an honoured age; and now in a moment, friendship, and peace of mind and the whole tenor of his life were wrecked. So great and unprepared a change pointed to madness; but in view of Lanyon's manner and words, there must lie for it some deeper ground.

A week afterwards Dr. Lanyon took to his bed, and in something less than a fortnight he was dead. The night after the funeral, at which he had been sadly affected, Utterson locked the door of his business room, and sitting there by the light of a melancholy candle, drew out and set before him an envelope addressed by the hand and sealed with the seal of his dead friend. "PRIVATE: for the hands of J. G. Utterson ALONE and in case of his predecease *to be destroyed unread*," so it was emphatically superscribed; and the lawyer dreaded to behold the contents. "I have buried one friend to-day," he thought: "what if this should cost me another?" And then he condemned the fear as a disloyalty, and broke the seal. Within there was another enclosure, likewise sealed, and marked upon the cover as "not to be opened till the death or disappearance of Dr. Henry Jekyll." Utterson could not trust his eyes. Yes, it was disappearance; here again, as in the mad will which he had long ago restored to its author, here again were the idea of a disappearance and the name of Henry Jekyll bracketed. But in the will, that idea had sprung from the sinister suggestion of the man Hyde; it was set there with a purpose all too plain

---

2. An echo of the line in Paul's First Epistle to Timothy, "Christ Jesus came into the world to save sinners; of whom I am chief" (I Timothy 1:15).

and horrible. Written by the hand of Lanyon, what should it mean?
A great curiosity came on the trustee, to disregard the prohibition
and dive at once to the bottom of these mysteries; but professional
honour and faith to his dead friend were stringent obligations; and
the packet slept in the inmost corner of his private safe.

It is one thing to mortify curiosity, another to conquer it; and it
may be doubted if, from that day forth, Utterson desired the society
of his surviving friend with the same eagerness. He thought of him
kindly; but his thoughts were disquieted and fearful. He went to call
indeed; but he was perhaps relieved to be denied admittance; perhaps, in his heart, he preferred to speak with Poole upon the door-
step and surrounded by the air and sounds of the open city, rather
than to be admitted into that house of voluntary bondage, and to sit
and speak with its inscrutable recluse. Poole had, indeed, no very
pleasant news to communicate. The doctor, it appeared, now more
than ever confined himself to the cabinet over the laboratory, where
he would sometimes even sleep; he was out of spirits, he had grown
very silent, he did not read; it seemed as if he had something on his
mind. Utterson became so used to the unvarying character of these
reports, that he fell off little by little in the frequency of his visits.

INCIDENT AT THE WINDOW.

It chanced on Sunday, when Mr. Utterson was on his usual walk
with Mr. Enfield, that their way lay once again through the by-street;
and that when they came in front of the door, both stopped to gaze
on it.

"Well," said Enfield, "that story's at an end at least. We shall never
see more of Mr. Hyde."

"I hope not," said Utterson. "Did I ever tell you that I once saw
him, and shared your feeling of repulsion?"

"It was impossible to do the one without the other," returned
Enfield. "And by the way what an ass you must have thought me,
not to know that this was a back way to Dr. Jekyll's! It was partly
your own fault that I found it out, even when I did."

"So you found it out, did you?" said Utterson.

"But if that be so, we may step into the court and take a look at
the windows. To tell you the truth, I am uneasy about poor Jekyll;
and even outside, I feel as if the presence of a friend might do him
good."

The court was very cool and a little damp, and full of premature
twilight, although the sky, high up overhead, was still bright with
sunset. The middle one of the three windows was half way open; and
sitting close beside it, taking the air with an infinite sadness of mien,
like some disconsolate prisoner, Utterson saw Dr. Jekyll.

"What! Jekyll!" he cried. "I trust you are better."

"I am very low, Utterson," replied the doctor drearily, "very low. It will not last long, thank God."

"You stay too much indoors," said the lawyer. "You should be out, whipping up the circulation like Mr. Enfield and me. (This is my cousin—Mr. Enfield—Dr. Jekyll.) Come now; get your hat and take a quick turn with us."

"You are very good," sighed the other. "I should like to very much; but no, no, no, it is quite impossible; I dare not. But indeed, Utterson, I am very glad to see you; this is really a great pleasure; I would ask you and Mr. Enfield up, but the place is really not fit."

"Why then," said the lawyer, good-naturedly, "the best thing we can do is to stay down here and speak with you from where we are."

"That is just what I was about to venture to propose," returned the doctor with a smile. But the words were hardly uttered, before the smile was struck out of his face and succeeded by an expression of such abject terror and despair, as froze the very blood of the two gentlemen below. They saw it but for a glimpse, for the window was instantly thrust down; but that glimpse had been sufficient, and they turned and left the court without a word. In silence, too, they traversed the by-street; and it was not until they had come into a neighbouring thoroughfare, where even upon a Sunday there were still some stirrings of life, that Mr. Utterson at last turned and looked at his companion. They were both pale; and there was an answering horror in their eyes.

"God forgive us, God forgive us," said Mr. Utterson.

But Mr. Enfield only nodded his head very seriously, and walked on once more in silence.

THE LAST NIGHT.

Mr. Utterson was sitting by his fireside one evening after dinner, when he was surprised to receive a visit from Poole.

"Bless me, Poole, what brings you here?" he cried; and then taking a second look at him, "What ails you?" he added, "is the doctor ill?"

"Mr. Utterson," said the man, "there is something wrong."

"Take a seat, and here is a glass of wine for you," said the lawyer. "Now, take your time, and tell me plainly what you want."

"You know the doctor's ways, sir," replied Poole, "and how he shuts himself up. Well, he's shut up again in the cabinet; and I don't like it, sir—I wish I may die if I like it. Mr. Utterson, sir, I'm afraid."

"Now, my good man," said the lawyer, "be explicit. What are you afraid of?"

"I've been afraid for about a week," returned Poole, doggedly disregarding the question, "and I can bear it no more."

The man's appearance amply bore out his words; his manner was altered for the worse; and except for the moment when he had first announced his terror, he had not once looked the lawyer in the face. Even now, he sat with the glass of wine untasted on his knee, and his eyes directed to a corner of the floor. "I can bear it no more," he repeated.

"Come," said the lawyer, "I see you have some good reason, Poole; I see there is something seriously amiss. Try to tell me what it is."

"I think there's been foul play," said Poole, hoarsely.

"Foul play!" cried the lawyer, a good deal frightened and rather inclined to be irritated in consequence. "What foul play? What does the man mean?"

"I daren't say, sir," was the answer; "but will you come along with me and see for yourself?"

Mr. Utterson's only answer was to rise and get his hat and great coat; but he observed with wonder the greatness of the relief that appeared upon the butler's face, and perhaps with no less, that the wine was still untasted when he set it down to follow.

It was a wild, cold, seasonable night of March, with a pale moon, lying on her back as though the wind had tilted her, and a flying wrack of the most diaphanous and lawny[1] texture. The wind made talking difficult, and flecked the blood into the face. It seemed to have swept the streets unusually bare of passengers, besides; for Mr. Utterson thought he had never seen that part of London so deserted. He could have wished it otherwise; never in his life had he been conscious of so sharp a wish to see and touch his fellow-creatures; for struggle as he might, there was borne in upon his mind a crushing anticipation of calamity. The square, when they got there, was all full of wind and dust, and the thin trees in the garden were lashing themselves along the railing. Poole, who had kept all the way a pace or two ahead, now pulled up in the middle of the pavement, and in spite of the biting weather, took off his hat and mopped his brow with a red pocket-handkerchief. But for all the hurry of his coming, these were not the dews of exertion that he wiped away, but the moisture of some strangling anguish; for his face was white and his voice, when he spoke, harsh and broken.

"Well, sir," he said, "here we are, and God grant there be nothing wrong."

"Amen, Poole," said the lawyer.

Thereupon the servant knocked in a very guarded manner; the door was opened on the chain; and a voice asked from within, "Is that you, Poole?"

"It's all right," said Poole. "Open the door."

---

1. Wrack: a layer or mound of clouds pushed by the wind; lawny: characteristic of the thin, fine-spun fabric known as lawn.

The hall, when they entered it, was brightly lighted up; the fire was built high; and about the hearth the whole of the servants, men and women, stood huddled together like a flock of sheep. At the sight of Mr. Utterson, the housemaid broke into hysterical whimpering; and the cook, crying out "Bless God! it's Mr. Utterson," ran forward as if to take him in her arms.

"What, what? Are you all here?" said the lawyer peevishly. "Very irregular, very unseemly; your master would be far from pleased."

"They're all afraid," said Poole.

Blank silence followed, no one protesting; only the maid lifted up her voice and now wept loudly.

"Hold your tongue!" Poole said to her, with a ferocity of accent that testified to his own jangled nerves; and indeed, when the girl had so suddenly raised the note of her lamentation, they had all started and turned towards the inner door with faces of dreadful expectation. "And now," continued the butler, addressing the knife-boy, "reach me a candle, and we'll get this through hands[2] at once." And then he begged Mr. Utterson to follow him, and led the way to the back garden.

"Now, sir," said he, "you come as gently as you can. I want you to hear, and I don't want you to be heard. And see here, sir, if by any chance he was to ask you in, don't go."

Mr. Utterson's nerves, at this unlooked-for termination, gave a jerk that nearly threw him from his balance; but he recollected his courage and followed the butler into the laboratory building and through the surgical theatre, with its lumber[3] of crates and bottles, to the foot of the stair. Here Poole motioned him to stand on one side and listen; while he himself, setting down the candle and making a great and obvious call on his resolution, mounted the steps and knocked with a somewhat uncertain hand on the red baize of the cabinet door.

"Mr. Utterson, sir, asking to see you," he called; and even as he did so, once more violently signed to the lawyer to give ear.

A voice answered from within: "Tell him I cannot see anyone," it said complainingly.

"Thank you, sir," said Poole, with a note of something like triumph in his voice; and taking up his candle, he led Mr. Utterson back across the yard and into the great kitchen, where the fire was out and the beetles were leaping on the floor.

"Sir," he said, looking Mr. Utterson in the eyes, "was that my master's voice?"

"It seems much changed," replied the lawyer, very pale, but giving look for look.

"Changed? Well, yes, I think so," said the butler. "Have I been

2. Disposed of.
3. A burdensome accumulation of stored or out-of-use materials.

twenty years in this man's house, to be deceived about his voice? No, sir; master's made away with; he was made away with, eight days ago, when we heard him cry out upon the name of God; and *who's* in there instead of him, and *why* it stays there, is a thing that cries to Heaven, Mr. Utterson!"

"This is a very strange tale, Poole; this is rather a wild tale, my man," said Mr. Utterson, biting his finger. "Suppose it were as you suppose, supposing Dr. Jekyll to have been—well, murdered, what could induce the murderer to stay? That won't hold water; it doesn't commend itself to reason."

"Well, Mr. Utterson, you are a hard man to satisfy, but I'll do it yet," said Poole. "All this last week (you must know) him, or it, or whatever it is that lives in that cabinet, has been crying night and day for some sort of medicine and cannot get it to his mind.[4] It was sometimes his way—the master's, that is—to write his orders on a sheet of paper and throw it on the stair. We've had nothing else this week back; nothing but papers, and a closed door, and the very meals left there to be smuggled in when nobody was looking. Well, sir, every day, ay, and twice and thrice in the same day, there have been orders and complaints, and I have been sent flying to all the whole-sale chemists in town. Every time I brought the stuff back, there would be another paper telling me to return it, because it was not pure, and another order to a different firm. This drug is wanted bitter bad, sir, whatever for."

"Have you any of these papers?" asked Mr. Utterson.

Poole felt in his pocket and handed out a crumpled note, which the lawyer, bending nearer to the candle, carefully examined. Its contents ran thus: "Dr. Jekyll presents his compliments to Messrs. Maw. He assures them that their last sample is impure and quite useless for his present purpose. In the year 18—, Dr. J. purchased a somewhat large quantity from Messrs. M. He now begs them to search with the most sedulous care, and should any of the same quality be left, to forward it to him at once. Expense is no consideration. The importance of this to Dr. J. can hardly be exaggerated." So far the letter had run composedly enough, but here with a sudden splutter of the pen, the writer's emotion had broken loose. "For God's sake," he had added, "find me some of the old."

"This is a strange note," said Mr. Utterson; and then sharply, "How do you come to have it open?"

"The man at Maw's was main[5] angry, sir, and he threw it back to me like so much dirt," returned Poole.

"This is unquestionably the doctor's hand, do you know?" resumed the lawyer.

4. To his liking.
5. Exceedingly (working-class dialect).

"I thought it looked like it," said the servant rather sulkily; and then, with another voice, "But what matters hand of write," he said. "I've seen him!"

"Seen him?" repeated Mr. Utterson. "Well?"

"That's it!" said Poole. "It was this way. I came suddenly into the theatre from the garden. It seems he had slipped out to look for this drug or whatever it is; for the cabinet door was open, and there he was at the far end of the room digging among the crates. He looked up when I came in, gave a kind of cry, and whipped upstairs into the cabinet. It was but for one minute that I saw him, but the hair stood upon my head like quills. Sir, if that was my master, why had he a mask upon his face? If it was my master, why did he cry out like a rat, and run from me? I have served him long enough. And then . . ." the man paused and passed his hand over his face.

"These are all very strange circumstances," said Mr. Utterson, "but I think I begin to see daylight. Your master, Poole, is plainly seized with one of those maladies that both torture and deform the sufferer; hence, for aught I know, the alteration of his voice; hence the mask and his avoidance of his friends; hence his eagerness to find this drug, by means of which the poor soul retains some hope of ultimate recovery—God grant that he be not deceived! There is my explanation; it is sad enough, Poole, ay, and appalling to consider; but it is plain and natural, hangs well together and delivers us from all exorbitant alarms."

"Sir," said the butler, turning to a sort of mottled pallor, "that thing was not my master, and there's the truth. My master"—here he looked round him and began to whisper—"is a tall fine build of a man, and this was more of a dwarf." Utterson attempted to protest. "O, sir," cried Poole, "do you think I do not know my master after twenty years? do you think I do not know where his head comes to in the cabinet door, where I saw him every morning of my life? No, sir, that thing in the mask was never Dr. Jekyll—God knows what it was, but it was never Dr. Jekyll; and it is the belief of my heart that there was murder done."

"Poole," replied the lawyer, "if you say that, it will become my duty to make certain. Much as I desire to spare your master's feelings, much as I am puzzled by this note which seems to prove him to be still alive, I shall consider it my duty to break in that door."

"Ah, Mr. Utterson, that's talking!" cried the butler.

"And now comes the second question," resumed Utterson: "Who is going to do it?"

"Why, you and me, sir," was the undaunted reply.

"That is very well said," returned the lawyer; "and whatever comes of it, I shall make it my business to see you are no loser."

"There is an axe in the theatre," continued Poole, "and you might take the kitchen poker for yourself."

The lawyer took that rude but weighty instrument into his hand, and balanced it. "Do you know, Poole," he said, looking up, "that you and I are about to place ourselves in a position of some peril?"

"You may say so, sir, indeed," returned the butler.

"It is well, then, that we should be frank," said the other. "We both think more than we have said; let us make a clean breast. This masked figure that you saw, did you recognise it?"

"Well, sir, it went so quick, and the creature was so doubled up, that I could hardly swear to that," was the answer. "But if you mean, was it Mr. Hyde?—why, yes, I think it was! You see, it was much of the same bigness; and it had the same quick light way with it; and then who else could have got in by the laboratory door? You have not forgot, sir, that at the time of the murder he had still the key with him? But that's not all. I don't know, Mr. Utterson, if ever you met this Mr. Hyde?"

"Yes," said the lawyer, "I once spoke with him."

"Then you must know as well as the rest of us that there was something queer about that gentleman—something that gave a man a turn—I don't know rightly how to say it, sir, beyond this: that you felt it in your marrow kind of cold and thin."

"I own I felt something of what you describe," said Mr. Utterson.

"Quite so, sir," returned Poole. "Well, when that masked thing like a monkey jumped from among the chemicals and whipped into the cabinet, it went down my spine like ice. O, I know it's not evidence, Mr. Utterson; I'm book-learned enough for that; but a man has his feelings, and I give you my bible-word it was Mr. Hyde!"

"Ay, ay," said the lawyer. "My fears incline to the same point. Evil, I fear, founded—evil was sure to come—of that connection. Ay, truly, I believe you; I believe poor Harry is killed; and I believe his murderer (for what purpose, God alone can tell) is still lurking in his victim's room. Well, let our name be vengeance. Call Bradshaw."

The footman came at the summons, very white and nervous.

"Pull yourself together, Bradshaw," said the lawyer. "This suspense, I know, is telling upon all of you; but it is now our intention to make an end of it. Poole, here, and I are going to force our way into the cabinet. If all is well, my shoulders are broad enough to bear the blame. Meanwhile, lest anything should really be amiss, or any malefactor seek to escape by the back, you and the boy must go round the corner with a pair of good sticks, and take your post at the laboratory door. We give you ten minutes, to get to your stations."

As Bradshaw left, the lawyer looked at his watch. "And now, Poole, let us get to ours," he said; and taking the poker under his arm, he led the way into the yard. The scud[6] had banked over the moon, and it was now quite dark. The wind, which only broke in puffs and draughts into that deep well of building, tossed the light of the candle to and fro about their steps, until they came into the shelter of the theatre, where they sat down silently to wait. London hummed solemnly all around; but nearer at hand, the stillness was only broken by the sound of a footfall moving to and fro along the cabinet floor.

"So it will walk all day, sir," whispered Poole; "ay, and the better part of the night. Only when a new sample comes from the chemist, there's a bit of a break. Ah, it's an ill-conscience that's such an enemy to rest! Ah, sir, there's blood foully shed in every step of it! But hark again, a little closer—put your heart in your ears, Mr. Utterson, and tell me, is that the doctor's foot?"

The steps fell lightly and oddly, with a certain swing, for all they went so slowly; it was different indeed from the heavy creaking tread of Henry Jekyll. Utterson sighed. "Is there never anything else?" he asked.

Poole nodded. "Once," he said. "Once I heard it weeping!"

"Weeping? how that?" said the lawyer, conscious of a sudden chill of horror.

"Weeping like a woman or a lost soul," said the butler. "I came away with that upon my heart, that I could have wept too."

But now the ten minutes drew to an end. Poole disinterred the axe from under a stack of packing straw; the candle was set upon the nearest table to light them to the attack; and they drew near with bated breath to where that patient foot was still going up and down, up and down, in the quiet of the night.

"Jekyll," cried Utterson, with a loud voice, "I demand to see you." He paused a moment, but there came no reply. "I give you fair warning, our suspicions are aroused, and I must and shall see you," he resumed; "if not by fair means, then by foul—if not of your consent, then by brute force!"

"Utterson," said the voice, "for God's sake, have mercy!"

"Ah, that's not Jekyll's voice—it's Hyde's!" cried Utterson. "Down with the door, Poole."

Poole swung the axe over his shoulder; the blow shook the building, and the red baize door leaped against the lock and hinges. A dismal screech, as of mere animal terror, rang from the cabinet. Up went the axe again, and again the panels crashed and the frame bounded; four times the blow fell; but the wood was tough and the fittings were of excellent workmanship; and it was not until the fifth, that the lock burst in sunder and the wreck of the door fell inwards on the carpet.

6. Wind-driven clouds.

The besiegers, appalled by their own riot and the stillness that had succeeded, stood back a little and peered in. There lay the cabinet before their eyes in the quiet lamplight, a good fire glowing and chattering on the hearth, the kettle singing its thin strain, a drawer or two open, papers neatly set forth on the business table, and nearer the fire, the things laid out for tea: the quietest room, you would have said, and, but for the glazed presses full of chemicals, the most commonplace that night in London.

Right in the midst there lay the body of a man sorely contorted and still twitching. They drew near on tiptoe, turned it on its back and beheld the face of Edward Hyde. He was dressed in clothes far too large for him, clothes of the doctor's bigness; the cords of his face still moved with a semblance of life, but life was quite gone; and by the crushed phial in the hand and the strong smell of kernels that hung upon the air, Utterson knew that he was looking on the body of a self-destroyer.[7]

"We have come too late," he said sternly, "whether to save or punish. Hyde is gone to his account; and it only remains for us to find the body of your master."

The far greater proportion of the building was occupied by the theatre, which filled almost the whole ground story and was lighted from above, and by the cabinet, which formed an upper story at one end and looked upon the court. A corridor joined the theatre to the door on the by-street; and with this, the cabinet communicated separately by a second flight of stairs. There were besides a few dark closets and a spacious cellar. All these they now thoroughly examined. Each closet needed but a glance, for all were empty and all, by the dust that fell from their doors, had stood long unopened. The cellar, indeed, was filled with crazy lumber, mostly dating from the times of the surgeon who was Jekyll's predecessor; but even as they opened the door, they were advertised of the uselessness of further search, by the fall of a perfect mat of cobweb which had for years sealed up the entrance. Nowhere was there any trace of Henry Jekyll, dead or alive.

Poole stamped on the flags of the corridor. "He must be buried here," he said, hearkening to the sound.

"Or he may have fled," said Utterson, and he turned to examine the door in the by-street. It was locked; and lying near by on the flags, they found the key, already stained with rust.

"This does not look like use," observed the lawyer.

"Use!" echoed Poole. "Do you not see, sir, it is broken? much as if a man had stamped on it."

"Ay," continued Utterson, "and the fractures, too, are rusty." The

7. Cyanide, an extremely fast-acting poison, has a characteristic smell of bitter almond kernels.

two men looked at each other with a scare. "This is beyond me, Poole," said the lawyer. "Let us go back to the cabinet."

They mounted the stair in silence, and still with an occasional awestruck glance at the dead body, proceeded more thoroughly to examine the contents of the cabinet. At one table, there were traces of chemical work, various measured heaps of some white salt being laid on glass saucers, as though for an experiment in which the unhappy man had been prevented.

"That is the same drug that I was always bringing him," said Poole; and even as he spoke, the kettle with a startling noise boiled over.

This brought them to the fireside, where the easy chair was drawn cosily up, and the tea things stood ready to the sitter's elbow, the very sugar in the cup. There were several books on a shelf; one lay beside the tea things open, and Utterson was amazed to find it a copy of a pious work, for which Jekyll had several times expressed a great esteem, annotated, in his own hand, with startling blasphemies.

Next, in the course of their review of the chamber, the searchers came to the cheval glass, into whose depths they looked with an involuntary horror. But it was so turned as to show them nothing but the rosy glow playing on the roof, the fire sparkling in a hundred repetitions along the glazed front of the presses, and their own pale and fearful countenances stooping to look in.

"This glass have seen some strange things, sir," whispered Poole.

"And surely none stranger than itself," echoed the lawyer in the same tones. "For what did Jekyll"—he caught himself up at the word with a start, and then conquering the weakness: "what could Jekyll want with it?" he said.

"You may say that!" said Poole.

Next they turned to the business table. On the desk among the neat array of papers, a large envelope was uppermost, and bore, in the doctor's hand, the name of Mr. Utterson. The lawyer unsealed it, and several enclosures fell to the floor. The first was a will, drawn in the same eccentric terms as the one which he had returned six months before, to serve as a testament in case of death and as a deed of gift in case of disappearance; but in place of the name of Edward Hyde, the lawyer, with indescribable amazement, read the name of Gabriel John Utterson. He looked at Poole, and then back at the paper, and last of all at the dead malefactor stretched upon the carpet.

"My head goes round," he said. "He has been all these days in possession; he had no cause to like me; he must have raged to see himself displaced; and he has not destroyed this document."

He caught up the next paper; it was a brief note in the doctor's hand and dated at the top. "O Poole!" the lawyer cried, "he was alive and here this day. He cannot have been disposed of in so short a space, he must be still alive, he must have fled! And then, why fled? and how? and in that case, can we venture to declare this suicide? O, we must be careful. I foresee that we may yet involve your master in some dire catastrophe."

"Why don't you read it, sir?" asked Poole.

"Because I fear," replied the lawyer solemnly. "God grant I have no cause for it!" And with that he brought the paper to his eyes and read as follows.

"My dear Utterson,—When this shall fall into your hands, I shall have disappeared, under what circumstances I have not the penetration to foresee, but my instinct and all the circumstances of my nameless situation tell me that the end is sure and must be early. Go then, and first read the narrative which Lanyon warned me he was to place in your hands; and if you care to hear more, turn to the confession of

"Your unworthy and unhappy friend,

"HENRY JEKYLL."

"There was a third enclosure?" asked Utterson.

"Here, sir," said Poole, and gave into his hands a considerable packet sealed in several places.

The lawyer put it in his pocket. "I would say nothing of this paper. If your master has fled or is dead, we may at least save his credit.[8] It is now ten; I must go home and read these documents in quiet; but I shall be back before midnight, when we shall send for the police."

They went out, locking the door of the theatre behind them; and Utterson, once more leaving the servants gathered about the fire in the hall, trudged back to his office to read the two narratives in which this mystery was now to be explained.

DR. LANYON'S NARRATIVE.

On the ninth of January, now four days ago, I received by the evening delivery a registered envelope, addressed in the hand of my colleague and old school-companion, Henry Jekyll. I was a good deal surprised by this; for we were by no means in the habit of correspondence; I had seen the man, dined with him, indeed, the night before; and I could imagine nothing in our intercourse that should justify the formality of registration. The contents increased my wonder; for this is how the letter ran:

10th December, 18—[1]

"Dear Lanyon,—You are one of my oldest friends; and although

---

8. I.e., reputation, good name.
1. This letter should be dated 9th January, 18—, judging not only by Lanyon's opening mention of having received the letter late on January 9 after seeing Jekyll the night before,

we may have differed at times on scientific questions, I cannot remember, at least on my side, any break in our affection. There was never a day when, if you had said to me, 'Jekyll, my life, my honour, my reason, depend upon you,' I would not have sacrificed my fortune or my left hand to help you. Lanyon, my life, my honour, my reason, are all at your mercy; if you fail me to-night, I am lost. You might suppose, after this preface, that I am going to ask you for something dishonourable to grant. Judge for yourself.

"I want you to postpone all other engagements for to-night—ay, even if you were summoned to the bedside of an emperor; to take a cab, unless your carriage should be actually at the door; and with this letter in your hand for consultation, to drive straight to my house. Poole, my butler, has his orders; you will find him waiting your arrival with a locksmith. The door of my cabinet is then to be forced; you are to go in alone; to open the glazed press (letter E) on the left hand, breaking the lock if it be shut; and to draw out, *with all its contents as they stand*, the fourth drawer from the top or (which is the same thing) the third from the bottom. In my extreme distress of mind, I have a morbid fear of misdirecting you; but even if I am in error, you may know the right drawer by its contents: some powders, a phial and a paper book. This drawer I beg of you to carry back with you to Cavendish Square exactly as it stands.

"That is the first part of the service: now for the second. You should be back, if you set out at once on the receipt of this, long before midnight; but I will leave you that amount of margin, not only in the fear of one of those obstacles that can neither be prevented nor foreseen, but because an hour when your servants are in bed is to be preferred for what will then remain to do. At midnight, then, I have to ask you to be alone in your consulting room, to admit with your own hand into the house a man who will present himself in my name, and to place in his hands the drawer that you will have brought with you from my cabinet. Then you will have played your part and earned my gratitude completely. Five minutes afterwards, if you insist upon an explanation, you will have understood that these arrangements are of capital importance; and that by the neglect of one of them, fantastic as they must appear, you might have charged your conscience with my death or the shipwreck of my reason.

"Confident as I am that you will not trifle with this appeal, my heart sinks and my hand trembles at the bare thought of such a possibility. Think of me at this hour, in a strange place, labouring under a blackness of distress that no fancy can exaggerate, and yet

---

but also by chronology established elsewhere in the story. Stevenson apparently simply slipped up in putting the December 10 date here, very likely as a result of what he later called the "white-hot haste" in which the story was initially drafted.

well aware that, if you will but punctually serve me, my troubles will roll away like a story that is told.[2] Serve me, my dear Lanyon, and save

"Your friend,

"H. J.

"P.S. I had already sealed this up when a fresh terror struck upon my soul. It is possible that the post office may fail me, and this letter not come into your hands until to-morrow morning. In that case, dear Lanyon, do my errand when it shall be most convenient for you in the course of the day; and once more expect my messenger at midnight. It may then already be too late; and if that night passes without event, you will know that you have seen the last of Henry Jekyll."

Upon the reading of this letter, I made sure[3] my colleague was insane; but till that was proved beyond the possibility of doubt, I felt bound to do as he requested. The less I understood of this farrago, the less I was in a position to judge of its importance; and an appeal so worded could not be set aside without a grave responsibility. I rose accordingly from table, got into a hansom,[4] and drove straight to Jekyll's house. The butler was awaiting my arrival; he had received by the same post as mine a registered letter of instruction, and had sent at once for a locksmith and a carpenter. The tradesmen came while we were yet speaking; and we moved in a body to old Dr. Denman's surgical theatre, from which (as you are doubtless aware) Jekyll's private cabinet is most conveniently entered. The door was very strong, the lock excellent; the carpenter avowed he would have great trouble and have to do much damage, if force were to be used; and the locksmith was near despair. But this last was a handy fellow, and after two hours' work, the door stood open. The press marked E was unlocked; and I took out the drawer, had it filled up with straw and tied in a sheet, and returned with it to Cavendish Square.

Here I proceeded to examine its contents. The powders were neatly enough made up, but not with the nicety of the dispensing chemist; so that it was plain they were of Jekyll's private manufacture; and when I opened one of the wrappers, I found what seemed to me a simple, crystalline salt of a white colour. The phial, to which I next turned my attention, might have been about half-full of a blood-red liquor, which was highly pungent to the sense of smell and seemed to me to contain phosphorus and some volatile ether. At the

2. Echoes but also inverts a biblical passage warning of lifelong moral accountability to God: "For all our days are passed in thy wrath: we spend our years as a tale that is told" (Psalms 90:9).
3. I.e., I felt sure.
4. A two-wheeled horsedrawn cab.

other ingredients, I could make no guess. The book was an ordinary version book[5] and contained little but a series of dates. These covered a period of many years, but I observed that the entries ceased nearly a year ago and quite abruptly. Here and there a brief remark was appended to a date, usually no more than a single word: "double" occurring perhaps six times in a total of several hundred entries; and once very early in the list and followed by several marks of exclamation, "total failure!!!" All this, though it whetted my curiosity, told me little that was definite. Here were a phial of some tincture, a paper of some salt, and the record of a series of experiments that had led (like too many of Jekyll's investigations) to no end[6] of practical usefulness. How could the presence of these articles in my house affect either the honour, the sanity, or the life of my flighty colleague? If his messenger could go to one place, why could he not go to another? And even granting some impediment, why was this gentleman to be received by me in secret? The more I reflected, the more convinced I grew that I was dealing with a case of cerebral disease; and though I dismissed my servants to bed, I loaded an old revolver that I might be found in some posture of self-defence.

Twelve o'clock had scarce rung out over London, ere the knocker sounded very gently on the door. I went myself at the summons, and found a small man crouching against the pillars of the portico.

"Are you come from Dr. Jekyll?" I asked.

He told me "yes" by a constrained gesture; and when I had bidden him enter, he did not obey me without a searching backward glance into the darkness of the square. There was a policeman not far off, advancing with his bull's eye open;[7] and at the sight, I thought my visitor started and made greater haste.

These particulars struck me, I confess, disagreeably; and as I followed him into the bright light of the consulting room, I kept my hand ready on my weapon. Here, at last, I had a chance of clearly seeing him. I had never set eyes on him before, so much was certain. He was small, as I have said; I was struck besides with the shocking expression of his face, with his remarkable combination of great muscular activity and great apparent debility of constitution, and—last but not least—with the odd, subjective disturbance caused by his neighbourhood.[8] This bore some resemblance to incipient rigor,[9] and was accompanied by a marked sinking of the pulse. At the time, I set it down to some idiosyncratic, personal distaste, and merely won-

---

5. A blank notebook designed for the school exercise of doing "versions," i.e., language translations (Scottish usage).
6. No outcome.
7. I.e., the sliding door of his lantern open (to emit light).
8. I.e., the odd disturbance within the perceiver caused by Hyde's physical nearness.
9. A medical term for a sudden chill or shivering; may also suggest *rigor mortis*, the stiffening of the body following death.

dered at the acuteness of the symptoms; but I have since had reason to believe the cause to lie much deeper in the nature of man, and to turn on some nobler hinge than the principle of hatred.

This person (who had thus, from the first moment of his entrance, struck in me what I can only describe as a disgustful curiosity) was dressed in a fashion that would have made an ordinary person laughable: his clothes, that is to say, although they were of rich and sober fabric, were enormously too large for him in every measurement— the trousers hanging on his legs and rolled up to keep them from the ground, the waist of the coat below his haunches, and the collar sprawling wide upon his shoulders. Strange to relate, this ludicrous accoutrement was far from moving me to laughter. Rather, as there was something abnormal and misbegotten in the very essence of the creature that now faced me—something seizing, surprising and revolting—this fresh disparity seemed but to fit in with and to reinforce it; so that to my interest in the man's nature and character, there was added a curiosity as to his origin, his life, his fortune and status in the world.

These observations, though they have taken so great a space to be set down in, were yet the work of a few seconds. My visitor was, indeed, on fire with sombre excitement.

"Have you got it?" he cried. "Have you got it?" And so lively was his impatience that he even laid his hand upon my arm and sought to shake me.

I put him back, conscious at his touch of a certain icy pang along my blood. "Come, sir," said I. "You forget that I have not yet the pleasure of your acquaintance. Be seated, if you please." And I showed him an example, and sat down myself in my customary seat and with as fair an imitation of my ordinary manner to a patient, as the lateness of the hour, the nature of my preoccupations, and the horror I had of my visitor, would suffer me to muster.

"I beg your pardon, Dr. Lanyon," he replied civilly enough. "What you say is very well founded; and my impatience has shown its heels to my politeness. I come here at the instance of your colleague, Dr. Henry Jekyll, on a piece of business of some moment; and I understood . . ." he paused and put his hand to his throat, and I could see, in spite of his collected manner, that he was wrestling against the approaches of the hysteria[1]—"I understood, a drawer . . ."

But here I took pity on my visitor's suspense, and some perhaps on my own growing curiosity.

"There it is, sir," said I, pointing to the drawer, where it lay on the

---

1. Hysteria was thought to rise to the throat in a ball of emotion. (Greek medical theory held that such manifestations of nervous excitement were a female ailment arising from a disorder of the womb, the Greek word for which is *hystera*. Victorian medicine regarded hysteria as primarily but not exclusively associated with women.)

floor behind a table and still covered with the sheet.

He sprang to it, and then paused, and laid his hand upon his heart; I could hear his teeth grate with the convulsive action of his jaws; and his face was so ghastly to see that I grew alarmed both for his life and reason.

"Compose yourself," said I.

He turned a dreadful smile to me, and as if with the decision of despair, plucked away the sheet. At sight of the contents, he uttered one loud sob of such immense relief that I sat petrified. And the next moment, in a voice that was already fairly well under control, "Have you a graduated glass?" he asked.

I rose from my place with something of an effort and gave him what he asked.

He thanked me with a smiling nod, measured out a few minims of the red tincture and added one of the powders. The mixture, which was at first of a reddish hue, began, in proportion as the crystals melted, to brighten in colour, to effervesce audibly, and to throw off small fumes of vapour. Suddenly and at the same moment, the ebullition ceased and the compound changed to a dark purple, which faded again more slowly to a watery green. My visitor, who had watched these metamorphoses with a keen eye, smiled, set down the glass upon the table, and then turned and looked upon me with an air of scrutiny.

"And now," said he, "to settle what remains. Will you be wise? will you be guided? will you suffer me to take this glass in my hand and to go forth from your house without further parley? or has the greed of curiosity too much command of you? Think before you answer, for it shall be done as you decide. As you decide, you shall be left as you were before, and neither richer nor wiser, unless the sense of service rendered to a man in mortal distress may be counted as a kind of riches of the soul. Or, if you shall so prefer to choose, a new province of knowledge and new avenues to fame and power shall be laid open to you, here, in this room, upon the instant; and your sight shall be blasted by a prodigy to stagger the unbelief of Satan."[2]

"Sir," said I, affecting a coolness that I was far from truly possessing, "you speak enigmas, and you will perhaps not wonder that I hear you with no very strong impression of belief. But I have gone too far in the way of inexplicable services to pause before I see the end."

"It is well," replied my visitor. "Lanyon, you remember your vows: what follows is under the seal of our profession.[3] And now, you who

---

2. I.e., a marvel to stun the godlessness of Satan.
3. The Hippocratic oath sworn by doctors at the time includes a vow of silence on "what I may see or hear in the course of the treatment or even outside of the treatment in regard to the life of men, which on no account one must spread abroad" (trans. Ludwig Edelstein, *The Hippocratic Oath* [Baltimore: The Johns Hopkins Press, 1943], p. 3).

have so long been bound to the most narrow and material views, you who have denied the virtue of transcendental medicine, you who have derided your superiors—behold!"

He put the glass to his lips and drank at one gulp. A cry followed; he reeled, staggered, clutched at the table and held on, staring with injected[4] eyes, gasping with open mouth; and as I looked there came, I thought, a change—he seemed to swell—his face became suddenly black and the features seemed to melt and alter—and the next moment, I had sprung to my feet and leaped back against the wall, my arm raised to shield me from that prodigy, my mind submerged in terror.

"O God!" I screamed, and "O God!" again and again; for there before my eyes—pale and shaken, and half fainting, and groping before him with his hands, like a man restored from death—there stood Henry Jekyll!

What he told me in the next hour, I cannot bring my mind to set on paper. I saw what I saw, I heard what I heard, and my soul sickened at it; and yet now when that sight has faded from my eyes, I ask myself if I believe it, and I cannot answer. My life is shaken to its roots; sleep has left me; the deadliest terror sits by me at all hours of the day and night; I feel that my days are numbered, and that I must die; and yet I shall die incredulous. As for the moral turpitude that man unveiled to me, even with tears of penitence, I cannot, even in memory, dwell on it without a start of horror. I will say but one thing, Utterson, and that (if you can bring your mind to credit it) will be more than enough. The creature who crept into my house that night was, on Jekyll's own confession, known by the name of Hyde and hunted for in every corner of the land as the murderer of Carew.

HASTIE LANYON.

HENRY JEKYLL'S FULL STATEMENT OF THE CASE.

I was born in the year 18— to a large fortune, endowed besides with excellent parts,[1] inclined by nature to industry, fond of the respect of the wise and good among my fellow-men, and thus, as might have been supposed, with every guarantee of an honourable and distinguished future. And indeed the worst of my faults was a certain impatient gaiety of disposition,[2] such as has made the happiness of

---

4. Swollen.
1. Abilities.
2. Victorian usages of "gay" do not shed much light on this vague phrase. "Gay" had not yet taken on what would later become its central slang association with homosexuality, but according to the OED, it could have either the straightforward meaning of "light-hearted, exuberantly cheerful, merry" or the sardonic sense of "addicted to social pleasures and dissipations" (with a slang application to a woman of "living by prostitution"). Even sup-

many, but such as I found it hard to reconcile with my imperious desire to carry my head high, and wear a more than commonly grave countenance before the public. Hence it came about that I concealed my pleasures; and that when I reached years of reflection, and began to look round me and take stock of my progress and position in the world, I stood already committed to a profound duplicity of life. Many a man would have even blazoned such irregularities as I was guilty of; but from the high views that I had set before me, I regarded and hid them with an almost morbid sense of shame. It was thus rather the exacting nature of my aspirations than any particular degradation in my faults, that made me what I was and, with even a deeper trench than in the majority of men, severed in me those provinces of good and ill which divide and compound man's dual nature. In this case, I was driven to reflect deeply and inveterately on that hard law of life,[3] which lies at the root of religion and is one of the most plentiful springs of distress. Though so profound a double-dealer, I was in no sense a hypocrite;[4] both sides of me were in dead earnest; I was no more myself when I laid aside restraint and plunged in shame, than when I laboured, in the eye of day, at the furtherance of knowledge or the relief of sorrow and suffering. And it chanced that the direction of my scientific studies, which led wholly towards the mystic and the transcendental, reacted and shed a strong light on this consciousness of the perennial war among my members.[5] With every day, and from both sides of my intelligence, the moral and the intellectual, I thus drew steadily nearer to that truth, by whose partial discovery I have been doomed to such a dreadful shipwreck: that man is not truly one, but truly two. I say two, because the state of my own knowledge does not pass beyond that point. Others will follow, others will outstrip me on the same lines; and I hazard the guess that man will be ultimately known for a mere polity of multifarious, incongruous and independent denizens. I for my part, from the nature of my life, advanced infallibly in one direction and in one direction only. It was on the moral side,

posing a relatively innocent meaning, however, Jekyll's categorization of his "impatient gaiety of disposition" as a "fault" needs to be understood in light of the Evangelical cast of Victorian Christianity, with its call for renunciation of soul-endangering levity in favor of self-disciplined moral earnestness.

3. Presumably the "law" which ordains that desires of the soul will often be pitted against desires of the body.

4. Jekyll may be straining the bounds of common word usage in claiming that someone who genuinely *desires* virtue is not a hypocrite, even if he pretends to a higher *level* of virtue than he really possesses. Compare Stevenson's language about Jekyll in his November 1887 letter to John Paul Bocock (excerpted on pp. 86–87 of this edition).

5. Conflict among parts of the self, especially between body and spirit. The phrase echoes James 4:1, "From whence come wars and fightings among you? come they not hence, even of your lusts that war in your members?" and, less directly, Romans 7:22–23, "For I delight in the law of God after the inward man: But I see another law in my members, warring against the law of my mind, and bringing me into captivity to the law of sin which is in my members."

and in my own person, that I learned to recognise the thorough and primitive duality of man; I saw that, of the two natures that contended in the field of my consciousness, even if I could rightly be said to be either, it was only because I was radically both; and from an early date, even before the course of my scientific discoveries had begun to suggest the most naked possibility of such a miracle, I had learned to dwell with pleasure, as a beloved daydream, on the thought of the separation of these elements. If each, I told myself, could but be housed in separate identities, life would be relieved of all that was unbearable; the unjust might go his way, delivered from the aspirations and remorse of his more upright twin; and the just could walk steadfastly and securely on his upward path, doing the good things in which he found his pleasure, and no longer exposed to disgrace and penitence by the hands of this extraneous evil.[6] It was the curse of mankind that these incongruous faggots[7] were thus bound together—that in the agonised womb of consciousness, these polar twins should be continuously struggling. How, then, were they dissociated?[8]

I was so far in my reflections when, as I have said, a side light began to shine upon the subject from the laboratory table. I began to perceive more deeply than it has ever yet been stated, the trembling immateriality, the mist-like transience, of this seemingly so solid body in which we walk attired. Certain agents I found to have the power to shake and to pluck back that fleshly vestment, even as a wind might toss the curtains of a pavilion.[9] For two good reasons, I will not enter deeply into this scientific branch of my confession. First, because I have been made to learn that the doom and burthen of our life is bound forever on man's shoulders, and when the attempt is made to cast it off, it but returns upon us with more unfamiliar and more awful pressure. Second, because as my narrative will make alas! too evident, my discoveries were incomplete. Enough, then, that I not only recognised my natural body for the mere aura and effulgence of certain of the powers that made up my spirit, but managed to compound a drug by which these powers should be dethroned from their supremacy, and a second form and countenance substituted, none the less natural to me because they

6. I.e., this alien evil. Various influences have been suggested for Stevenson's interest in the mental condition which divorces the sinful from the virtuous self. Among them are the biblical text of Romans (e.g., 7:20, "Now if I do that I would not, it is no more I that do it, but sin that dwelleth in me"); the Edinburgh legend of Deacon Brodie (1741–88, master craftsman by day and burglar by night); and James Hogg's novel, *The Private Memoirs and Confessions of a Justified Sinner* (1824), in which a young Scotch Calvinist puffed up by a conviction of being among the Elect falls under the spell of a double whom he fails to recognize as the devil.
7. A faggot is a collection of twigs or sticks bundled together for use as fuel; or, figuratively, a collection of things not forming any genuine unity.
8. I.e., How, then, were they to be dissociated?
9. A large, often stately tent.

were the expression, and bore the stamp, of lower elements in my soul.

I hesitated long before I put this theory to the test of practice. I knew well that I risked death; for any drug that so potently controlled and shook the very fortress of identity, might by the least scruple of an overdose or at the least inopportunity in the moment of exhibition, utterly blot out that immaterial tabernacle[1] which I looked to it to change. But the temptation of a discovery so singular and profound, at last overcame the suggestions of alarm. I had long since prepared my tincture; I purchased at once, from a firm of wholesale chemists, a large quantity of a particular salt which I knew, from my experiments, to be the last ingredient required; and late one accursed night, I compounded the elements, watched them boil and smoke together in the glass, and when the ebullition had subsided, with a strong glow of courage, drank off the potion.

The most racking pangs succeeded: a grinding in the bones, deadly nausea, and a horror of the spirit that cannot be exceeded at the hour of birth or death. Then these agonies began swiftly to subside, and I came to myself as if out of a great sickness. There was something strange in my sensations, something indescribably new and, from its very novelty, incredibly sweet. I felt younger, lighter, happier in body; within I was conscious of a heady recklessness, a current of disordered sensual images running like a mill race in my fancy, a solution[2] of the bonds of obligation, an unknown but not an innocent freedom of the soul. I knew myself, at the first breath of this new life, to be more wicked, tenfold more wicked, sold a slave to my original evil; and the thought, in that moment, braced and delighted me like wine. I stretched out my hands, exulting in the freshness of these sensations; and in the act, I was suddenly aware that I had lost in stature.

There was no mirror, at that date, in my room; that which stands beside me as I write, was brought there later on and for the very purpose of these transformations. The night, however, was far gone into the morning—the morning, black as it was, was nearly ripe for the conception of the day—the inmates of my house were locked in the most rigorous hours of slumber; and I determined, flushed as I was with hope and triumph, to venture in my new shape as far as to my bedroom. I crossed the yard, wherein the constellations looked down upon me, I could have thought, with wonder, the first creature of that sort that their unsleeping vigilance had yet disclosed to them;

1. Scruple: a very small unit of weight or measurement (20 grams or 1/24th ounce); tabernacle: i.e., the body (a usage found in 2 Corinthians 5:1–4 and 2 Peter 1:13–14, where the body, as a perishable abode for the soul, is likened to the "tabernacle," or tent sanctuary, used for religious worship during the Israelite wandering in the wilderness).
2. Mill race: the current of water that drives a mill-wheel; solution: dissolving.

I stole through the corridors, a stranger in my own house; and coming to my room, I saw for the first time the appearance of Edward Hyde.

I must here speak by theory alone, saying not that which I know, but that which I suppose to be most probable. The evil side of my nature, to which I had now transferred the stamping efficacy,[3] was less robust and less developed than the good which I had just deposed. Again, in the course of my life, which had been, after all, nine tenths a life of effort, virtue and control, it had been much less exercised and much less exhausted. And hence, as I think, it came about that Edward Hyde was so much smaller, slighter and younger than Henry Jekyll. Even as good shone upon the countenance of the one, evil was written broadly and plainly on the face of the other. Evil besides (which I must still believe to be the lethal side of man) had left on that body an imprint of deformity and decay. And yet when I looked upon that ugly idol[4] in the glass, I was conscious of no repugnance, rather of a leap of welcome. This, too, was myself. It seemed natural and human. In my eyes it bore a livelier image of the spirit, it seemed more express[5] and single, than the imperfect and divided countenance, I had been hitherto accustomed to call mine. And in so far I was doubtless right. I have observed that when I wore the semblance of Edward Hyde, none could come near to me at first without a visible misgiving of the flesh. This, as I take it, was because all human beings, as we meet them, are commingled out of good and evil: and Edward Hyde, alone in the ranks of mankind, was pure evil.

I lingered but a moment at the mirror: the second and conclusive experiment had yet to be attempted; it yet remained to be seen if I had lost my identity beyond redemption and must flee before daylight from a house that was no longer mine; and hurrying back to my cabinet, I once more prepared and drank the cup, once more suffered the pangs of dissolution, and came to myself once more with the character, the stature and the face of Henry Jekyll.

That night I had come to the fatal cross roads. Had I approached my discovery in a more noble spirit, had I risked the experiment while under the empire of generous or pious aspirations, all must have been otherwise, and from these agonies of death and birth, I had come forth an angel instead of a fiend. The drug had no discriminating action; it was neither diabolical nor divine; it but shook the

---

3. I.e., the shape-giving power.
4. Carries the specialized meaning of "a visible but unsubstantial appearance, an image caused by reflexion as in a mirror" (OED, which quotes this usage by Stevenson), but also suggests the more familiar meaning of an image or representation of a deity, especially as an object of false worship.
5. Truly depicted; exactly resembling.

doors of the prisonhouse of my disposition; and like the captives of Philippi, that which stood within ran forth.[6] At that time my virtue slumbered; my evil, kept awake by ambition, was alert and swift to seize the occasion; and the thing that was projected was Edward Hyde. Hence, although I had now two characters as well as two appearances, one was wholly evil, and the other was still the old Henry Jekyll, that incongruous compound of whose reformation and improvement I had already learned to despair. The movement was thus wholly toward the worse.

Even at that time, I had not yet conquered my aversion to the dryness of a life of study. I would still be merrily disposed at times; and as my pleasures were (to say the least) undignified, and I was not only well known and highly considered, but growing towards the elderly man, this incoherency of my life was daily growing more unwelcome. It was on this side that my new power tempted me until I fell in slavery. I had but to drink the cup, to doff at once the body of the noted professor, and to assume, like a thick cloak, that of Edward Hyde. I smiled at the notion; it seemed to me at the time to be humorous; and I made my preparations with the most studious care. I took and furnished that house in Soho, to which Hyde was tracked by the police; and engaged as housekeeper a creature whom I well knew to be silent and unscrupulous. On the other side, I announced to my servants that a Mr. Hyde (whom I described) was to have full liberty and power about my house in the square; and to parry mishaps, I even called and made myself a familiar object, in my second character. I next drew up that will to which you so much objected; so that if anything befell me in the person of Dr. Jekyll, I could enter on that of Edward Hyde without pecuniary loss. And thus fortified, as I supposed, on every side, I began to profit by the strange immunities of my position.

Men have before hired bravos[7] to transact their crimes, while their own person and reputation sat under shelter. I was the first that ever did so for his pleasures. I was the first that could thus plod in the public eye with a load of genial respectability, and in a moment, like a schoolboy, strip off these lendings[8] and spring headlong into the sea of liberty. But for me, in my impenetrable mantle, the safety was complete. Think of it—I did not even exist! Let me but escape into my laboratory door, give me but a second or two to mix and swallow

---

6. As recounted in Acts 16:26, when God visited an earthquake upon the prison in Philippi where the apostle Paul and his companion Silas were being held captive, "immediately all the doors were opened, and every one's bands were loosed." Paul and Silas, however, rather than fleeing, honorably turned themselves over to their captors.
7. Paid desperadoes or assassins.
8. Something lent, here referring to clothes in an echo of King Lear's line, "Off, off, you lendings!" as he tears off his garments on the heath in a sudden access of fellow-feeling for the naked madman he encounters there (*King Lear*, 3.4.114).

the draught that I had always standing ready; and whatever he had done, Edward Hyde would pass away like the stain of breath upon a mirror; and there in his stead, quietly at home, trimming the midnight lamp in his study, a man who could afford to laugh at suspicion, would be Henry Jekyll.

The pleasures which I made haste to seek in my disguise were, as I have said, undignified; I would scarce use a harder term. But in the hands of Edward Hyde, they soon began to turn towards the monstrous. When I would come back from these excursions, I was often plunged into a kind of wonder at my vicarious depravity. This familiar that I called out of my own soul, and sent forth alone to do his good pleasure,[9] was a being inherently malign and villainous; his every act and thought centered on self; drinking pleasure with bestial avidity from any degree of torture to another; relentless like a man of stone. Henry Jekyll stood at times aghast before the acts of Edward Hyde; but the situation was apart from ordinary laws, and insidiously relaxed the grasp of conscience. It was Hyde, after all, and Hyde alone, that was guilty. Jekyll was no worse; he woke again to his good qualities seemingly unimpaired; he would even make haste, where it was possible, to undo the evil done by Hyde. And thus his conscience slumbered.

Into the details of the infamy at which I thus connived (for even now I can scarce grant that I committed it)[1] I have no design of entering; I mean but to point out the warnings and the successive steps with which my chastisement approached. I met with one accident which, as it brought on no consequence, I shall no more than mention. An act of cruelty to a child aroused against me the anger of a passer by, whom I recognised the other day in the person of your kinsman; the doctor and the child's family joined him; there were moments when I feared for my life; and at last, in order to pacify their too just resentment, Edward Hyde had to bring them to the door, and pay them in a cheque drawn in the name, of Henry Jekyll. But this danger was easily eliminated from the future, by opening an account at another bank in the name of Edward Hyde himself; and when, by sloping my own hand backward, I had supplied my double with a signature, I thought I sat beyond the reach of fate.

Some two months before the murder of Sir Danvers, I had been out for one of my adventures, had returned at a late hour, and woke the next day in bed with somewhat odd sensations. It was in vain I

9. Familiar: a spirit or demon supposed to be in association with or under the power of a particular person; his good pleasure: i.e., pleasure that is satisfying or suitable to him (the phrase occurs frequently in the Bible in reference to God's "good pleasure," e.g., Psalms 51:18, Luke 12:32, Philippians 2:13).
1. This parenthesis makes more sense in light of what the OED defines as the ordinary meaning at the time of "connive": "to shut one's eyes to an action that one ought to oppose, but which one covertly sympathizes with; to wink at, be secretly privy or accessory."

looked about me; in vain I saw the decent furniture and tall propor-
tions of my room in the square; in vain that I recognised the pattern
of the bed curtains and the design of the mahogany frame; something
still kept insisting that I was not where I was, that I had not wakened
where I seemed to be, but in the little room in Soho where I was
accustomed to sleep in the body of Edward Hyde. I smiled to myself,
and, in my psychological way, began lazily to inquire into the elements of this illusion, occasionally, even as I did so, dropping back
into a comfortable morning doze. I was still so engaged when, in one
of my more wakeful moments, my eye fell upon my hand. Now the
hand of Henry Jekyll (as you have often remarked) was professional
in shape and size: it was large, firm, white and comely. But the hand
which I now saw, clearly enough, in the yellow light of a mid-London
morning, lying half shut on the bed clothes, was lean, corded,
knuckly, of a dusky pallor and thickly shaded with a swart[2] growth
of hair. It was the hand of Edward Hyde.

I must have stared upon it for near half a minute, sunk as I was
in the mere stupidity of wonder, before terror woke up in my breast
as sudden and startling as the crash of cymbals; and bounding from
my bed, I rushed to the mirror. At the sight that met my eyes, my
blood was changed into something exquisitely thin and icy. Yes, I
had gone to bed Henry Jekyll, I had awakened Edward Hyde. How
was this to be explained? I asked myself; and then, with another
bound of terror—how was it to be remedied? It was well on in the
morning; the servants were up; all my drugs were in the cabinet—a
long journey, down two pair of stairs, through the back passage,
across the open court and through the anatomical theatre, from
where I was then standing horror-struck. It might indeed be possible
to cover my face; but of what use was that, when I was unable to
conceal the alteration in my stature? And then with an overpowering
sweetness of relief, it came back upon my mind that the servants
were already used to the coming and going of my second self. I had
soon dressed, as well as I was able, in clothes of my own size: had
soon passed through the house, where Bradshaw stared and drew
back at seeing Mr. Hyde at such an hour and in such a strange array;
and ten minutes later, Dr. Jekyll had returned to his own shape and
was sitting down, with a darkened brow, to make a feint of break-
fasting.

Small indeed was my appetite. This inexplicable incident, this
reversal of my previous experience, seemed, like the Babylonian finger on the wall, to be spelling out the letters of my judgment;[3] and

2. Swarthy, dark.
3. Refers to the biblical episode in which King Belshazzar of Babylon sees "fingers of a man's
hand" writing onto the wall of his palace a mysterious message, which the prophet Daniel
reveals to be a sign of God's imminent punishment of Belshazzar for having "lifted" himself
"up against the Lord of heaven" (Daniel 5:5 and 5:23).

I began to reflect more seriously than ever before on the issues and possibilities of my double existence. That part of me which I had the power of projecting, had lately been much exercised and nourished; it had seemed to me of late as though the body of Edward Hyde had grown in stature, as though (when I wore that form) I were conscious of a more generous tide of blood; and I began to spy a danger that, if this were much prolonged, the balance of my nature might be permanently overthrown, the power of voluntary change be forfeited, and the character of Edward Hyde become irrevocably mine. The power of the drug had not been always equally displayed. Once, very early in my career, it had totally failed me; since then I had been obliged on more than one occasion to double, and once, with infinite risk of death, to treble the amount; and these rare uncertainties had cast hitherto the sole shadow on my contentment. Now, however, and in the light of that morning's accident, I was led to remark that whereas, in the beginning, the difficulty had been to throw off the body of Jekyll, it had of late, gradually but decidedly transferred itself to the other side. All things therefore seemed to point to this: that I was slowly losing hold of my original and better self, and becoming slowly incorporated with my second and worse.

Between these two, I now felt I had to choose. My two natures had memory in common, but all other faculties were most unequally shared between them. Jekyll (who was composite) now with the most sensitive apprehensions, now with a greedy gusto, projected and shared in the pleasures and adventures of Hyde; but Hyde was indifferent to Jekyll, or but remembered him as the mountain bandit remembers the cavern in which he conceals himself from pursuit. Jekyll had more than a father's interest; Hyde had more than a son's indifference. To cast in my lot with Jekyll, was to die to those appetites which I had long secretly indulged and had of late begun to pamper. To cast it in with Hyde, was to die to a thousand interests and aspirations, and to become, at a blow and forever, despised and friendless. The bargain might appear unequal; but there was still another consideration in the scales; for while Jekyll would suffer smartingly in the fires of abstinence, Hyde would be not even conscious of all that he had lost. Strange as my circumstances were, the terms of this debate are as old and commonplace as man; much the same inducements and alarms cast the die for any tempted and trembling sinner; and it fell out with me, as it falls with so vast a majority of my fellows, that I chose the better part and was found wanting in the strength to keep to it.

Yes, I preferred the elderly and discontented doctor, surrounded by friends and cherishing honest hopes; and bade a resolute farewell to the liberty, the comparative youth, the light step, leaping pulses and secret pleasures, that I had enjoyed in the disguise of Hyde. I made this choice perhaps with some unconscious reservation, for I neither gave up the house in Soho, nor destroyed the clothes of Edward Hyde, which still lay ready in my cabinet. For two months, however, I was true to my determination; for two months, I led a life of such severity as I had never before attained to, and enjoyed the compensations of an approving conscience. But time began at last to obliterate the freshness of my alarm; the praises of conscience began to grow into a thing of course; I began to be tortured with throes and longings, as of Hyde struggling after freedom; and at last, in an hour of moral weakness, I once again compounded and swallowed the transforming draught.

I do not suppose that, when a drunkard reasons with himself upon his vice, he is once out of five hundred times affected by the dangers that he runs through his brutish, physical insensibility; neither had I, long as I had considered my position, made enough allowance for the complete moral insensibility and insensate readiness to evil, which were the leading characters of Edward Hyde. Yet it was by these that I was punished. My devil had been long caged, he came out roaring. I was conscious, even when I took the draught, of a more unbridled, a more furious propensity to ill. It must have been this, I suppose, that stirred in my soul that tempest of impatience with which I listened to the civilities of my unhappy victim; I declare at least, before God, no man morally sane[4] could have been guilty of that crime upon so pitiful a provocation; and that I struck in no more reasonable spirit than that in which a sick child may break a plaything. But I had voluntarily stripped myself of all those balancing instincts, by which even the worst of us continues to walk with some degree of steadiness among temptations; and in my case, to be tempted, however slightly, was to fall.

Instantly the spirit of hell awoke in me and raged. With a transport of glee, I mauled the unresisting body, tasting delight from every blow; and it was not till weariness had begun to succeed,[5] that I was suddenly, in the top fit of my delirium, struck through the heart by a cold thrill of terror. A mist dispersed; I saw my life to be forfeit; and fled from the scene of these excesses, at once glorying and trembling, my lust of evil gratified and stimulated, my love of life screwed to the topmost peg.[6] I ran to the house in Soho, and (to make assurance doubly sure) destroyed my papers; thence I set out through the

---

4. Moral insanity was proposed as a category of medical diagnosis by Dr. James Prichard in 1835 ("a morbid perversion of the natural feelings, affections, inclinations, temper, habits, moral dispositions, and natural impulses, without any remarkable disorder or defect of the intellect or knowing and reasoning faculties, and particularly without any insane illusion or hallucination") and subsequently was sometimes used in court as a criminal defense plea. (See article by Mary Rosner cited in the bibliography of this edition.)
5. Follow.
6. Raised to its highest pitch (as in tuning a string instrument).

lamplit streets, in the same divided ecstasy of mind, gloating on my crime, light-headedly devising others in the future, and yet still hastening and still hearkening in my wake for the steps of the avenger. Hyde had a song upon his lips as he compounded the draught, and as he drank it, pledged the dead man. The pangs of transformation had not done tearing him, before Henry Jekyll, with streaming tears of gratitude and remorse, had fallen upon his knees and lifted his clasped hands to God. The veil of self-indulgence was rent from head to foot, I saw my life as a whole: I followed it up from the days of childhood, when I had walked with my father's hand, and through the self-denying toils of my professional life, to arrive again and again, with the same sense of unreality, at the damned horrors of the evening. I could have screamed aloud; I sought with tears and prayers to smother down the crowd of hideous images and sounds with which my memory swarmed against me; and still, between the petitions, the ugly face of my iniquity stared into my soul. As the acuteness of this remorse began to die away, it was succeeded by a sense of joy. The problem of my conduct was solved. Hyde was thenceforth impossible; whether I would or not, I was now confined to the better part of my existence; and O, how I rejoiced to think it! with what willing humility, I embraced anew the restrictions of natural life! with what sincere renunciation, I locked the door by which I had so often gone and come, and ground the key under my heel!

The next day, came the news that the murder had been overlooked,[7] that the guilt of Hyde was patent to the world, and that the victim was a man high in public estimation. It was not only a crime, it had been a tragic folly. I think I was glad to know it; I think I was glad to have my better impulses thus buttressed and guarded by the terrors of the scaffold. Jekyll was now my city of refuge; let but Hyde peep out an instant, and the hands of all men would be raised to take and slay him.[8]

I resolved in my future conduct to redeem the past; and I can say with honesty that my resolve was fruitful of some good. You know yourself how earnestly in the last months of last year, I laboured to relieve suffering; you know that much was done for others, and that the days passed quietly, almost happily for myself. Nor can I truly say that I wearied of this beneficent and innocent life; I think instead that I daily enjoyed it more completely; but I was still cursed with my duality of purpose; and as the first edge of my penitence wore off, the lower side of me, so long indulged, so recently chained down,

---

7. Seen from above (by the maidservant at the upstairs window).
8. City of refuge: in the Bible, a city set aside to provide safe haven for someone guilty of an accidental killing (see Numbers 35:9–34; Deuteronomy 4:41–43; Joshua 20:1–9); hands of all men . . . slay him: echoes the prophecy in Genesis about the "wild man," Ishmael, that "his hand will be against every man, and every man's hand against him" (Genesis 16:12).

began to growl for license. Not that I dreamed of resuscitating Hyde; the bare idea of that would startle me to frenzy: no, it was in my own person, that I was once more tempted to trifle with my conscience; and it was as an ordinary secret sinner, that I at last fell before the assaults of temptation.

There comes an end to all things; the most capacious measure is filled at last; and this brief condescension to my evil finally destroyed the balance of my soul. And yet I was not alarmed; the fall seemed natural, like a return to the old days before I had made my discovery. It was a fine, clear, January day, wet under foot where the frost had melted, but cloudless overhead; and the Regent's Park[9] was full of winter chirrupings and sweet with Spring odours. I sat in the sun on a bench; the animal within me licking the chops of memory; the spiritual side a little drowsed, promising subsequent penitence, but not yet moved to begin. After all, I reflected, I was like my neighbours; and then I smiled, comparing myself with other men, comparing my active goodwill with the lazy cruelty of their neglect. And at the very moment of that vainglorious thought, a qualm came over me, a horrid nausea and the most deadly shuddering. These passed away, and left me faint; and then as in its turn the faintness subsided, I began to be aware of a change in the temper of my thoughts, a greater boldness, a contempt of danger, a solution of the bonds of obligation. I looked down; my clothes hung formlessly on my shrunken limbs; the hand that lay on my knee was corded and hairy. I was once more Edward Hyde. A moment before I had been safe of all men's respect, wealthy, beloved—the cloth laying for me in the dining room at home; and now I was the common quarry of mankind, hunted, houseless, a known murderer, thrall to the gallows.

My reason wavered, but it did not fail me utterly. I have more than once observed that, in my second character, my faculties seemed sharpened to a point and my spirits more tensely elastic; thus it came about that, where Jekyll perhaps might have succumbed, Hyde rose to the importance of the moment. My drugs were in one of the presses of my cabinet; how was I to reach them? That was the problem that (crushing my temples in my hands) I set myself to solve. The laboratory door I had closed. If I sought to enter by the house, my own servants would consign me to the gallows. I saw I must employ another hand, and thought of Lanyon. How was he to be reached? how persuaded? Supposing that I escaped capture in the streets, how was I to make my way into his presence? and how should I, an unknown and displeasing visitor, prevail on the famous physician to rifle the study of his colleague, Dr. Jekyll? Then I remembered that of my original character, one part remained to me: I could write

---

9. A large public park just north of the west-central London neighborhood where Dr. Lanyon lives.

my own hand; and once I had conceived that kindling spark, the way that I must follow became lighted up from end to end.

Thereupon, I arranged my clothes as best I could, and summoning a passing hansom, drove to an hotel in Portland Street, the name of which I chanced to remember. At my appearance (which was indeed comical enough, however tragic a fate these garments covered) the driver could not conceal his mirth. I gnashed my teeth upon him with a gust of devilish fury; and the smile withered from his face— happily for him—yet more happily for myself, for in another instant I had certainly dragged him from his perch. At the inn, as I entered, I looked about me with so black a countenance as made the attendants tremble; not a look did they exchange in my presence; but obsequiously took my orders, led me to a private room, and brought me wherewithal to write. Hyde in danger of his life was a creature new to me: shaken with inordinate anger, strung to the pitch of murder, lusting to inflict pain. Yet the creature was astute; mastered his fury with a great effort of the will; composed his two important letters, one to Lanyon and one to Poole; and that he might receive actual evidence of their being posted, sent them out with directions that they should be registered.

Thenceforward, he sat all day over the fire in the private room, gnawing his nails; there he dined, sitting alone with his fears, the waiter visibly quailing before his eye; and thence, when the night was fully come, he set forth in the corner of a closed cab, and was driven to and fro about the streets of the city. He, I say—I cannot say, I. That child of Hell had nothing human; nothing lived in him but fear and hatred. And when at last, thinking the driver had begun to grow suspicious, he discharged the cab and ventured on foot, attired in his misfitting clothes, an object marked out for observation, into the midst of the nocturnal passengers, these two base passions raged within him like a tempest. He walked fast, hunted by his fears, chattering to himself, skulking through the less frequented thoroughfares, counting the minutes that still divided him from midnight. Once a woman spoke to him, offering, I think, a box of lights.[1] He smote her in the face, and she fled.

When I came to myself at Lanyon's, the horror of my old friend perhaps affected me somewhat: I do not know; it was at least but a drop in the sea to the abhorrence with which I looked back upon these hours. A change had come over me. It was no longer the fear of the gallows, it was the horror of being Hyde that racked me. I received Lanyon's condemnation partly in a dream; it was partly in a dream that I came home to my own house and got into bed. I slept after the prostration of the day, with a stringent and profound slum-

1. Matches.

ber which not even the nightmares that wrung me could avail to break. I awoke in the morning shaken, weakened, but refreshed. I still hated and feared the thought of the brute that slept within me, and I had not of course forgotten the appalling dangers of the day before; but I was once more at home, in my own house and close to my drugs; and gratitude for my escape shone so strong in my soul that it almost rivalled the brightness of hope.

I was stepping leisurely across the court after breakfast, drinking the chill of the air with pleasure, when I was seized again with those indescribable sensations that heralded the change; and I had but the time to gain the shelter of my cabinet, before I was once again raging and freezing with the passions of Hyde. It took on this occasion a double dose to recall me to myself; and alas, six hours after, as I sat looking sadly in the fire, the pangs returned, and the drug had to be re-administered. In short, from that day forth it seemed only by a great effort as of gymnastics, and only under the immediate stimulation of the drug, that I was able to wear the countenance of Jekyll. At all hours of the day and night, I would be taken with the premonitory shudder; above all, if I slept, or even dozed for a moment in my chair, it was always as Hyde that I awakened. Under the strain of this continually impending doom and by the sleeplessness to which I now condemned myself, ay, even beyond what I had thought possible to man, I became, in my own person, a creature eaten up and emptied by fever, languidly weak both in body and mind, and solely occupied by one thought: the horror of my other self. But when I slept, or when the virtue of the medicine wore off, I would leap almost without transition (for the pangs of transformation grew daily less marked) into the possession of a fancy brimming with images of terror, a soul boiling with causeless hatreds, and a body that seemed not strong enough to contain the raging energies of life. The powers of Hyde seemed to have grown with the sickliness of Jekyll. And certainly the hate that now divided them was equal on each side. With Jekyll, it was a thing of vital instinct. He had now seen the full deformity of that creature that shared with him some of the phenomena of consciousness, and was co-heir with him to death: and beyond these links of community, which in themselves made the most poignant part of his distress, he thought of Hyde, for all his energy of life, as of something not only hellish but inorganic. This was the shocking thing; that the slime of the pit seemed to utter cries and voices; that the amorphous dust gesticulated and sinned; that what was dead, and had no shape, should usurp the offices of life.[2]

---

2. I.e., functions of life. Jekyll's vision of "amorphous dust" masquerading as life invites comparison with Genesis 2:7, where "the dust of the ground" is made man only when God gives it shape, breath, and immortal soul. The notion of a godless creation of life

And this again, that that insurgent horror was knit to him closer than a wife, closer than an eye; lay caged in his flesh, where he heard it mutter and felt it struggle to be born; and at every hour of weakness, and in the confidence of slumber, prevailed against him, and deposed him out of life. The hatred of Hyde for Jekyll, was of a different order. His terror of the gallows drove him continually to commit temporary suicide, and return to his subordinate station of a part instead of a person; but he loathed the necessity, he loathed the despondency into which Jekyll was now fallen, and he resented the dislike with which he was himself regarded. Hence the apelike tricks that he would play me, scrawling in my own hand blasphemies on the pages of my books, burning the letters and destroying the portrait of my father; and indeed, had it not been for his fear of death, he would long ago have ruined himself in order to involve me in the ruin. But his love of life is wonderful; I go further: I, who sicken and freeze at the mere thought of him, when I recall the abjection and passion of this attachment, and when I know how he fears my power to cut him off by suicide, I find it in my heart to pity him.

It is useless, and the time awfully fails me, to prolong this description; no one has ever suffered such torments, let that suffice; and yet even to these, habit brought—no, not alleviation—but a certain callousness of soul, a certain acquiescence of despair; and my punishment might have gone on for years, but for the last calamity which has now fallen, and which has finally severed me from my own face and nature. My provision of the salt, which had never been renewed since the date of the first experiment, began to run low. I sent out for a fresh supply, and mixed the draught; the ebullition followed, and the first change of colour, not the second; I drank it and it was without efficiency. You will learn from Poole how I have had London ransacked; it was in vain; and I am now persuaded that my first supply was impure, and that it was that unknown impurity which lent efficacy to the draught.

About a week has passed, and I am now finishing this statement under the influence of the last of the old powders. This, then, is the last time, short of a miracle, that Henry Jekyll can think his own thoughts or see his own face (now how sadly altered!) in the glass. Nor must I delay too long to bring my writing to an end; for if my narrative has hitherto escaped destruction, it has been by a combination of great prudence and great good luck. Should the throes of change take me in the act of writing it, Hyde will tear it in pieces;

---

from brute matter held painful resonance for a generation struggling to come to terms with the new scientific account of man's origins emerging around the middle of the nineteenth century from the combined findings of geologists and evolutionists, most notably Charles Darwin.

but if some time shall have elapsed after I have laid it by, his wonderful selfishness and circumscription to the moment[3] will probably save it once again from the action of his apelike spite. And indeed the doom that is closing on us both, has already changed and crushed him. Half an hour from now, when I shall again and forever reindue[4] that hated personality, I know how I shall sit shuddering and weeping in my chair, or continue, with the most strained and fearstruck ecstasy[5] of listening, to pace up and down this room (my last earthly refuge) and give ear to every sound of menace. Will Hyde die upon the scaffold? or will he find the courage to release himself at the last moment? God knows; I am careless;[6] this is my true hour of death, and what is to follow concerns another than myself. Here then, as I lay down the pen and proceed to seal up my confession, I bring the life of that unhappy Henry Jekyll to an end.

---

3. I.e., his astonishing selfishness and limitation of attention to each present moment.
4. Put on again.
5. Transport; frenzy.
6. Indifferent.

Textual Appendix

I. Selected Manuscript Variations

The manuscript fragments surviving from Stevenson's composition of *Strange Case of Dr. Jekyll and Mr. Hyde* offer an intriguing array of clues about the evolution of the tale through several stages of the drafting process.

The largest fragment consists of thirty-four closely written long pages (8" × 13") belonging to the manuscript used by Stevenson's London publisher, Longmans, Green, and Co., for the first edition of the tale. The text is entirely in Stevenson's handwriting; notations by the compositors setting up the type are occasionally to be found in the margins or alongside chapter headings. Thirty-three of these thirty-four final draft pages are held by the Morgan Library in New York; the remaining page is at the Silverado Museum in California. Collectively, these thirty-four pages cover, in two unbroken segments, the first quarter and final third of the tale. Much of their interest lies in the fact that they bear a substantial number of on-the-page insertions and deletions, especially in the opening paragraphs of "Henry Jekyll's Full Statement of the Case." Deleted words usually remain readable beneath Stevenson's line-through cancellations. On the reverse of one of the pages there is a crossed-out unfinished half-page version of a scene from the middle section of the story.

The remaining autograph manuscript material consists of twenty-seven relatively small-sized pages (approximately 6" × 8") generally supposed to be part of an intermediate second draft.[1] This supposition is based on Stevenson's own statement in a letter that the story had gone through three versions and the testimony of his wife and stepson after his death that the first draft had been destroyed.[2]

The twenty-seven pages fall into two groups. Twenty-five pages,

---

1. See Roger Swearingen, *The Prose Writings of Robert Louis Stevenson: A Guide* (Hamden, Connecticut: Archon Books, 1980), pp. 98–101; and William Veeder, "The Texts in Question," in *Dr Jekyll and Mr Hyde after One Hundred Years* (Chicago: University of Chicago Press, 1988), pp. 3–11.
2. See Stevenson's letter to F. W. H. Myers, 1 March 1886, and Graham Balfour's summary of composition in the Composition and Production section of this Norton Critical Edition.

all but one of which are held by the Beinecke Library at Yale University (here again the remaining page is at the Silverado Museum), contain mostly continuous text belonging to the second half of the story. The material these twenty-five pages contain is in rough draft form. It varies in noticeable ways from the final text, and insertions and deletions abound, but all the material on these pages can readily be matched to corresponding passages in the first edition. The other two pages, in the holding of Princeton Library, represent rejected experimentation from the first half of the story. Numbered 33 and 48, they are each crossed out with one or two full-page diagonal penstrokes, and the material they contain varies so far from the final form of the tale that it can only loosely be placed in relation to the plot as we know it. These two pages survive because Stevenson used their blank reverse sides (describing them as "ancient scraps of MS") on which to write a letter to his cousin Bob, apparently in mid-October 1885 while at work on the tale's final version.[3]

Some mysteries remain about the dating of the two cancelled Princeton pages. They are on the same type of lined notebook paper as the twenty-five Beinecke-Silverado rough-draft pages and the two groups are connected by common mention of a later-expunged character, Mr. Lemsome (or "Lewsome"[4]). On the other hand, the two Princeton pages bear some puzzling anomalies: they carry their page numbers in a different place on the page than the other twenty-five pages (all page numbers are in Stevenson's handwriting) and their content speaks for a configuration and pacing of plot far more divergent from the published text than what we see in the other twenty-five pages. Various theories might be put forward to account for this: the two cancelled pages might, for example, belong to an aborted early experimental phase of the second draft; or conceivably they might have been written and set aside as reject material in the course of the first draft and thereby escaped its reported wholesale destruction.

In any case, for purposes of tracing the development of Stevenson's artistry, the attraction of these two pages is that they take us closer to the inception of the tale than any other of the existing manuscript fragments. On one page, we get a fleeting glimpse of a version of the story in which Utterson first hears of Hyde not from Enfield, but from the "incurable cad," Mr. Lemsome. On the other

3. In referring to these recycled manuscript pages as "ancient" (see *Letters* 5:133), Stevenson speaks hyperbolically: Yale *Letters* editor, Ernest Mehew, gives mid-October 1885 as an estimated composition date for this undated letter to Bob; he also provides evidence establishing the fact that Stevenson began writing the tale only a few weeks earlier, in late September or the opening days of October 1885 (see *Letters* 5:128, n. 2).

4. Stevenson's hasty scrawling of this name in its two appearances in the manuscript fragments allows for reading the third letter as either an "m" or a "w"; in the remainder of this appendix, I adopt "Lemsome" for the sake of consistency with the transcription offered by William Veeder (see next note).

page, we see Utterson after the murder in a moment of moral revulsion unmatched by anything in the final text, reeling with the vision of a ubiquitous potential for human evil flourishing in the "monstrous seething mud-pot" of London.

The remaining manuscript materials, while not as dramatically divergent from the final text, have their own interesting angles to offer on Stevenson's ongoing adjustment of the tale's conception and execution. At no stage of composition are Jekyll's secret pleasures distinctly specified, but the Beinecke-Silverado second draft fragment gives a stronger suggestion of vice and addictive habit formed in early youth than appears in the published text. In the corresponding portion of the printer's copy manuscript, deletions and insertions show Stevenson wrestling up until the last minute with the question of how far to soften that connotation of vice. By the final draft, Stevenson has dropped the specificity in dating which in the second draft fragment gives Jekyll a birth year of 1830 and a full fifteen or twenty years of controlled transformations into Hyde before the capacity for involuntary transformation begins wreaking the havoc to which the events of the tale are witness. Hyde's murder victim shifts over the course of revisions from Mr. Lemsome to Sir Danvers Carew. Utterson's speculations as to whether Hyde could be Jekyll's illegitimate son are deleted. Mood and symbolism are carefully built up in the description of the suicide scene Utterson and Poole encounter when they break into Jekyll's cabinet in "The Last Night." Taken as a whole, the alterations can usefully be studied for what insights they yield about the way Stevenson might have been aiming to strengthen allegory, increase indeterminacy, or reduce what might be perceived as offensive sordidness—to name only a few examples of possible goals for revision.

In selecting the manuscript variations featured below, I have sought to bring to the fore what seem to me the most interesting or significant details of change among the many to be noted.[5] The two cancelled Princeton pages are transcribed in full as the first items in this list. I then move on to the remaining variations. The format used to display those variations begins by citing the text, referenced by page and line number in the present edition of the tale, towards which a particular change develops. Then, after a left-facing arrow, the manuscript variant of the text is transcribed, including Stevenson's on-the-page insertions and deletions. In cases where an overlap

5. For a complete transcript of the manuscript pages, see William Veeder's "Collated Fractions of the Manuscript Drafts of Strange Case of Dr Jekyll and Mr Hyde" in his co-edited Dr Jekyll and Mr Hyde after One Hundred Years. I am indebted to William Veeder for his work. I have also been helped by consultation on manuscript matters with Richard Dury, currently at work on a scholarly edition of Strange Case of Dr. Jekyll and Mr. Hyde forthcoming from Edinburgh University Press, and with Ernest Mehew, editor of the Stevenson Letters.

in textual coverage across manuscript fragments allows us to trace a change back through two stages of drafting, the entry works backwards in compositional time, with the printer's copy version being presented before the earlier notebook draft version. The complete set of visual symbols used is as follows:

. . . ← . . .	words left of arrow replaced those on right
PC, followed by roman script	variation found in printer's copy manuscript
ND, followed by *italic script*	variation found in the Beinecke-Silverado notebook draft
\ . . . /	words between slashes inserted in manuscript
< . . . >	words within angled brackets deleted
{ . . . }	words within braces inserted, then deleted
[. . .]	editor's comments, not Stevenson's revisions

Symbols are doubled when there are deletions within deletions (thus: < . . . << . . . >> . . . >).

Cancelled Princeton page 33[6]

ten years old. For ten years he had kept that preposterous document in his safe; and here was the first <external proof> \independent sign/ that such a man as Mr Hyde existed<.>—here, <on> \from/ the lips of a creature who had come to him bleating for help under the most ignoble and deserved misfortunes, he <found> \heard/ the name of the man to whom Henry Jekyll had left everything and whom, <in that> he named his "friend and benefactor." He studied Mr Lemsome covertly. He was <still> a <youngish> man of about twenty eight, with a fine forehead and good features; anæmically pale; shielding a pair of <faint> suffering eyes under blue spectacles; and dressed with that sort of <external> \outward/ decency that implies \both/ a lack of means and a defect of taste. By his own confession, Mr Utterson knew him to be a bad fellow; <in this short scrutiny, he <<read him through and through>> \made {out very

---

6. The following transcription of cancelled manuscript leaves 33 and 48, from the Morris L. Parrish Collection of Victorian Novelists, Manuscripts Division, Department of Rare Books and Special Collections, Princeton University Library is published with permission of the Princeton University Library.

plainly that}/ him out to be a bad fellow of the> he now saw for himself that he was an incurable cad.

"Sit down," said he. "I will take your business."

No one was more astonished than the client; but as he had been speaking uninterruptedly for some three minutes, he set down the success to the score of his own eloquence. <And> there never was a client who did less credit to his lawyer; but still Mr Utterson stuck to him on the chance that something might

Cancelled Princeton page 48:

Thereupon, Mr Utterson, conceiving he had done <the> all and more than could be asked of him, went home to his rooms and lay down upon his bed, <mentally> \like one/ sick. <The last words of the public officer had been the last straw on his overtaxed endurance; there was something in the beaming air {, as of a man who said a pleasant and witty thing,} with which that deadly truth had been communicated that finally unmanned the lawyer.> He had been dragged all day through scenes and among characters that made his gorge rise; hunting a low murderer, and himself hag-ridden by the thought that this murderer was the chosen heir \and/ the secret ally <and the so-called benefactor of the <<good,>> learned and well beloved Henry Jekyll> \of his friend/; and now, at the end of that experience, an honest man and active public servant <tells him with a smile> \spoke out in words what had been for Mr Utterson the haunting moral and unspoken refrain of the day's journeyings:/ that all men, high and low, are of the same \pattern/. He lay on the outside <side> \of/ his bed in the fall of the foggy night; and <he> heard the pattering of countless thousands of feet, all, as he now told himself, making haste to do evil, and the rush of the wheels of countless cabs and carriages conveying men <to deadly yet> {still} \yet/ more expeditiously to sin and punishment; and the horror of that monstrous seething mud-pot of a city, and of that kindred <monster> monster—man's soul, rose up within \him/ to the

Variations from rough-draft notebook pages and printer's copy manuscript[7]

10:3   faces; and ← **PC** faces; <I declare we looked like fiends> and

---

7. All passages in the following transcriptions headed ND (notebook draft) are, with one exception, found on manuscript pages in the holding of the Beinecke Rare Book and Manuscript Library, Yale University, and are published with permission of that library. All passages headed PC (printer's copy) are, again with one exception, found on manuscript pages in the holding of the Pierpont Morgan Library, New York (accession number PML 133614) and are published with permission of that library. The two excepted passages,

14:30   besieged by questions. [paragraph break] Six o'clock ←
PC besieged by questions. <How could such a man as Henry Jekyll
be bound up with such a man as Edward Hyde? How should he have
chosen as his heir one who was unknown to his oldest intimates? If
it were a case of terrorism, why the will? Or again, if Hyde were
Jekyll's son, why the proviso of the disappearance?> Six o'clock

14:31–15:29   digging at the problem . . . "If he be Mr. Hyde,"
[The following eight sentences coming after "digging at the problem"
were deleted in the printer's copy manuscript to allow the insertion,
as page 8A, of Utterson's troubled night visions of Hyde.[8]] ← PC
digging at the problem. <And for all that, he had no sooner swallowed his breakfast, than he must put on his hat and greatcoat and
set forth eastward <<of a>> \in/ the teeth of a fine, driving rain,
coming iced out of Siberia, with no more sensible purpose than to
stand awhile on the opposite pavement and look awhile at the door
with the knocker. . . . This excursion, once taken, seemed to have
laid a spell on the methodical gentleman. In the morning before
office hours, at noon when business was plenty and time scarce, at
night under the glimpses of the fogged city moon or by the cheap
glare of the lamps, a spirit in his feet kept still drawing and guiding
the lawyer to that door in the by street of shops. <<He saw it thus
under all sorts of illumination, and occupied by all kinds of passing
tenants.>> He made long stages on the pavement opposite, studying the bills of fare stuck on the sweating windows of the cookshop,
reading the labels on the various lotions or watching the bust of the
proud lady swing stonily round upon him on her \velvet/ pedestal at
the perfumers; but <<all the time>> \still/ with one eye over his
shoulder, spying at the door. And all the time the door remained
inexorably closed; none entered in, none came forth; <<it>> the
high tides of the town swarmed close by, but did not touch it. Yet
the lawyer was not to be beaten. He had made a solemn agreement
with himself <<and>> \to/ penetrate this mystery of Mr Hyde.>
"If he be Mr Hyde,"

18:39   deep waters! He was wild ← PC deep waters! <That could
never be the face of his son, never in this world. No, there is a secret
at the root of it; <<Jekyll>>> \He/ was wild

one belonging to the notebook draft and the other to the printer's copy, are located on
manuscript pages in the holding of the Robert Louis Stevenson Silverado Museum, St.
Helena, California. They are identified by footnotes where they occur in this list of manuscript variations, and they are published with permission of that museum.
8. The first of the eight sentences occurs on the bottom of Morgan Library's p. 8 of the
printer's copy manuscript. The remaining seven sentences, beginning with an ellipsis
which is Stevenson's own, occur on Silverado Museum's p. 9 of the printer's copy manuscript.

19:13   like sunshine. Things cannot ← **PC** like sunshine. <I think we might turn the tables; I am sure, if Harry will but let me, that I ought to try. For> Things cannot

40:7–40:29   glass saucers, as though . . . the business table ← **PC discarded draft** [The immediately following variation comes from the cancelled, discontinuous half-page found on the reverse of a printer's copy manuscript page, as described in the headnote to this section.] glass saucers, as if for <some> \an/ experiment in which the unhappy man had been prevented. <At another, as has been said, tea was set out> The kettle had by this time boiled over; and they were obliged to take it off the fire; but the tea things were still set forth with a comfortable orderliness that was in strange contrast to the tumbled corpse upon the floor. <Indeed the> Several books were on a shelf <beside> \near/ the fire; one lay <beside> beside the tea things open, and Utterson was <amazed> {somewhat surprised} \amazed/ to find it <[? illegible word]> \pious/. Next, in the course of their review of the chamber, the searchers came to the cheval glass.
     "This glass have seen some queer doings, \sir,/ no doubt," whispered Poole.
     "And none stranger than itself," echoed the lawyer \in the same tones/. "What did—what did Jekyll do with a glass?"
     "<I can't tell you> \That's what I have/ often asked myself," returned the butler.
     Then they found a prayer in the doctor's writing, very eloquently put in words but breathing a spirit of despair and horror worthy of the cells of Bedlam, and the sight of this so ← **ND** *glass saucers <; and>, <these Poole recognised> as if for some purpose in which the unhappy man had been interrupted. On the desk of the business table*

44:2   no guess. The book was an ordinary version book and contained little but a series of dates. These covered a period of many years, but I observed that the entries ceased nearly a year ago and quite abruptly. Here and there ← **ND** *no guess. The dates in the version \book/ covered <a consider-> many years, fifteen I think or twenty, but I observed that they had ceased some months before \that day, on about April 1884/.*[9] *Here and there*

44:33   small, as I have said; I was struck ← **ND** *small, I have said; he had besides a slight shortening of some of the cords of the neck which tilted his head upon one side; I was struck*

9. The concluding nine words of this sentence, beginning with "some months," occur on Silverado Museum's p. 68 of the notebook draft manuscript.

46:23   with an air of scrutiny. ← **ND** *with a great air of scrutiny and hesitation.*

47:16–47:30   to set on paper . . . HASTIE LANYON ← **ND** *to place on paper. In spite of what I saw, my mind revolts* <from> *against belief; the shock of that moment has, I feel sure, struck at the very roots of my life, but it has not bowed the pride of my scepticism; I shall die, but I shall die incredulous. As for the moral turpitude that man unveiled to me, it is matter that I disdain to handle. He found me an elderly, a useful and a happy man; that he has blighted and shortened what remains to me of life, is but a small addendum to the monstrous tale of his misdeeds. Hastie Lanyon.*

47:32   I was born in the year 18—to ← **ND** *I was born in the year 1830 to*

47:35–48:4   distinguished future. And indeed . . . my pleasures; and that when I reached ← **PC** distinguished future. <From an early age, however, I became in secret the slave of certain appetites;> \And indeed the worst of my faults was a certain impatient gaiety of disposition, such as has made the happiness of many, but such as I found it hard to reconcile with my imperious desire to carry my head high, and wear a more than commonly grave countenance before the public. Hence it came about that I concealed my pleasures;/ and \that when/ I reached ← **ND** *distinguished future. From a very early age, however, I became* <add> *in secret/ the slave of disgraceful pleasures;* <*my life was double;* <<*outwardly*>> *absorbed in scientific toil,* <<*and [?two illegible words]*>> *never indifferent to any noble* <<*opinion*>> *cause or*> *and when I reached*

48:6–48:11   duplicity of life. Many a man . . . and with an even deeper trench ← **PC** duplicity of life. <On the one side, I was what you have known me, a man of some note, immersed in toils, open to \all/ generous sympathies, never slow to befriend struggling virtue, never backward in <<an honour>> \the course/ of honour; on the other, as soon as night released me from my engagements and <<covered>> \hid/ me from the <<espial>> \notice/ of my friends, <<the iron hand>> indurated habit plunged me again into the mire of my vices. I will trouble you with these no further than to say that they were, at that period, no worse than those of many who have lived and died with credit. It was rather the somewhat high aspiration of my life by daylight> \Many a man would have even blazoned such irregularities as I was guilty of; but from the high views <of conduct> \that I had/ set before me I regarded and hid them with an almost morbid sense of shame, and it was thus rather the exacting nature of my aspirations/ than any particular degradation in my faults, that made me what I was; and with even a deeper trench ← **ND** *duplicity of life. On the one side, I was what you have known me, a man of distinction, immersed in toils, open to generous sympathies, never slow to befriend struggling virtue, never backward in an honourable cause; on the other, as soon as night had fallen and I could shake off my friends, the iron hand of indurated habit plunged me once again into the mire of my vices. I will trouble you with these no further than to say that they were at once criminal in the sight of the law and abhorrent in themselves. They cut me off from the sympathy of those whom I otherwise respected; and with even a deeper trench*

52:8–52:22   already learned to despair. The movement . . . On the other side I announced to my servants ← **ND** *already learned to despair. You can see now what was the result; for days, I would, <[? two words illegible]> \as of yore,/ preserve and obey my better <nature> \instincts/; and then when evil triumphed, I would again drink the cup and, impenetrably disguised as <Henry> \Edward/ Hyde, pass \privately/ out of the laboratory door and roll myself in infamy.*

The temptation of my present power can hardly be overestimated. As <Henry> \Edward/ Hyde (, for I had so dubbed <myself> \my second self—God help me—/ in pleasantry), I was secure of an immunity that never <man> before was attained by any criminal. Think of it—I did not exist! Let me but escape into my laboratory door, give me but a second to \mix and/ swallow <that> the draft that I had always standing ready, and whatever <I> he had done, Edward Hyde had vanished like a wreath of smoke, and there, in his stead, quietly at home and trimming the midnight lamp in his laborious study, was the well-known, the spotless, the benevolent and the beloved Dr Jekyll!

I made my preparations with the most studious care. I announced to my servants

52:28–53:24   And thus fortified . . . I mean but to point out ← **ND** *And thus fortified as I fondly supposed on every side, I began to plunge into a career of cruel, soulless and degrading vice.*

Into the details of <this> my shame, I scorn to enter; I mean but to point out

53:25   chastisement approached. I met ← **PC** chastisement approached <, and the halter of social responsibility, which I had so long eluded, \was/ once more tightened about my neck>. I met

52:36–53:30   shall no more than mention . . . in order to pacify
their too just resentment ← **ND** *mention only in passing: detected in
an act of infamy, I had to bribe a party of young fools to set me free,
and in order to <find [?] the money> \satisfy their demands/*

53:37   Some two months before the murder of Sir Danvers, I ←
ND *About <five> \a/ month <s> before the Lemsome murder, I*

54:5   but in the little room in Soho where ← **ND** *but in the iron
bed and the somewhat dreary and exiguous rooms off Gray's Inn Road,
where*

54:10   Now the hand of Henry Jekyll (as you have often
remarked) was professional in shape and size: it was large, firm, white
and comely. But ← **ND** *Now the hand of Henry Jekyll, as we have
often jocularly said, was eminently professional in shape and size: it
was large, firm, white and comely, the hand of a lady's doctor, in a
word. <Now> But*

57:31   slay him ← **PC** *slay him. <The long drawn hum of anger
and horror that sounded through society upon the fall of their favourite [crew? For Carew?] was>*

59:25–59:42   driven to and fro about the streets of the city . . .
came home to my own house ← **ND** *driven to a remote part of London
<, where> \. Here/ I stopped \the driver/ at a door, asked for the first
name that came into my head, was of course refused admittance, and
was then driven back to the neighbourhood of Cavendish Square not
very long before the hour of my appointment.*
        *You know already what occurred. Lanyon threw me off from him
with horror; it scarcely moved me; I was still so full of my immediate
joy. I was already so conscious of the perpetual doom that hung above
my head; and when I returned home*

60:35   to death: and beyond these links of community, which ←
PC *to death: <more bonds he could not now recognise; the thought
of him, like the <<sight of something odious>> \killing smell of
ammonia/> \and beyond these links of community,/ <he did not
stoop to recognise him> which*

II. Variations in Wording between Printer's Copy Fragment and First Edition

The thirty-four extant pages of printer's copy manuscript vary from the corresponding portion of the first edition in some details of wording, punctuation, and spelling. The most mechanical of these changes are likely to have been introduced by the publisher and printer, since it was normal procedure for nineteenth-century publishers and printers to correct an author's spelling, regularize or standardize punctuation, and sometimes change what were taken to be errors in grammar or syntax. Stevenson read the proofs,[1] so we can assume that he acquiesced in these changes. The more significant changes in wording, however, were almost certainly introduced by Stevenson himself at the proofreading stage. They are in keeping with the direction of changes he made in the manuscript as well as with his known practice in other work. I have chosen to list below only unambiguous changes of wording between the printer's copy manuscript pages and the corresponding portion of the first edition.[2]

Page:line	Printer's copy manuscript	This edition, following first edition
7:18	I rather incline	I incline
7:22	And to these, as long as	And to such as these, so long as
8:7	set	put
8:28	into its shelter	into the recess
10:11	but that place	but to that place
10:28	it, sir.	it.
11:29	Yes, sir, I	Yes, I
12:35	it; and it	it; it
13:8	offended him as	offended him both as
14:5	will be	must be
14:37	the nocturnal city	a nocturnal city
16:31	look me in the face	let me see your face
17:10	cried Mr Hyde, "never, never told you."	cried Mr. Hyde, with a flush of anger.
19:8	had so near	had come so near

1. See *Letters* 5:150, n. 1, and 153, n. 2.
2. Differences from the list compiled by William Veeder in *Dr Jekyll and Mr Hyde after One Hundred Years*, pp. 54–56, are chiefly due to two things: his having compared the manuscript with a version of the text following but not identical to the first British edition; and his having interpreted as viable final copy a cancelled half-page of what I construe as a piece of rejected draft material on the reverse side of one page of printer's copy manuscript (see headnote to section I of this appendix).

44:21	I opened it, of course, myself	I went myself at the summons
44:37	incipient rigor or what is called goose-flesh; and	incipient rigor, and
45:12	far from tickling the cacchinatory impulse	far from moving me to laughter
45:38	the hysteric ball	the hysteria
47:18	has melted	has faded
47:28	and now hunted	and hunted
48:9	shame. And it was thus	shame. It was thus
48:24	and both sides	and from both sides
51:8	deposed. And again	deposed. Again
51:39	diabolic	diabolical
52:2	hour	time
52:36	safety was complete, and I could snap my fingers. Think of it—	safety was complete. Think of it—
53:9	I soon began to be plunged	I was often plunged
53:26	I mention only in passing	I shall no more than mention
53:38	out on one of	out for one of
55:38	every tempted	any tempted
57:5	pledged the dead man by name.	pledged the dead man.
57:11	self-denying days	self-denying toils
57:19	I was compelled to my better life	I was now confined to the better part of my existence
58:18	came upon me	came over me
58:33	of the occasion	of the moment
61:21	yet even to this	yet even to these

BACKGROUNDS AND CONTEXTS

Composition and Production

GRAHAM BALFOUR

[Summary of Composition and Early Reception]†

* * *

A subject much in his [Stevenson's] thoughts at this time [early autumn, 1885] was the duality of man's nature and the alternation of good and evil; and he was for a long while casting about for a story to embody this central idea. Out of this frame of mind had come the sombre imagination of "Markheim," but that was not what he required. The true story still delayed, till suddenly one night he had a dream. He awoke, and found himself in possession of two, or rather three, of the scenes in the *Strange Story* [sic] *of Dr. Jekyll and Mr. Hyde.*

Its waking existence, however, was by no means without incident. He dreamed these scenes in considerable detail, including the circumstance of the transforming powders, and so vivid was the impression that he wrote the story off at a red heat, just as it had presented itself to him in his sleep.

"In the small hours of one morning," says Mrs. Stevenson, "I was awakened by cries of horror from Louis. Thinking he had a nightmare, I awakened him. He said angrily: 'Why did you wake me? I was dreaming a fine bogey tale.' I had awakened him at the first transformation scene."

Mr. Osbourne[1] writes: "I don't believe that there was ever such a literary feat before as the writing of *Dr. Jekyll.* I remember the first reading as though it were yesterday. Louis came downstairs in a fever; read nearly half the book aloud; and then, while we were still gasping, he was away again, and busy writing. I doubt if the first draft took so long as three days."

---

† From *The Life of Robert Louis Stevenson*, vol. 2 (London: Methuen and Co., 1901), pp. 12–14. Footnotes are by the editor of this Norton Critical Edition. Seven years after Stevenson's death, his cousin Graham Balfour produced this account of the writing of *Strange Case of Dr. Jekyll and Mr. Hyde*, incorporating recollections obtained from Stevenson's widow and stepson as well as from the publisher Charles Longman.

1. Lloyd Osbourne, Stevenson's stepson. He was seventeen in the fall of 1885.

He had lately had a hemorrhage, and was strictly forbidden all discussion or excitement. No doubt the reading aloud was contrary to the doctor's orders; at any rate Mrs. Stevenson, according to the custom then in force, wrote her detailed criticism of the story as it then stood, pointing out her chief objection—that it was really an allegory, whereas he had treated it purely as if it were a story. In the first draft Jekyll's nature was bad all through, and the Hyde change was worked only for the sake of a disguise. She gave the paper to her husband and left the room. After a while his bell rang; on her return she found him sitting up in bed (the clinical thermometer in his mouth), pointing with a long denunciatory finger to a pile of ashes. He had burned the entire draft. Having realised that he had taken the wrong point of view, that the tale was an allegory and not another "Markheim," he at once destroyed his manuscript, acting not out of pique, but from a fear that he might be tempted to make too much use of it, and not rewrite the whole from a new stand-point.[2]

It was written again in three days ("I drive on with Jekyll: bank-ruptcy at my heels"); but the fear of losing the story altogether pre-vented much further criticism. The powder was condemned as too material an agency, but this he could not eliminate, because in the dream it had made so strong an impression upon him.

"The mere physical feat," Mr. Osbourne continues, "was tremen-dous; and instead of harming him, it roused and cheered him inex-pressibly." Of course it must not be supposed that these three days represent all the time that Stevenson spent upon the story, for after this he was working hard for a month or six weeks in bringing it into its present form.[3]

---

2. Because accounts of Fanny Stevenson's criticism and Stevenson's consequent destruction of the first draft can be neither confirmed nor denied on the basis of any known first-hand evidence from Stevenson himself, this part of composition history remains a matter of speculation and controversy among critics. For arguments that Fanny's objections to the first draft may have had more to do with what she considered off-color sexual content than with the issue of allegory as such, see Malcolm Elwin, *The Strange Case of Robert Louis Stevenson* (1950) and William Veeder, "The Texts in Question" in *Dr Jekyll and Mr Hyde after One Hundred Years* (1988). For a claim that the tale of the burning itself deserves to be questioned, see Christopher Frayling, *Nightmare: The Birth of Horror* (London: BBC Books, 1996).

3. This conclusion is strengthened by evidence in the Yale *Letters* that Stevenson's comment about "driving on with Jekyll," which Balfour assigns to the first week of composition, in fact belongs to at least the third week of composition, since the comment occurs in a letter to Fanny dated October 20, 1885. The *Letters* tell us also that the completed man-uscript was delivered to Longmans on October 31, 1885, and that page proofs were avail-able by mid-November (*Letters* 5:150). Writing on March 1, 1886, to F. W. H. Myers, Stevenson estimated that the overall process of composition and production for the tale, including typesetting, proofreading, and first-run printing, was completed in under ten weeks. In a June 8, 1888, San Francisco *Examiner* article, he is quoted as saying that the basic work of composition involved three days' initial drafting and six weeks' further writing (see Roger Swearingen, *The Prose Writings of Robert Louis Stevenson* [Hamden, Conn.: Archon Books, 1980]).

The manuscript was then offered to Messrs. Longmans for their magazine; and on their judgment the decision was taken not to break it up into monthly sections, but to issue it as a shilling book in paper covers.[4] The chief drawbacks of this plan to the author were the loss of immediate payment and the risk of total failure, but these were generously met by an advance payment from the publishers on account of royalties. "The little book was printed," says Mr. Charles Longman, "but when it was ready the bookstalls were already full of Christmas numbers etc., and the trade would not look at it.[5] We therefore withdrew it till after Christmas. In January it was launched—not without difficulty. The trade did not feel inclined to take it up, till a review appeared in the *Times*[6] calling attention to the story. This gave it a start, and in the next six months close on forty thousand copies were sold in this country alone." Besides the authorised edition in America, the book was widely pirated, and probably not less than a quarter of a million copies in all have been sold in the United States.[7]

Its success was probably due rather to the moral instincts of the public than to any conscious perception of the merits of its art. It was read by those who never read fiction, it was quoted in pulpits, and made the subject of leading articles in religious newspapers.* * *

But as literature also it was justly received with enthusiasm.* * *

4. When the book came out in Britain and America, it was offered not only as a paperback priced to sell in quantity (a shilling in Britain, twenty-five cents in America), but also clothbound at a higher price (a shilling and sixpence in Britain, a dollar in America). (Prices derived from book advertisement sections of *The Saturday Review* and *The Literary World* for January 9, 1886.)
5. For background on the role of tales of the macabre and the supernatural in the Christmas book trade, as well as Stevenson's previous experience with that market niche, see pp. 120–23 in this edition.
6. *The Times* of London, January 25, 1886 (reprinted on pp. 96–98 in this edition).
7. The authorized American edition, made up from page sheets sent ahead from Longmans, but using separate typesetting and pagination, was put out by Charles Scribner's Sons on January 5, 1886. The date was set four days ahead of British publication to give the American edition a brief monopoly on U.S. sales before the inevitable American piracies began. The sales figures Balfour gives are as of his time of writing, i.e., 1901.

ROBERT LOUIS STEVENSON

Selected Letters†

To Sidney Colvin

[Late September/early October 1885]¹   [Skerryvore]²

* * * The world is too much with us; and coin it grows so sparsely
on the tree! (Scotch Ballad) I am pouring forth a penny (12 penny)
dreadful; it is dam dreadful; they call it the Abbot George of Shaw
(beg pardon: Scottish poesie)—I mean, they call it Doctor Jekyll,³
but they also call it Mr Hyde, Mr Hyde, but they also, also call it Mr
Hyde. I seem to bloom by nature—oh, by nature, into song; but for
all my tale is silly it shall not be very long.* * *

---

† Except where otherwise noted, the text for these letters is taken from *The Letters of Robert
Louis Stevenson*, ed. Bradford Booth and Ernest Mehew, 8 vols. (New Haven: Yale University Press, 1994–95). I have devised my own notes to meet the needs of this edition,
but I am indebted to the excellent Yale notes on various points of content. Publication
permissions for letters other than those published by 1911 in the second of Sidney Colvin's
four editions of Stevenson's letters are as acknowledged in the first footnotes to individual
letters. References to page numbers in this Norton Critical Edition appear in square brackets [Editor].

1. Letter located in the Manuscripts Division, Department of Rare Books and Special Collections, Princeton University Library. This excerpt is published by permission of Princeton University Library. Sidney Colvin: an art critic and man of letters who was a beloved
   friend and literary mentor to Stevenson. [Late September/early October 1885]: bracketed
   date headings for letters represent Yale *Letters* editor Ernest Mehew's best estimate on
   the date of composition for a letter which Stevenson himself left undated. (As confirming
   evidence for the estimated date on this letter, Mehew notes that Stevenson's wife and
   stepson can be found in correspondence at this time reporting on Stevenson's immersion
   in the composition of a new tale, referred to by his stepson as "a most terrible story which
   he said occurred to him in the night." See *Letters* 5:128, n. 2.)
2. The Stevensons called their home in Bournemouth "Skerryvore" in honor of the Scottish
   lighthouse by that name built by Stevenson's uncle, Alan Stevenson. Brackets around a
   location heading signal that the heading is supplied by the editors of the Yale *Letters*.
3. Dreadful: a sensationalized tale of crime, horror, or boy's adventure produced for mass
   market consumption. Usually issued by weekly installments in periodicals costing a penny,
   the dreadful also sometimes appeared full-length in paperbacks costing a shilling, i.e.,
   twelve pence. Doctor Jekyll: Stevenson's own pronunciation of the name, now rarely
   observed, was "Jee-kill," not "Jek-ill," he told an interviewer for the San Francisco *Examiner* in 1888, adding, "Jekyll is a very good family name in England, and over there it is
   pronounced in the manner stated." (Article dated June 8, 1888, in Stevenson Scrapbook
   2, p. 64, Stevenson House Collection, Monterey State Historic Park, California Department of Parks and Recreation; hereafter referred to as the Monterey Stevenson Museum
   Scrapbooks.)

To his Wife

[*Postmark 20 October 1885*][4]   *Skerryvore*

Dear Pig, * * * I am all right, but the coins are gone to hell. * * * Do for God's sake amuse yourself: I am as happy as fits. Dear Pig, I am, Yours   The Parker

I drive on with *Jekyll*, bankruptcy at my heels.

To Andrew Lang

[*Early December 1885*][5]   [*Skerryvore*]

Dear Lang, Yes, I knew William Wilson; but I now hear for the first time (and with chagrin) of the Chevalier Double. Who in hell was he? I hope he didn't shoot over my preserves. My point is the identity with difficulty preserved; I thought it was quite original * * *

*   *   *

To Katharine de Mattos

1 January 1886[6]   [*Skerryvore*]

Dearest Katharine, Here, on a very little book and accompanied with your lame verses, I have put your name. Our kindness is now getting well on in years; it must be nearly of age; and it gets more valuable to me with every time I see you. It is not possible to express any sentiment, and it is not necessary to try at least between us. You know very well that I love you dearly, and that I always will. I only wish the verses were better, but at least you like the story; and it is sent to you by the one that loves you—Jekyll and not Hyde. R.L.S.

4. Published with permission of the Beinecke Rare Book and Manuscript Library, Yale University. *To his Wife*: Stevenson's wife Fanny had gone to visit their friends Anna and William Ernest Henley in London.
5. Letter located in the Huntington Library (call number 2490). This excerpt is reproduced by permission of the Huntington Library, San Marino, California. Andrew Lang: a prolific writer, reviewer, and mythologist who was a friend of Stevenson's. Having read the tale in manuscript, Lang had written to ask about Stevenson's familiarity with two stories that Lang saw as possible influences on *Strange Case of Dr. Jekyll and Mr. Hyde*: Edgar Allan Poe's "William Wilson" (1839), in which a dissolute young man is repeatedly shamed by a same-name, same-age look-alike whom he finally murders; and Théophile Gautier's "Le Chevalier Double" (1863), the tale of a medieval knight born with a split personality whose best self eventually vanquishes his malignant mirror image on the field of battle. For Lang's review of *Strange Case of Dr. Jekyll and Mr. Hyde*, praising its originality in relation to these same two texts, see pp. 93–94 in this edition.
6. To the cousin to whom *Strange Case of Dr. Jekyll and Mr. Hyde* is dedicated, Stevenson is sending a pre-publication copy. Though the dedicatory poem is of his own composition (hence the self-deprecating adjective, "lame"), he speaks of it as "your . . . verses" because he knows she will recognize it as an adapted version of the poem he had written for her on a family occasion the previous spring.

To Will H. Low

2 January 1886[7]

*   *   *

Skerryvore

* * * I send you herewith a gothic gnome for your Greek nymph; but the gnome is interesting I think and he came out of a deep mine, where he guards the fountain of tears. It is not always the time to rejoice. Yours ever

R.L.S.

The gnome's name is *Jekyll and Hyde*; I believe you will find he is likewise quite willing to answer to the name of Low or Stevenson.

To F. W. H. Myers

[c. 23] February 1886[8]

Skerryvore

My dear Sir, Many thanks for your kind letter; it contains expressions at which I can only wonder and be well pleased. I hope you do not deceive yourself; but I confess I was pretty fond of *Jekyll* from the first, and the good opinions of many—and now yours—have increased the fondness.

You were so kind as offer to explain your suggestions: will you? I do not know that I can promise to give effect to them; simply because some time has past, the clay is no longer plastic in my hands—nay, and the very hand has changed; but I should much like to understand your views, and it is possible I may find the courage to tamper with the work. I do not know if you understand my difficulty; until a book is published, I can turn it inside out or upside down at a moment's notice; once it is published, I relax the effort, that part of my mind crystallises, and except the least details, the thing becomes irrevocable.

*   *   *

7. Will H. Low: an artist friend of Stevenson's. Low had just sent him a new edition of Keats's *Lamia* (1820) containing illustrations by Low himself, among which Stevenson's favorite was Low's depiction of a Greek nymph bathing in a forest stream. *2 January 1886*: postscript attaching to letter dated 26 December 1885 (see *Letters* 5: 161–63).
8. Published with permission of the Master and Fellows of Trinity College Cambridge. F. W. H. Myers: a literary man with connections to several of Stevenson's friends. He had written offering to spell out suggestions for revising what he saw as a few weak points in *Strange Case of Dr. Jekyll and Mr. Hyde*, so as to render more secure what he enthusiastically predicted would be the tale's future place in the ranks of English literature. Myers' interest in the tale was related to his self-directed research into questions of multiple personality and divided streams of consciousness. Years later Stevenson was to send him a description of his experience of fever episodes in which his mind seemed to divide between a sane and a hallucinatory self (*Letters* 7:331–34).

To J. R. Vernon

25 February 1886[9]   *Skerryvore*

My dear Sir, I am gratified by your letter and wish to answer two points.

First, as to a key, I conceive I could not make my allegory better, nay, that I could not fail to weaken it, if I tried. I have said my say as I was best able: others must look for what was meant; the allegorist is one, the commentator is another; I conceive they are two parts.

Second, I would not for the world have you suppose the parodies in *Punch* are dictated by spite, or are taken in ill part. If it were only a little funnier, I should set down the parody of *Jekyll*[1] to one of my own friends, and a great admirer of that particular book. * * * What appears spite, both in reviews and parodies, is usually our humble human friend—stupidity.

I have written some other slighter things in a more or less allegorical vein; but they have not yet been collected.

I am glad you think the book may be useful, and remain, truly yours,

                                        Robert Louis Stevenson

To Edward Purcell

27 February 1886[2]   *Skerryvore*

                        *   *   *

* * * What you say about the confusion of my ethics, I own to be all too true. It is, as you say, where I fall, and fall almost consciously. I have the old Scotch Presbyterian preoccupation about these problems; itself morbid; I have alongside of that a second, perhaps more—possibly less—morbid element—the dazzled incapacity to choose, of an age of transition.[3] The categorical imperative is ever

9. Published with permission of the Robert Louis Stevenson Museum, St. Helena, California. J. R. Vernon: a clergyman and author of religious books with whom Stevenson evidently had no previous personal acquaintance, though he speaks warmly of one of Vernon's books in a postscript to this letter.
1. A heavy-handed parody entitled "The Strange Case of Dr T. and Mr H." had appeared in the February 6, 1886, issue of the British humor magazine *Punch*.
2. The last known owner of this letter was Brigadier J. A. C. Pennycuick of Horam, East Sussex. Purcell: a clergyman and leading reviewer who had published an article on Stevenson's work in *The Academy* (February 27, 1886), suggesting that the effectiveness of Stevenson's genius as a writer was hindered by his "puzzling enigmatic ethics." Stevenson in response wrote this letter outlining his dilemma as one of moral intensity balked by intellectual uncertainty.
3. Scotch Presbyterian preoccupation: an anxiety about the soul's liability to sin and damnation such as Stevenson elsewhere speaks of being haunted by in his Edinburgh childhood. Age of transition: introduced in an 1858 *Edinburgh Review* article, "age of transition" became a catch phrase encoding Victorian awareness of the way that rapidly advancing scientific discovery, industrialization, urbanization, and democratization were

with me, but utters dark oracles.[4] This is a ground almost of pity. The Scotch side came out plain in *Dr Jekyll*; the XIXth century side probably baffled me even there, and in most other places baffles me entirely. Ethics are my veiled mistress; I love them, but I know not what they are. Is this my fault? Partly, of course, it is; because I love my sins like other people. Partly my merit, because I do not take, and rest contented in, the first subterfuge.[5]

* * *

To F. W. H. Myers

1 March 1886[6]

Skerryvore

My dear Sir, I know not how to thank you: this is as handsome as it is clever. With almost every word I agree—much of it I even knew before—much of it, I must confess, would never have been, if I had been able to do what I like, and lay the thing by for the matter of a year. But the wheels of Byles the Butcher drive exceeding swiftly,[7] and *Jekyll* was conceived, written, rewritten, re-rewritten, and printed inside ten weeks. Nothing but this white-hot haste would explain the gross error of Hyde's speech at Lanyon's.[8] Your point

---

not only transforming everyday life, but also radically unsettling previously established systems of ethical and religious thought.

4. I.e., the sense that there is an unquestionable moral law dictated by pure reason (the "categorical imperative" of philosopher Immanuel Kant) is ever with me, but the content of that law remains unfathomable.

5. Whether "the first subterfuge" refers to using confusion of ethics or to using satisfaction in one's sins as an excuse for evading moral issues, Stevenson's point in this knotty sentence seems to be that his merit is that he refuses to accept moral evasion, even if he also lacks moral answers.

6. In response to Stevenson's letter of [c. 23] February, Myers had sent a document entitled "Notes on 'Dr. Jekyll and Mr. Hyde,'" praising the strengths of some passages in the tale and pointing out in precise detail what he saw as weaknesses in the logic of plot or characterization in others. See n. 8 below.

7. A reference to the pressure of bills needing to be paid; the allusion is to a passage in George Eliot's *Middlemarch* (ch. 71) where we hear of a large debt owed to "Mr. Byles the butcher."

8. Myers had suggested that Hyde's speech to Lanyon ("Will you be wise? will you be guided?") is in a "style too elevated" to fit Hyde, sounding instead more like Jekyll. The remaining points from Myers' list to which Stevenson responds in this letter may be summarized as follows: a) Stevenson may have slipped into making Hyde "a generalized fiend" (the embodiment of all evil) rather than a "specialized" one (the underside of Jekyll)— because when the concealed, pleasure-loving side of the gentlemanly Jekyll turns to crime, wouldn't his acts of cruelty logically reflect motives of lust, rather than the mere madness and savagery reflected in murdering a total stranger on a whim? b) Is it logical to suppose, as Utterson does, that Jekyll would have chosen to make a present to Hyde of the "good picture" Utterson sees in Hyde's Soho apartment, especially when it would presumably have involved Jekyll's using his servants to convey the picture to a place that he wanted no one in his household to know about? c) The orderly room set for tea that Utterson and Poole encounter when they break into Jekyll's cabinet is "surely not a true point," since "neither J. nor H. would prepare in that minute way for comfort" and servants would hardly have been allowed in to do the work. (The full text of Myers' "Notes on 'Dr. Jekyll and Mr. Hyde'" can be found in Maixner, 214–19, along with Myers' two ensuing letters to Stevenson, doggedly—and unsuccessfully—pursuing the case for revision.)

about the specialised fiend is more subtle, but not less just; I had not seen it.—About the picture, I rather meant that Hyde had bought it himself; and Utterson's hypothesis of the gift (p. 42)[24] an error.—The tidiness of the room, I thought, but I dare say my psychology is here too ingenious to be sound, was due to the dread weariness and horror of the imprisonment. Something has to be done; he would tidy the room. But I dare say it is false.

I shall keep your paper; and if ever my works come to be collected, I will put my back into these suggestions. In the meanwhile, I do truly lack words in which to express my sense of gratitude for the trouble you have taken. The receipt of such a paper is more than a reward for my labours. I have read it with pleasure, and as I say, I hope to use it with profit. Believe me, Your most obliged

Robert Louis Stevenson

To John Addington Symonds

[Early March 1886][9]   Skerryvore

*   *   *

Jekyll is a dreadful thing, I own; but the only thing I feel dreadful about is that damned old business of the war in the members.[1] This time it came out; I hope it will stay in, in future.

*   *   *

To Thomas Russell Sullivan

[Postmark 27 January 1887][2]   Skerryvore

My dear Sir, I have to thank you again for a kind letter, and to assure you that I am not in the least struck by the liberties you have taken; on the contrary, had I tried to make a play of it, I should have been driven to take more: I should have had *Jekyll married*; it is true it would no longer have been a one part play, and that is what is wanted no doubt. Actors are very hopeful, when they have plenty of "fat"[3]—if you have that expression on your side; and their hopefulness is jus-

9. Stevenson's friend Symonds, a writer and critic, had written to say that he found the story both brilliant and painful (see excerpt on pp. 98–99 of this edition).
1. A variation on the biblically derived phrase Jekyll uses in the text to describe inner conflicts, especially between spirit and flesh.
2. Letter located at the American Antiquarian Society, Worcester, Massachusetts; not included in the Yale *Letters*. This excerpt is published with permission of the American Antiquarian Society. Thomas Russell Sullivan: an American playwright. Sullivan had written on behalf of both himself and the American actor-manager Richard Mansfield, to inform Stevenson of the liberty they proposed to take by including a fiancée for Jekyll in their collaborative stage adaptation of the novel (a venture Stevenson had approved the preceding June).
3. The opportunity that a good part in a play affords for capturing an audience's attention.

tified by the languor and indifference of the public. I should imagine your actor *may* carry you (and me) on his back;[4] and yet I wonder. The spectacle I fear will be unlovely at the best. But I wish well to all.

Pray pardon me the delay and present brevity; both of which are referable to my health, always a sore stumbling block; and believe me with my thanks, Yours very truly

Robert Louis Stevenson

T. R. Sullivan Esq.

Will your actor *change* coram publico?[5] I wonder: it would be a fine effect, if he could do it. Fechter did something like.[6]   R.L.S.

To John Paul Bocock

[? *Mid-November 1887*][7]   *Saranac Lake*

Private   *   *   *

* * *Your prominent dramatic critic, writing like a journalist, has written like a braying ass; what he meant is probably quite different and true enough—that the book is ugly and the allegory too like the usual pulpit fudge and not just enough to the modesty of facts. You are right as to Mansfield: Hyde was the younger of the two.[8] He was not good looking however; and not, Great Gods! a mere voluptuary. There is no harm in a voluptuary; and none, with my hand on my heart and in the sight of God, none—no harm whatever—in what prurient fools call "immorality." The harm was in Jekyll, because he was a hypocrite—not because he was fond of women; he says so himself; but people are so filled full of folly and inverted lust, that they can think of nothing but sexuality. The Hypocrite let out the beast Hyde—who is no more sexual than another, but who is the essence of cruelty and malice, and selfishness and cowardice: and these are the diabolic in man—not this poor wish to have a woman, that they make such a cry about. I know, and I dare to say, you know as well as I, that bad and good, even to our human eyes, has no more connection with what is called dissipation than it has with flying

4. I.e., may carry off the dual role with enough virtuosity to ensure your success (and mine).
5. Before the eyes of the public.
6. Presumably a reference to an on-stage role transformation achieved by internationally renowned actor Charles Albert Fechter (1824–79), playing twin brothers Fabien and Louis dei Franchi in the play, *The Corsican Brothers*.
7. Letter located in the Huntington Library (call number 2414). This excerpt is reproduced by permission of the Huntington Library, San Marino, California. John Paul Bocock: an American journalist who began corresponding with Stevenson shortly after Stevenson came to America in the fall of 1887. Stevenson is here responding to a report Bocock had sent on the reception given to the Sullivan-Mansfield stage adaptation which had played at New York's Madison Square Theatre from September 12 to October 1, 1887.
8. In his stage portrayal, Richard Mansfield had made Hyde older than Jekyll, reversing the order of ages shown in the novel.

kites. But the sexual field and the business field are perhaps the two best fitted for the display of cruelty and cowardice and selfishness. That is what people see; and these they confound.

* * *

ROBERT LOUIS STEVENSON

[The Dream Origin of the Tale]†

* * *

* * *there are some among us who claim to have lived longer and more richly than their neighbors; when they lay asleep they claim they were still active; and among the treasures of memory that all men review for their amusement, these count in no second place the harvests of their dreams. There is one of this kind whom I have in my eye, and whose case is perhaps unusual enough to be described. He was from a child an ardent and uncomfortable dreamer. * * * His dreams were at times commonplace enough, at times very strange: at times they were almost formless, he would be haunted, for instance, by nothing more definite than a certain hue of brown, which he did not mind in the least while he was awake, but feared and loathed while he was dreaming; at times, again, they took on every detail of circumstance, as when once he supposed he must swallow the populous world, and awoke screaming with the horror of the thought. The two chief troubles of his very narrow existence—the practical and every-day trouble of school tasks and the ultimate and airy one of hell and judgment—were often confounded together into one appalling nightmare. He seemed to himself to stand before the Great White Throne; he was called on, poor little devil, to recite some form of words, on which his destiny depended; his tongue stuck, his memory was blank, hell gaped for him; and he would awake, clinging to the curtain-rod with his knees to his chin.

* * * But presently, in the course of his growth, the cries and physical contortions passed away, seemingly forever * * * . The look of the world beginning to take hold on his attention, scenery came to play a part in his sleeping as well as in his waking thoughts, so that he would take long, uneventful journeys and see strange towns and

---

† From "A Chapter on Dreams," *Scribner's Magazine* (January 1888): 122–28. Reprinted in Robert Louis Stevenson, *Across the Plains* (1892). These selections touch on what Stevenson relates in the essay of the ungovernable nightmares of his youth as well as the development of the facility for artistically productive unconscious creation that helped create *Strange Case of Dr. Jekyll and Mr. Hyde*.

beautiful places as he lay in bed. * * * About the same time, he began
to read in his dreams—tales, for the most part, and for the most part
after the manner of G. P. R. James,[1] but so incredibly more vivid and
moving than any printed book, that he has ever since been malcon-
tent with literature.

And then, while he was yet a student, there came to him a dream-
adventure which he has no anxiety to repeat; he began, that is to say,
to dream in sequence and thus to lead a double life—one of the day,
one of the night—one that he had every reason to believe was the
true one, another that he had no means of proving to be false. I
should have said he studied, or was by way of studying, at Edinburgh
College, which (it may be supposed) was how I came to know him.
Well, in his dream-life, he passed a long day in the surgical theatre,
his heart in his mouth, his teeth on edge, seeing monstrous malfor-
mations and the abhorred dexterity of surgeons. In a heavy, rainy,
foggy evening he came forth into the South Bridge, turned up the
High Street, and entered the door of a tall *land*,[2] at the top of which
he supposed himself to lodge. All night long, in his wet clothes, he
climbed the stairs, stair after stair in endless series, and at every
second flight a flaring lamp with a reflector. All night long, he
brushed by single persons passing downward—beggarly women of
the street, great, weary, muddy laborers, poor scarecrows of men,
pale parodies of women—but all drowsy and weary like himself, and
all single, and all brushing against him as they passed. In the end,
out of a northern window, he would see day beginning to whiten over
the Firth, give up the ascent, turn to descend, and in a breath be
back again upon the streets, in his wet clothes, in the wet, haggard
dawn, trudging to another day of monstrosities and operations. * * *
The poor gentleman has since been troubled by nothing of the
sort; indeed, his nights were for some while like other men's, now
blank, now checkered with dreams, and these sometimes charming,
sometimes appalling, but except for an occasional vividness, of no
extraordinary kind. I will just note one of these occasions, ere I pass
on to what makes my dreamer truly interesting. It seemed to him
that he was in the first floor of a rough hill-farm. * * * There was no
sign of the farm folk or of any live stock, save for an old, brown, curly
dog of the retriever breed, who sat close in against the wall of the
house and seemed to be dozing. Something about this dog disquieted
the dreamer; it was quite a nameless feeling, for the beast looked
right enough—indeed, he was so old and dull and dusty and broken-
down, that he should rather have awakened pity; and yet the conviction came and grew upon the dreamer that this was no proper dog

---

1. George Payne Rainsford James (1799–1860), British statesman and writer of romantic
   novels, biographies and popular histories.
2. One of the steep walk-up apartment buildings for which Old Town Edinburgh was famous.

at all, but something hellish. A great many dozing summer flies
hummed about the yard; and presently the dog thrust forth his paw,
caught a fly in his open palm, carried it to his mouth like an ape,
and looking suddenly up at the dreamer in the window, winked to
him with one eye. The dream went on, it matters not how it went; it
was a good dream as dreams go; but there was nothing in the sequel
worthy of that devilish brown dog. And the point of interest for me
lies partly in that very fact: that having found so singular an incident,
my imperfect dreamer should prove unable to carry the tale to a fit
end and fall back on indescribable noises and indiscriminate horrors.
It would be different now; he knows his business better!

For, to approach at last the point: This honest fellow had long
been in the custom of setting himself to sleep with tales, and so had
his father before him; but these were irresponsible inventions, told
for the teller's pleasure, with no eye to the crass public or the thwart
reviewer: Tales where a thread might be dropped, or one adventure
quitted for another, on fancy's least suggestion. So that the little
people who manage man's internal theatre had not as yet received a
very rigorous training; and played upon their stage like children who
should have slipped into the house and found it empty, rather than
like drilled actors performing a set piece to a huge hall of faces. But
presently my dreamer began to turn his former amusement of story-
telling to (what is called) account; by which I mean that he began
to write and sell his tales. Here was he, and here were the little people
who did that part of his business, in quite new conditions. The stories
must now be trimmed and pared and set upon all fours, they must
run from a beginning to an end and fit (after a manner) with the
laws of life; the pleasure, in one word, had become a business; and
that not only for the dreamer, but for the little people of his theatre.
These understood the change as well as he. When he lay down to
prepare himself for sleep, he no longer sought amusement, but print-
able and profitable tales; and after he had dozed off in his box-seat,
his little people continued their evolutions with the same mercantile
design. * * *

                              *   *   *

* * *Who are the Little People? They are near connections of the
dreamer's * * * ; they have plainly learned like him to build the
scheme of a considerate story and to arrange emotion in progressive
order: only I think they have more talent; and one thing is beyond
doubt, they can tell him a story piece by piece, like a serial, and keep
him all the while in ignorance of where they aim. Who are they,
then? and who is the dreamer?

Well, as regards the dreamer, I can answer that, for he is no less
a person than myself;—as I might have told you from the beginning,

only that the critics murmur over my consistent egotism;—and as I am positively forced to tell you now, or I could advance but little further with my story. And for the Little People, what shall I say they are but just my Brownies, God bless them! who do one-half my work for me while I am fast asleep, and in all human likelihood, do the rest for me as well, when I am wide awake and fondly suppose I do it for myself. That part which is done while I am sleeping is the Brownies' part beyond contention; but that which is done when I am up and about is by no means necessarily mine, since all goes to show the Brownies have a hand in it even then. Here is a doubt that much concerns my conscience. For myself—what I call I, my conscious ego, the denizen of the pineal gland unless he has changed his residence since Descartes,[3] the man with the conscience and the variable bank-account, the man with the hat and the boots, and the privilege of voting and not carrying his candidate at the general elections—I am sometimes tempted to suppose he is no story-teller at all, but a creature as matter of fact as any cheesemonger or any cheese, and a realist bemired up to the ears in actuality; so that, by that account, the whole of my published fiction should be the single-handed product of some Brownie, some Familiar, some unseen collaborator, whom I keep locked in a back garret, while I get all the praise and he but a share (which I cannot prevent him getting) of the pudding.[4] * * *

I can but give an instance or so of what part is done sleeping and what part awake, and leave the reader to share what laurels there are, at his own nod, between myself and my collaborators; and to do this I will first take a book that a number of persons have been polite enough to read, the *Strange Case of Dr. Jekyll and Mr. Hyde.* I had long been trying to write a story on this subject, to find a body, a vehicle for that strong sense of man's double being which must at times come in upon and overwhelm the mind of every thinking creature.[5] I had even written one, *The Travelling Companion*, which was returned by an editor on the plea that it was a work of genius and indecent, and which I burned the other day on the ground that it was not a work of genius, and that *Jekyll* had supplanted it. Then

---

3. French philosopher and mathematician René Descartes (1596–1650) believed that the pineal gland was the seat of the soul, and hence the place wherein our conscious sense of self resides.

4. Alludes to the description in Alexander Pope's *The Dunciad* (1728), I:53–54, of Poetic Justice lifting a scale "Where, in nice balance, truth with gold she weighs, / And solid pudding against empty praise."

5. Fanny Stevenson, in a prefatory note for Scribner's 1905 Biographical Edition of Stevenson's work, proposes a genealogy of her husband's interest in double being. She suggests that his longstanding fascination with Deacon Brodie (respected Edinburgh craftsman by day and burglar by night) combined with his discovery of an article in a French scientific journal on subconsciousness (never identified) to stimulate his 1879 co-authoring with W. E. Henley of the play *Deacon Brodie or the Double Life*, followed by the 1884 writing of "Markheim," and then the 1885 dream of Jekyll and Hyde.

came one of those financial fluctuations to which (with an elegant modesty) I have hitherto referred in the third person. For two days I went about racking my brains for a plot of any sort; and on the second night I dreamed the scene at the window, and a scene afterward split in two, in which Hyde, pursued for some crime, took the powder and underwent the change in the presence of his pursuers. All the rest was made awake, and consciously, although I think I can trace in much of it the manner of my Brownies. The meaning of the tale is therefore mine, and had long pre-existed in my garden of Adonis,[6] and tried one body after another in vain; indeed, I do most of the morality, worse luck! and my Brownies have not a rudiment of what we call a conscience. Mine, too, is the setting, mine the characters. All that was given me was the matter of three scenes, and the central idea of a voluntary change becoming involuntary. Will it be thought ungenerous, after I have been so liberally ladling out praise to my unseen collaborators, if I here toss them over, bound hand and foot, into the arena of the critics? For the business of the powders, which so many have censured, is, I am relieved to say, not mine at all but the Brownies'. * * * sometimes I cannot but suppose my Brownies have been aping Bunyan,[7] and yet in no case with what would possibly be called a moral in a tract; never with the ethical narrowness; conveying hints instead of life's larger limitations and that sort of sense which we seem to perceive in the arabesque of time and space.

For the most part, it will be seen, my Brownies are somewhat fantastic, like their stories hot and hot, full of passion and the picturesque, alive with animating incident; and they have no prejudice against the supernatural. * * *

6. The reference is to Edmund Spenser's version of the garden of Adonis in *The Faerie Queene* (1590), III:vi; a place where all created essences of things wrought out of chaos reside while awaiting their mortal embodiment in the world.
7. The allegorist John Bunyan (1628–88), author of *The Pilgrim's Progress* (1678; Second Part 1684).

"I am, Yours, RLS": A Stevenson Signature†

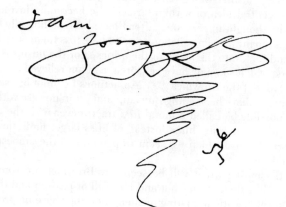

† From Robert Louis Stevenson to Edmund Gosse [26 March 1886], as featured in *The Letters of Robert Louis Stevenson*, ed. Booth and Mehew, 5:239, from the facsimile in Sotheby Catalogue of 26 February 1929 (306). Reprinted by permission of Sotheby's. This signature, with its agitated—or exhilarated—falling man, is one of a number of cartoonish doodles found in Stevenson's letters which are enjoyably reproduced in the Booth and Mehew edition of his letters. It appears at the end of a brief note Stevenson wrote to his literary friend Gosse, accepting an invitation to dine in London several months after the publication of *Strange Case of Dr. Jekyll and Mr. Hyde*.

Reception

[ANDREW LANG]

[Mr. Stevenson's Originality of Treatment]†

Mr. Stevenson's *Prince Otto* was, no doubt, somewhat disappointing to many of his readers. They will be hard to please if they are disappointed in his *Strange Case of Dr. Jekyll and Mr. Hyde*. To adopt a recent definition of some of Mr. Stevenson's tales, this little shilling work is like "Poe with the addition of a moral sense." * * *

Mr. Stevenson's idea, his secret (but a very open secret) is that of the double personality in every man. The mere conception is familiar enough. Poe used it in *William Wilson*, and Gautier in *Le Chevalier Double*. Yet Mr. Stevenson's originality of treatment remains none the less striking and astonishing. The double personality does not in his romance take the form of a personified conscience, the *doppel ganger* of the sinner, a "double" like his own double which Goethe is fabled to have seen: No; the "separable self" in this "strange case" is all unlike that in *William Wilson*, and, with its unlikeness to its master, with its hideous caprices, and appalling vitality, and terrible power of growth and increase, is, to our thinking, a notion as novel as it is terrific. We would welcome a spectre, a ghoul, or even a vampire gladly, rather than meet Mr. Edward Hyde. * * *

It is a proof of Mr. Stevenson's skill that he has chosen the scene for his wild "Tragedy of a Body and a Soul," as it might have been called, in the most ordinary and respectable quarters of London. His heroes (surely *this* is original) are all successful middle-aged professional men. No woman appears in the tale (as in *Treasure Island*), and we incline to think that Mr. Stevenson always does himself most justice in novels without a heroine. It may be regarded by some critics as a drawback to the tale that it inevitably disengages a powerful

† From *The Saturday Review* (January 9, 1886): 55–56. Brackets around the reviewer's name mark an attribution of authorship to what was originally an unsigned review. In this case, Lang can be identified as the author partly by the recurrence of the reference he had made to "William Wilson" and "Le Chevalier Double" when writing to Stevenson about *Strange Case of Dr. Jekyll and Mr. Hyde* some six weeks earlier (see p. 81, n. 5 in this edition).

lesson in conduct. It is not a moral allegory, of course; but you cannot help reading the moral into it, and recognizing that, just as every one of us, according to Mr. Stevenson, travels through life with a donkey (as he himself did in the Cevennes),[1] so every Jekyll among us is haunted by his own Hyde. But it would be most unfair to insist on this, as there is nothing a novel-reader hates more than to be done good to unawares. Nor has Mr. Stevenson, obviously, any didactic purpose. The moral of the tale is its natural soul, and no more separable from it than, in ordinary life, Hyde is separable from Jekyll.

* * *

FROM THE *BIRMINGHAM DAILY POST*

[A Mere Bit of Catch-Penny Sensationalism]†

The attempt which is made here to unite strange men—the strangeness of a Frankenstein story or an old Greek myth—with modern science, leaves no stranger impression on the mind than a sense of the ingenuity of the writer. One thrills before the ghost in "Hamlet" or the weird sisters in "Macbeth," for one believes in them; we only smile in the presence of Mr. Jekyll and Mr. Hyde, for we know they are a mere clever invention. The story turns upon the supposition that there is a duality in man's nature, a better and a worse self, which are separable. Dr. Jekyll discovers a drug by means of which he can effect the change. * * * But a new terror comes into his life, for the transformation which he had first effected by an effort of his will takes place involuntarily, and this involuntary change from the better to the worse self becomes more and more frequent. At last— and this is really a comic touch which shows what great things Mr. Stevenson may do in the laughter-provoking way—his stock of the drug becomes exhausted, and he cannot get it renewed, for, as he discovers too late, his first supply had been adulterated, and it was the unknown adulteration which gave it its strange power. So Dr. Jekyll has perforce to become Edward Hyde, brutal murderer and mean scoundrel, in which capacity he has yet enough of common sense to commit suicide, and so end the book. Mr. Stevenson is a man of such great ability and artistic faculty that even this repulsive theme is made fascinating in his hands; but surely it is unworthy of him—a mere bit of catch-penny sensationalism. It is as though a

1. In the dedication to his *Travels with a Donkey in the Cévennes* (1879), Stevenson wrote, "we are all . . . in what John Bunyan calls the wilderness of this world . . . travellers with a donkey."

† From the *Birmingham Daily Post* (January 19, 1886): 7.

great sculptor should spend his time in making bogie turnip-lanterns to frighten children.

[JAMES ASHCROFT NOBLE]

[The Place of Honour]†

The *Strange Case of Dr. Jekyll and Mr. Hyde* is not an orthodox three-volume novel; it is not even a one-volume novel of the ordinary type; it is simply a paper-covered shilling story, belonging, so far as external appearance goes, to a class of literature familiarity with which has bred in the minds of most readers a certain measure of contempt. Appearances, it has been once or twice remarked, are deceitful; and in this case they are very deceitful indeed, for, in spite of the paper cover and the popular price, Mr. Stevenson's story distances so unmistakably its three-volume and one-volume competitors, that its only fitting place is the place of honour. It is, indeed, many years since English fiction has been enriched by any work at once so weirdly imaginative in conception and so faultlessly ingenious in construction as this little tale, which can be read with ease in a couple of hours. * * * And, indeed, the story has a much larger and deeper interest than that belonging to a mere skilful narrative. It is a marvellous exploration into the recesses of human nature; and though it is more than possible that Mr. Stevenson wrote with no ethical intent, its impressiveness as a parable is equal to its fascination as a work of art. I do not ignore the many differences between the genius of the author of *The Scarlet Letter* and that of the author of *Dr. Jekyll and Mr. Hyde* when I say that the latter story is worthy of Hawthorne.

[E. T. COOK]

[Not Merely Strange, But Impossible]‡

Mr. R. L. Stevenson's proved ability in the invention of exciting stories is by no means at fault in his *Strange Case of Dr. Jekyll and Mr. Hyde* (Longmans & Co.). It is certainly a very strange case, and one

---

† From *The Academy* (January 23, 1886): 55. Noble was a writer and critic who contributed regularly to a group of well-reputed London journals.
‡ From *The Athenaeum* (January 23, 1886): 100. (Sir) Edward Tyas Cook had a distinguished career in journalism, eventually becoming chief editor of several major London periodicals.

which would be extremely difficult to see through from the beginning. It has also the first requisite of such a story—it is extremely clearly narrated, and it holds one's interest. It overshoots the mark, however, by being not merely strange, but impossible, and even absurd when the explanation is given. So good an artist in fanciful mysteries as Mr. Stevenson should have avoided the mistake of a lengthy rationalization which in the nature of things is no rationalization at all. In the effective part of the story two points strike the reader as weak: the first incident which is meant to show the diabolical character of Mr. Hyde is inadequate, and the terms of Dr. Jekyll's will would have been inoperative. Mr. Stevenson has overlooked the fact that a man's will does not come into force until he is dead, and that the fact that he has not been heard of for three months would not enable his executor to carry out his testamentary directions.

* * *

FROM *THE TIMES* OF LONDON

[His Very Original Genius]†

Nothing Mr. Stevenson has written as yet has so strongly impressed us with the versatility of his very original genius as this sparsely-printed little shilling volume. * * * every connoisseur who reads the story once must certainly read it twice. He will read it the first time, passing from surprise to surprise, in a curiosity that keeps growing, because it is never satisfied. For the life of us, we cannot make out how such an incident can possibly be explained on grounds that are intelligible or in any way plausible. Yet all the time the seriousness of the tone assures us that explanations are forthcoming. In our impatience we are hurried towards the denouement, which accounts for everything upon strictly scientific grounds, though the science be the science of problematical futurity. Then, having drawn a sigh of relief at having found even a fantastically speculative issue from our embarrassments, we begin reflectively to call to mind how systematically the writer has been working towards it. Never for a moment, in the most startling situations, has he lost his grasp of the grand ground-facts of a wonderful and supernatural problem. Each apparently incredible or insignificant detail has been thoughtfully

† From *The Times* of London (January 25, 1886). This is the review that Stevenson's publisher Charles Longman said gave the book its real "start."

subordinated to his purpose. And if we say, after all, on a calm retrospect, that the strange case is absurdly and insanely improbable, Mr. Stevenson might answer in the words of Hamlet, that there are more things in heaven and in earth than are dreamed of in our philosophy. For we are still groping by doubtful lights on the dim limits of boundless investigation; and it is always possible that we may be on the brink of a new revelation as to the unforeseen resources of the medical art. And, at all events, the answer should suffice for the purposes of Mr. Stevenson's sensational *tour d'esprit.*[1]

* * * Naturally, we compare it with the sombre masterpieces of Poe, and we may say at once that Mr. Stevenson has gone far deeper. Poe embroidered richly in the gloomy grandeur of his imagination upon themes that were but too material, and not very novel—on the sinister destiny overshadowing a doomed family, on a living and breathing man kept prisoner in a coffin or vault, on the wild whirling of a human waif in the boiling eddies of the Maelstrom—while Mr. Stevenson evolves the ideas of his story from the world that is unseen, enveloping everything in weird mystery, till at last it pleases him to give us the password. We are not going to tell his strange story, though we might well do so, and only excite the curiosity of our readers. We shall only say that we are shown the shrewdest of lawyers hopelessly puzzled by the inexplicable conduct of a familiar friend. All the antecedents of a life of virtue and honour seem to be belied by the discreditable intimacy that has been formed with one of the most callous and atrocious of criminals. A crime committed under the eyes of a witness goes unavenged, though the notorious criminal has been identified, for he disappears as absolutely as if the earth had swallowed him. He reappears in due time where we should least expect to see him, and for some miserable days he leads a charmed life, while he excites the superstitious terrors—of all about him. Indeed, the strongest nerves are shaken by stress of sinister circumstances, as well they may be, for the worthy Dr. Jekyll—the benevolent physician—has likewise vanished amid events that are enveloped in impalpable mysteries; nor can any one surmise what has become of him. So with overwrought feelings and conflicting anticipations we are brought to the end, where all is accounted for, more or less credibly.

Nor is it the mere charm of the story, strange as it is, which fascinates and thrills us. Mr. Stevenson is known for a master of style, and never has he shown his resources more remarkably than on this occasion. We do not mean that the book is written in excellent English—that must be a matter of course; but he has weighed his words and turned his sentences so as to sustain and excite through-

1. Feat of wit.

out the sense of mystery and of horror. The mere artful use of an "it" for a "he" may go far in that respect, and Mr. Stevenson has carefully chosen his language and missed no opportunity. And if his style is good, his motive is better, and shows a higher order of genius. Slight as is the story, and supremely sensational, we remember nothing better since George Eliot's "Romola" than this delineation of a feeble but kindly nature steadily and inevitably succumbing to the sinister influences of besetting weaknesses.[2] With no formal preaching and without a touch of Pharisaism, he works out the essential power of Evil, which, with its malignant patience and unwearying perseverance, gains ground with each casual yielding to temptation, till the once well-meaning man may actually become a fiend, or at least wear the reflection of the fiend's image. But we have said enough to show our opinion of the book, which should be read as a finished study in the art of fantastic literature.

JOHN ADDINGTON SYMONDS

Letter to Robert Louis Stevenson, March 3, 1886†

At last I have read Dr Jekyll. It makes me wonder whether a man has the right so to scrutinize "the abysmal deeps of personality." It is indeed a dreadful book, most dreadful because of a certain moral callousness, a want of sympathy, a shutting out of hope. The art is burning and intense. The Peau de Chagrin[1] disappears; Poe is as water. As a piece of literary work, this seems to me the finest you have done—in all that regards style, invention, psychological analysis, exquisite fitting of parts, and admirable employment of motives to realize the abnormal. But it has left such a deeply painful impression on my heart that I do not know how I am ever to turn to it again.

The fact is that, viewed as an allegory, it touches one too closely. Most of us at some epoch of our lives have been upon the verge of developing a Mr Hyde.[2]

---

2. The character in *Romola* (1862–63) is the handsome, well-educated, disastrously weak-willed husband of Romola, Tito Melema.

† From *The Letters of John Addington Symonds*, ed. Herbert M. Schueller and Robert L. Peters (Detroit: Wayne State University Press, 1969) 3: 120–22. Reprinted by permission of Robert L. Peters. Footnotes are by the editor of this Norton Critical Edition. For Stevenson's response to this letter, see p. 85 in this edition.

1. Honoré de Balzac's 1831 story of a young man fatally seduced by power and pleasure through the gift of a magic ass' skin which reduces his life with every wish it grants.

2. Critic Elaine Showalter cites these sentences as evidence that "Symonds . . . may have read the book as a signing to the male community" of Stevenson's awareness of painful self-divisions fostered in men by Victorian dread of homosexuality (see Showalter, *Sexual Anarchy* [New York: Viking, 1990], p. 115). Symonds was to describe his own battle with homosexuality in a memoir which, to protect his family, he arranged to have kept out of

Physical and biological Science on a hundred lines is reducing individual freedom to zero, and weakening the sense of responsibility. I doubt whether the artist should lend his genius to this grim argument. Your Dr Jekyll seems to me capable of loosening the last threads of self-control in one who should read it while wavering between his better and worse self. It is like the Cave of Despair in the Faery Queen.[3]

I had the great biologist Lauder Brunton[4] with me a fortnight back. He was talking about Dr Jekyll and a book by W. O. Holmes, in wh atavism is played with. I could see that, though a Christian, he held very feebly to the theory of human liberty; and these two works of fiction interested him, as Dr Jekyll does me, upon that point at issue.[5]

I understand now thoroughly how much a sprite you are. Really there is something not quite human in your genius!

The denouement would have been finer, I think, if Dr Jekyll by a last supreme effort of his lucid self had given Mr Hyde up to justice— wh might have been arranged after the scene in Lanyon's study. Did you ever read Raskolnikow?[6] How fine is that ending! Had you made your hero act thus, you would at least have saved the sense of human dignity. The doors of Broadmoor[7] would have closed on Mr Hyde.

---

public view until long after his death. (An excerpt from it appears on pp. 138–40 of this edition.)

3. Where Despair lures men to suicide by persuading them that life holds no hope of relief from their sins and sufferings (*The Faerie Queene*. I:ix).

4. An eminent London physician as well as biologist; Stevenson had had a medical consultation with him in July 1884 (see *Letters* 5:1).

5. W. O. Holmes: i.e., Oliver Wendell Holmes, Sr. (1809–1894), American doctor and writer. That point at issue: i.e., the point of whether biology is so determinative of our beings as to preclude the possibility of free will. The book in question is probably either Holmes' *Elsie Venner* (1861), about a girl with a partially "envenomed" nature as a result of a snakebite her mother received in pregnancy, or else his *The Guardian Angel* (1867), about a girl whose personality mingles ancestral strains of native American "savage" and spiritualized Protestant martyr.

6. I.e., the 1866 novel by Fyodor Dostoyevsky later to be translated into English as *Crime and Punishment*. Symonds had recommended the French translation to Stevenson in a letter of February 27, 1885; by early November of that year, Stevenson had read it and was writing excitedly to W. E. Henley, "Dostoieffsky is of course simply immense: it is not reading a book, it is having a brain fever, to read it" (*Letters* 5:151). He speaks of the novel just as warmly to Symonds when he responds to this letter, calling it "the greatest book I have read easily in ten years . . . a room, a house of life, into which [readers] themselves enter, and are tortured and purified" (*Letters* 5:220–21).

7. A state asylum for the criminally insane built in 1862 in southeast England.

[JULIA WEDGWOOD]

[The Individualizing Influence of Modern Democracy]†

* * *

By far the most remarkable work we have to notice this time is "The Strange Case of Dr. Jekyll and Mr. Hyde," a shilling story, which the reader devours in an hour, but to which he may return again and again, to study a profound allegory and admire a model of style. * * * Mr. Stevenson has set before himself the psychical problem of Hawthorne's "Transformation," viewed from a different and perhaps an opposite point of view, and has dealt with it with more vigour if with less grace.[1] Here it is not the child of Nature who becomes manly by experience of sin, but a fully-developed man who goes through a different form of the process, and if the delineation is less associated with beautiful imagery, the parable is deeper, and, we would venture to add, truer. Mr. Stevenson represents the individualizing influence of modern democracy in its more concentrated form. Whereas most fiction deals with the relation between man and woman (and the very fact that its scope is so much narrowed is a sign of the atomic character of our modern thought), the author of this strange tale takes an even narrower range, and sets himself to investigate the meaning of the word *self*. No woman's name occurs in the book, no romance is even suggested in it; it depends on the interest of an idea; but so powerfully is this interest worked out that the reader feels that the same material might have been spun out to cover double the space, and still have struck him as condensed and close-knit workmanship. It is one of those rare fictions which make one understand the value of temperance in art. * * *

---

† From *The Contemporary Review* (April 1886): 594–5. Frances Julia Wedgwood was a frequent contributor to London periodicals and author of several books on morality and religion.
1. Nathaniel Hawthorne's *Transformation* (1860; American title *The Marble Faun*) investigates the effects of remorse for a crime of passion on the soul of a childishly simple, animalistically high-spirited young man.

GERARD MANLEY HOPKINS

Letter to Robert Bridges, October 28, 1886†

* * *

This sour severity blinds you to his great genius. *Jekyll and Hyde* I have read. You speak of "the gross absurdity" of the interchange.[1] Enough that it is impossible and might perhaps have been a little better masked: it must be connived at, and it gives rise to a fine situation. It is not more impossible than fairies, giants, heathen gods, and lots of things that literature teems with—and none more than yours. You are certainly wrong about Hyde being overdrawn: my Hyde is worse. The trampling scene is perhaps a convention: he was thinking of something unsuitable for fiction.

I can by no means grant that the characters are not characterised, though how deep the springs of their surface action are I am not yet clear. But the superficial touches of character are admirable: how can you be so blind as not to see them? e.g. Utterson frowning, biting the end of his finger, and saying to the butler "This is a strange tale you tell me, my man, a very strange tale." And Dr Lanyon: "I used to like it; sir [life]; yes, sir, I liked it. Sometimes I think if we knew all" etc. These are worthy of Shakespeare. * * *

* * * Stevenson is master of a consummate style and each phrase is finished as in poetry. It will not do at all, your treatment of him.

HENRY JAMES

[The Art of the Presentation]†

* * *

Is "Dr. Jekyll and Mr. Hyde" a work of high philosophic intention, or simply the most ingenious and irresponsible of fictions? It has the stamp of a really imaginative production, that we may take it in dif-

---

† From *Gerard Manley Hopkins: Selected Letters*, ed. Catherine Phillips (Oxford: Clarendon Press, 1990), pp. 243–44. Footnotes are by the editor of this Norton Critical Edition. Reprinted by permission of Oxford University Press. Hopkins, poet and priest, maintained a lifetime friendship with fellow-poet Robert Bridges following the meeting of the two as students at Oxford in the 1860s.

1. I.e., the transformation from Jekyll to Hyde.

† From *Century Magazine* (April 1888): 877–78. These comments appear as part of a lengthy essay by James reviewing all of Stevenson's work to date ("Robert Louis Stevenson"; reprinted in James' *Partial Portraits*, 1888). Much as Stevenson and James differed from one another as novelists, they had a great appreciation for one another's art. That appreciation developed into a warm personal friendship shortly after Stevenson published "A Humble Remonstrance" (*Longman's Magazine*, December 1884) as a cordially respectful response to James' "The Art of Fiction."

ferent ways, but I suppose it would be called the most serious of the
author's tales. It deals with the relation of the baser parts of man to
his nobler—of the capacity for evil that exists in the most generous
natures, and it expresses these things in a fable which is a wonder-
fully happy invention. The subject is endlessly interesting, and rich
in all sorts of provocation, and Mr. Stevenson is to be congratulated
on having touched the core of it. I may do him injustice, but it is,
however, here, not the profundity of the idea which strikes me so
much as the art of the presentation—the extremely successful form.
There is a genuine feeling for the perpetual moral question, a fresh
sense of the difficulty of being good and the brutishness of being
bad, but what there is above all is a singular ability in holding the
interest. I confess that that, to my sense, is the most edifying thing
in the short, rapid, concentrated story, which is really a masterpiece
of concision. There is something almost impertinent in the way, as
I have noticed, in which Mr. Stevenson achieves his best effects
without the aid of the ladies, and "Dr. Jekyll" is a capital example of
his heartless independence. It is usually supposed that a truly poignant impression cannot be made without them, but in the drama of
Mr. Hyde's fatal ascendency they remain altogether in the wing. It
is very obvious—I do not say it cynically—that they must have played
an important part in his development. The gruesome tone of the tale
is, no doubt, deepened by their absence; it is like the late afternoon
light of a foggy winter Sunday, when even inanimate objects have a
kind of wicked look. * * *

FROM THE *LEAMINGTON SPA COURIER*

The Rev. Dr. Nicholson on "Dr. Jekyll and Mr. Hyde"†

*   *   *

An overflowing congregation was attracted to St. Alban's Church, on
Sunday evening, by an announcement, made in the early part of the
week, that the Rev. Dr. Nicholson would preach upon "Dr. Jekyll
and Mr. Hyde," a sensational novel, which has of late attracted much
attention, and a dramatised version of which was produced last week,
at the Theatre Royal. The preacher selected as his text the last verse

† From the *Leamington Spa Courier* (November 24, 1888) This piece of local reporting gives
the flavor of the sermonizing uses made of *Strange Case of Dr. Jekyll and Mr. Hyde* in a
society where, as mentioned by Graham Balfour, "it was read by those who never read
fiction, it was quoted in pulpits, and made the subject of leading articles in religious
newspapers" (Balfour 2:17–18).

of the 7th chapter of St. Paul's Epistle to the Romans: "So then, with the mind I myself serve the Lord God, but with the flesh the Lord sin.[1] He said he took it for granted that his hearers were acquainted with the case of Dr. Jekyll and Mr. Hyde, and he would not, therefore, proceed to a minute account of the incidents of it. It had taken a firm hold of the public mind. The copy of the book which he held in his hand was one of the fifth edition, and it had been dramatised. * * * About two years ago, it fell into his hands, and he took to reading it; and before he had got beyond the first half of the book, he was reminded of the 7th chapter of Romans—not that the author referred to it—and he concluded the book with the opinion that it was one of the most moral sermons ever preached, or, at all events, ever written. Let them not take it for a sensational story. What was a sensational story? It was a story which appealed to the feelings, to the sensations, as they called them; to the emotions, and to the nervous system, and to nothing more. It had no purpose beyond that. Idle people, who had nothing else to do, and morbid people, took a great delight in reading such stories; they delighted in reading "shockers," as they called them, and "penny dreadfuls," and so on, and those people did their lives and nerves a great deal of harm. Such books were full of all that was altogether imaginative, and of pernicious nonsense. * * * The account that the writer gave them was metaphysically and morally true. He told them, which was true of human nature, that it was a duality; that there was a higher nature within them and a lower nature; that by power of will they could, if they would, surrender their higher natures to their lower natures; and that if they did that too frequently, return was impossible, and that all that would be left to them of the higher nature was the capacity for remorse. That was good logic, good metaphysics, and good theology. * * * in reading the fiction, or in observing the drama—for he had been told it was dramatised—let them take care they did not bestow their sympathies in the wrong direction. Who did they sympathise with, Jekyll or Hyde? Hyde for him. Hyde was wrong, if they were to look upon those characters as they moved before them as individuals in that book, it was the poor animal that was wrong. What then was the cultured philosopher, the man of refinement and knowledge? According to his own showing, he sent forth that animal, without moral sense or goodness, upon the world. Who was to blame, who was the more guilty—that poor animal that ravened through the world? It must be destroyed of course, but they could almost weep for it while they destroyed it. The guilty man was the philosopher. It was his will that had done all, and his will was

---

1. Either the reporter or the Reverend faltered here; in the King James version of the Bible, this verse reads, "So then with the mind I myself serve the law of God; but with the flesh the law of sin."

guilty of all. * * * In that story they had seen the enswining of a nature. How did it come about? Why, by habit. He first took a dose of oblivion, and then descended. For one reason or another, he wished to get back again, and he took another dose and he returned. He continued thus until the drug was exhausted, that was to say until the human being was exhausted and he could not get back. What had they learned from the book? * * * They could no more trifle with sin, than they could spring into the water and gambol with an octopus. One man had one besetting sin, one another, but that sin would be their ruin which took them away from God. They were all one in so far as they had to do with a very slippery nature, but they had also, thank God, to do with a spirit of God, and in that spirit, they could do all things. If Christ was in their hearts, they would gain the victory and spiritualise even there on earth, that poor fallen nature, and triumph over sin, and over death, through Jesus Christ their Lord.

"Markheim" and the Victorian Market for Sensation Fiction

ROBERT LOUIS STEVENSON

Markheim.†

"Yes," said the dealer, "our windfalls are of various kinds. Some customers are ignorant, and then I touch a dividend on my superior knowledge. Some are dishonest," and here he held up the candle, so that the light fell strongly on his visitor, "and in that case," he continued, "I profit by my virtue."

Markheim had but just entered from the daylight streets, and his eyes had not yet grown familiar with the mingled shine and darkness in the shop. At these pointed words, and before the near presence of the flame, he blinked painfully and looked aside.

The dealer chuckled. "You come to me on Christmas Day," he resumed, "when you know that I am alone in my house, put up my shutters, and make a point of refusing business. Well, you will have to pay for that; you will have to pay for my loss of time, when I should be balancing my books; you will have to pay, besides, for a kind of manner that I remark in you to-day very strongly. I am the essence of discretion, and ask no awkward questions; but when a customer cannot look me in the eye, he has to pay for it." The dealer once more chuckled; and then, changing to his usual business voice,

---

† "Markheim" was written a year before *Strange Case of Dr. Jekyll and Mr. Hyde* to fulfill a commission from the *Pall Mall Gazette* for a Christmas ghost story. However, when finished, "Markheim" proved too short for the magazine's length requirement. Another story was supplied in its place and "Markheim" was not published until a year later, in *Unwin's Annual, 1886: The Broken Shaft* (London: T. Fisher Unwin, given date 1886; publication release date December 1885). Stevenson slightly revised the tale when he republished it in *The Merry Men and Other Tales and Fables* in 1887. His opinion of the story rose over time: just after he had written it, he worried that its quality suffered from the haste with which it was composed; by 1887, he had come to the judgment that "Markheim" was "true" in a way some of his more painstakingly produced stories were not (see *Letters* 5: 39 and 365). While a slighter piece than *Strange Case of Dr. Jekyll and Mr. Hyde*, "Markheim" provides an interesting antecedent to it, as a horror story taking us with great psychological intensity from the event of a crime into the fractured consciousness of the man of culture and education who committed it. The text seen here is taken from the first edition of *The Merry Men* (London: Chatto and Windus, 1887).

though still with a note of irony, "You can give, as usual, a clear account of how you came into the possession of the object?" he continued. "Still your uncle's cabinet? A remarkable collector, sir!"

And the little pale, round-shouldered dealer stood almost on tip-toe, looking over the top of his gold spectacles, and nodding his head with every mark of disbelief. Markheim returned his gaze with one of infinite pity, and a touch of horror.

"This time," said he, "you are in error. I have not come to sell, but to buy. I have no curios to dispose of; my uncle's cabinet is bare to the wainscot;[1] even were it still intact, I have done well on the Stock Exchange, and should more likely add to it than otherwise, and my errand to-day is simplicity itself. I seek a Christmas present for a lady," he continued, waxing more fluent as he struck into the speech he had prepared; "and certainly I owe you every excuse for thus disturbing you upon so small a matter. But the thing was neglected yesterday; I must produce my little compliment at dinner; and, as you very well know, a rich marriage is not a thing to be neglected."

There followed a pause, during which the dealer seemed to weigh this statement incredulously. The ticking of many clocks among the curious lumber of the shop, and the faint rushing of the cabs in a near thoroughfare, filled up the interval of silence.

"Well, sir," said the dealer, "be it so. You are an old customer after all; and if, as you say, you have the chance of a good marriage, far be it from me to be an obstacle. Here is a nice thing for a lady now," he went on, "this hand glass[2]—fifteenth century, warranted; comes from a good collection, too; but I reserve the name, in the interests of my customer, who was just like yourself, my dear sir, the nephew and sole heir of a remarkable collector."

The dealer, while he thus ran on in his dry and biting voice, had stooped to take the object from its place; and, as he had done so, a shock had passed through Markheim, a start both of hand and foot, a sudden leap of many tumultuous passions to the face. It passed as swiftly as it came, and left no trace beyond a certain trembling of the hand that now received the glass.

"A glass," he said hoarsely, and then paused, and repeated it more clearly. "A glass? For Christmas? Surely not?"

"And why not?" cried the dealer. "Why not a glass?"

Markheim was looking upon him with an indefinable expression. "You ask me why not?" he said. "Why, look here—look in it—look at yourself! Do you like to see it? No! nor I —nor any man."

The little man had jumped back when Markheim had so suddenly confronted him with the mirror; but now, perceiving there was noth-

1. Wood-paneled lining in a piece of furniture or on a wall.
2. Mirror.

ing worse on hand, he chuckled. "Your future lady, sir, must be pretty hard favoured," said he.

"I ask you," said Markheim, "for a Christmas present, and you give me this—this damned reminder of years, and sins and follies—this hand-conscience! Did you mean it? Had you a thought in your mind? Tell me. It will be better for you if you do. Come, tell me about yourself. I hazard a guess now, that you are in secret a very charitable man?"

The dealer looked closely at his companion. It was very odd, Markheim did not appear to be laughing; there was something in his face like an eager sparkle of hope, but nothing of mirth.

"What are you driving at?" the dealer asked.

"Not charitable?" returned the other, gloomily. "Not charitable; not pious; not scrupulous; unloving, unbeloved; a hand to get money, a safe to keep it. Is that all? Dear God, man, is that all?"

"I will tell you what it is," began the dealer, with some sharpness, and then broke off again into a chuckle. "But I see this is a love match of yours, and you have been drinking the lady's health."

"Ah!" cried Markheim, with a strange curiosity. "Ah, have you been in love? Tell me about that."

"I," cried the dealer. "I in love! I never had the time, nor have I the time to-day for all this nonsense. Will you take the glass?"

"Where is the hurry?" returned Markheim. "It is very pleasant to stand here talking; and life is so short and insecure that I would not hurry away from any pleasure—no, not even from so mild a one as this. We should rather cling, cling to what little we can get, like a man at a cliff's edge. Every second is a cliff, if you think upon it—a cliff a mile high—high enough, if we fall, to dash us out of every feature of humanity. Hence it is best to talk pleasantly. Let us talk of each other: why should we wear this mask? Let us be confidential. Who knows, we might become friends?"

"I have just one word to say to you," said the dealer. "Either make your purchase, or walk out of my shop!"

"True, true," said Markheim. "Enough fooling. To business. Show me something else."

The dealer stooped once more, this time to replace the glass upon the shelf, his thin blond hair falling over his eyes as he did so. Markheim moved a little nearer, with one hand in the pocket of his great-coat; he drew himself up and filled his lungs; at the same time many different emotions were depicted together on his face—terror, horror, and resolve, fascination and a physical repulsion; and through a haggard lift of his upper lip, his teeth looked out.

"This, perhaps, may suit," observed the dealer: and then, as he began to re-arise, Markeim bounded from behind upon his victim.

The long, skewerlike dagger flashed and fell. The dealer struggled like a hen, striking his temple on the shelf, and then tumbled on the floor in a heap.

Time had some score of small voices in that shop, some stately and slow as was becoming to their great age; others garrulous and hurried. All these told out the seconds in an intricate chorus of tickings. Then the passage of a lad's feet, heavily running on the pavement, broke in upon these smaller voices and startled Markheim into the consciousness of his surroundings. He looked about him awfully.[3] The candle stood on the counter, its flame solemnly wagging in a draught; and by that inconsiderable movement, the whole room was filled with noiseless bustle and kept heaving like a sea: the tall shadows nodding, the gross blots of darkness swelling and dwindling as with respiration, the faces of the portraits and the china gods changing and wavering like images in water. The inner door stood ajar, and peered into that leaguer of shadows with a long slit of daylight like a pointing finger.

From these fear-stricken rovings, Markheim's eyes returned to the body of his victim, where it lay both humped and sprawling, incredibly small and strangely meaner than in life. In these poor, miserly clothes, in that ungainly attitude, the dealer lay like so much sawdust. Markheim had feared to see it, and, lo! it was nothing. And yet, as he gazed, this bundle of old clothes and pool of blood began to find eloquent voices. There it must lie; there was none to work the cunning hinges or direct the miracle of locomotion—there it must lie till it was found. Found! ay, and then? Then would this dead flesh lift up a cry that would ring over England, and fill the world with the echoes of pursuit. Ay, dead or not, this was still the enemy. "Time was that when the brains were out,"[4] he thought; and the first word struck into his mind. Time, now that the deed was accomplished—time, which had closed for the victim, had become instant and momentous for the slayer.

The thought was yet in his mind, when, first one and then another, with every variety of pace and voice—one deep as the bell from a cathedral turret, another ringing on its treble notes the prelude of a waltz—the clocks began to strike the hour of three in the afternoon.

The sudden outbreak of so many tongues in that dumb chamber staggered him. He began to bestir himself, going to and fro with the candle, beleaguered by moving shadows, and startled to the soul by chance reflections. In many rich mirrors, some of home design, some

3. With dread.
4. Alludes to lines spoken by Shakespeare's Macbeth, distraught at the sight of the ghost who haunts him after his murder of King Duncan: "The time has been, / That, when the brains were out, the man would die, / And there an end. But now they rise again, / With twenty mortal murders on their crowns, / And push us from our stools" (*Macbeth*, 3.4. 78–82).

from Venice or Amsterdam, he saw his face repeated and repeated, as it were an army of spies; his own eyes met and detected him; and the sound of his own steps, lightly as they fell, vexed the surrounding quiet. And still, as he continued to fill his pockets, his mind accused him with a sickening iteration, of the thousand faults of his design. He should have chosen a more quiet hour; he should have prepared an alibi; he should not have used a knife; he should have been more cautious, and only bound and gagged the dealer, and not killed him; he should have been more bold, and killed the servant also; he should have done all things otherwise: poignant regrets, weary, incessant toiling of the mind to change what was unchangeable, to plan what was now useless, to be the architect of the irrevocable past. Meanwhile, and behind all this activity, brute terrors, like the scurrying of rats in a deserted attic, filled the more remote chambers of his brain with riot; the hand of the constable would fall heavy on his shoulder, and his nerves would jerk like a hooked fish; or he beheld, in galloping defile, the dock,[5] the prison, the gallows, and the black coffin.

Terror of the people in the street sat down before his mind like a besieging army. It was impossible, he thought, but that some rumour[6] of the struggle must have reached their ears and set on edge their curiosity; and now, in all the neighbouring houses, he divined them sitting motionless and with uplifted ear—solitary people, condemned to spend Christmas dwelling alone on memories of the past, and now startingly recalled from that tender exercise; happy family parties, struck into silence round the table, the mother still with raised finger: every degree and age and humour, but all, by their own hearths, prying and hearkening and weaving the rope that was to hang him. Sometimes it seemed to him he could not move too softly; the clink of the tall Bohemian goblets rang out loudly like a bell; and alarmed by the bigness of the ticking, he was tempted to stop the clocks. And then, again, with a swift transition of his terrors, the very silence of the place appeared a source of peril, and a thing to strike and freeze the passer-by; and he would step more boldly, and bustle aloud among the contents of the shop, and imitate, with elaborate bravado, the movements of a busy man at ease in his own house.

But he was now so pulled about by different alarms that, while one portion of his mind was still alert and cunning, another trembled on the brink of lunacy. One hallucination in particular took a strong hold on his credulity. The neighbour hearkening with white face beside his window, the passer-by arrested by a horrible surmise on the pavement—these could at worst suspect, they could not know; through the brick walls and shuttered windows only sounds could

5. Defile: line of march; dock: the enclosure in a criminal court in which the prisoner is placed at his trial.
6. Noise.

penetrate. But here, within the house, was he alone? He knew he was; he had watched the servant set forth sweet-hearting, in her poor best, "out for the day" written in every ribbon and smile. Yes, he was alone, of course; and yet, in the bulk of empty house above him, he could surely hear a stir of delicate footing—he was surely conscious, inexplicably conscious of some presence. Ay, surely; to every room and corner of the house his imagination followed it; and now it was a faceless thing, and yet had eyes to see with; and again it was a shadow of himself; and yet again behold the image of the dead dealer, reinspired with cunning and hatred.

At times, with a strong effort, he would glance at the open door which still seemed to repel his eyes. The house was tall, the skylight small and dirty, the day blind with fog; and the light that filtered down to the ground story was exceedingly faint, and showed dimly on the threshold of the shop. And yet, in that strip of doubtful brightness, did there not hang wavering a shadow?

Suddenly, from the street outside, a very jovial gentleman began to beat with a staff on the shop-door, accompanying his blows with shouts and railleries in which the dealer was continually called upon by name. Markheim, smitten into ice, glanced at the dead man. But no! he lay quite still; he was fled away far beyond earshot of these blows and shoutings; he was sunk beneath seas of silence; and his name, which would once have caught his notice above the howling of a storm, had become an empty sound. And presently the jovial gentleman desisted from his knocking and departed.

Here was a broad hint to hurry what remained to be done, to get forth from this accusing neighbourhood, to plunge into a bath of London multitudes, and to reach, on the other side of day, that haven of safety and apparent innocence—his bed. One visitor had come: at any moment another might follow and be more obstinate. To have done the deed, and yet not to reap the profit, would be too abhorrent a failure. The money, that was now Markheim's concern; and as a means to that, the keys.

He glanced over his shoulder at the open door, where the shadow was still lingering and shivering; and with no conscious repugnance of the mind, yet with a tremor of the belly, he drew near the body of his victim. The human character had quite departed. Like a suit half-stuffed with bran, the limbs lay scattered, the trunk doubled, on the floor; and yet the thing repelled him. Although so dingy and inconsiderable to the eye, he feared it might have more significance to the touch. He took the body by the shoulders, and turned it on its back. It was strangely light and supple, and the limbs, as if they had been broken, fell into the oddest postures. The face was robbed of all expression; but it was as pale as wax, and shockingly smeared with blood about one temple. That was, for Markheim, the one displeasing circumstance. It carried him back, upon the instant, to a certain fair-day in a fishers' village: a gray day, a piping wind, a crowd upon the street, the blare of brasses, the booming of drums, the nasal voice of a ballad singer; and a boy going to and fro, buried over head in the crowd and divided between interest and fear, until, coming out upon the chief place of concourse, he beheld a booth and a great screen with pictures, dismally designed, garishly coloured: Brownrigg with her apprentice; the Mannings with their murdered guest; Weare in the death-grip of Thurtell; and a score besides of famous crimes.[7] The thing was as clear as an illusion; he was once again that little boy; he was looking once again, and with the same sense of physical revolt, at these vile pictures; he was still stunned by the thumping of the drums. A bar of that day's music returned upon his memory; and at that, for the first time, a qualm came over him, a breath of nausea, a sudden weakness of the joints, which he must instantly resist and conquer.

He judged it more prudent to confront than to flee from these considerations; looking the more hardily in the dead face, bending his mind to realise the nature and greatness of his crime. So little a while ago that face had moved with every change of sentiment, that pale mouth had spoken, that body had been all on fire with governable energies; and now, and by his act, that piece of life had been arrested, as the horologist,[8] with interjected finger, arrests the beating of the clock. So he reasoned in vain; he could rise to no more remorseful consciousness; the same heart which had shuddered before the painted effigies of crime, looked on its reality unmoved. At best, he felt a gleam of pity for one who had been endowed in vain with all those faculties that can make the world a garden of enchantment, one who had never lived and who was now dead. But of penitence, no, not a tremor.

With that, shaking himself clear of these considerations, he found the keys and advanced towards the open door of the shop. Outside, it had begun to rain smartly; and the sound of the shower upon the roof had banished silence. Like some dripping cavern, the chambers of the house were haunted by an incessant echoing, which filled the ear and mingled with the ticking of the clocks. And, as Markheim approached the door, he seemed to hear, in answer to his own cautious tread, the steps of another foot withdrawing up the stair. The

---

7. London midwife Elizabeth Brownrigg in 1767 killed a young maidservant through a series of tortures which included stringing the girl up naked and savagely flogging her. London railway worker Frederic Manning and his wife Marie in 1849 invited a friend to dinner, murdered him for his money, and buried him in quicklime under their kitchen floor. John Thurtell, a young rake of early nineteenth-century London, in 1823 revenged himself on gambling companion William Weare by waylaying him in a desolate country lane, killing him in a violent struggle, and dumping his body in a nearby slough.
8. A clock- or watch-maker.

shadow still palpitated loosely on the threshold. He threw a ton's weight of resolve upon his muscles, and drew back the door.

The faint, foggy daylight glimmered dimly on the bare floor and stairs; on the bright suit of armour posted, halbert[9] in hand, upon the landing; and on the dark wood-carvings, and framed pictures that hung against the yellow panels of the wainscot. So loud was the beating of the rain through all the house that, in Markheim's ears, it began to be distinguished into many different sounds. Footsteps and sighs, the tread of regiments marching in the distance, the chink of money in the counting, and the creaking of doors held stealthily ajar, appeared to mingle with the patter of the drops upon the cupola and the gushing of the water in the pipes. The sense that he was not alone grew upon him to the verge of madness. On every side he was haunted and begirt by presences. He heard them moving in the upper chambers; from the shop, he heard the dead man getting to his legs; and as he began with a great effort to mount the stairs, feet fled quietly before him and followed stealthily behind. If he were but deaf, he thought, how tranquilly he would possess his soul! And then again, and hearkening with ever fresh attention, he blessed himself for that unresting sense which held the outposts and stood a trusty sentinel upon his life. His head turned continually on his neck; his eyes, which seemed starting from their orbits, scouted on every side, and on every side were half-rewarded as with the tail of something nameless vanishing. The four-and-twenty steps to the first floor were four-and-twenty agonies.

On that first storey, the doors stood ajar, three of them like three ambushes, shaking his nerves like the throats of cannon. He could never again, he felt, be sufficiently immured and fortified from men's observing eyes; he longed to be home, girt in by walls, buried among bedclothes, and invisible to all but God. And at that thought he wondered a little, recollecting tales of other murderers and the fear they were said to entertain of heavenly avengers. It was not so, at least, with him. He feared the laws of nature, lest, in their callous and immutable procedure, they should preserve some damning evidence of his crime. He feared tenfold more, with a slavish, superstitious terror, some scission[1] in the continuity of man's experience, some wilful illegality of nature. He played a game of skill, depending on the rules, calculating consequence from cause; and what if nature, as the defeated tyrant overthrew the chess-board, should break the mould of their succession? The like had befallen Napoleon (so writers said) when the winter changed the time of its appear-

9. I.e., halberd, a military weapon consisting of a blade and spearhead mounted on a five-to-seven foot-long handle.
1. Schism or break.

ance.[2] The like might befall Markheim: the solid walls might become transparent and reveal his doings like those of bees in a glass hive; the stout planks might yield under his foot like quicksands and detain him in their clutch; ay, and there were soberer accidents that might destroy him: if, for instance, the house should fall and imprison him beside the body of his victim; or the house next door should fly on fire, and the firemen invade him from all sides. These things he feared; and, in a sense, these things might be called the hands of God reached forth against sin. But about God himself he was at ease; his act was doubtless exceptional, but so were his excuses, which God knew; it was there, and not among men, that he felt sure of justice.[3]

When he had got safe into the drawing-room, and shut the door behind him, he was aware of a respite from alarms. The room was quite dismantled, uncarpeted besides, and strewn with packing cases and incongruous furniture; several great pier-glasses, in which he beheld himself at various angles, like an actor on a stage; many pictures, framed and unframed, standing, with their faces to the wall; a fine Sheraton sideboard, a cabinet of marquetry, and a great old bed, with tapestry hangings. The windows opened to the floor; but by great good fortune the lower part of the shutters had been closed, and this concealed him from the neighbours. Here, then, Markheim drew in a packing case before the cabinet, and began to search among the keys. It was a long business, for there were many; and it was irksome, besides; for, after all, there might be nothing in the cabinet, and time was on the wing. But the closeness of the occupation sobered him. With the tail of his eye he saw the door—even glanced at it from time to time directly, like a besieged commander pleased to verify the good estate of his defences. But in truth he was at peace. The rain falling in the street sounded natural and pleasant. Presently, on the other side, the notes of a piano were wakened to the music of a hymn, and the voices of many children took up the air and words. How stately, how comfortable was the melody! How fresh the youthful voices! Markheim gave ear to it smilingly, as he sorted out the keys; and his mind was thronged with answerable

2. Napoleon was hurried into his 1812 retreat from Moscow, according to the 1830 biography by William Hazlitt that may have been Stevenson's source, because "the winter set-in this year a fortnight or three weeks sooner than it had almost ever been known to do" (Hazlitt, *The Life of Napoleon Buonaparte*, 4 vols., 1828–30 [Philadelphia: J. P. Lippincott & Co., 1875], 3:96).

3. This sense of secret justification in overruling the ordinary laws of man, emerging as the facilitating condition for an impoverished, well-educated, once tender-hearted man's murder and robbery of an avaricious pawnbroker, contributes to the parallels critics have noticed between this story and Dostoyevsky's *Crime and Punishment*. From the Stevenson *Letters*, we can be sure only that Stevenson's reading of *Crime and Punishment* in its 1884 French translation took place sometime in the months just before or after his writing of "Markheim" (see *Letters* 5:151).

ideas and images; church-going children and the pealing of the high organ; children afield, bathers by the brookside, ramblers on the brambly common, kite-flyers in the windy and cloud-navigated sky; and then, at another cadence of the hymn, back again to church, and the somnolence of summer Sundays, and the high genteel voice of the parson (which he smiled a little to recall) and the painted Jacobean tombs, and the dim lettering of the Ten Commandments in the chancel.

And as he sat thus, at once busy and absent, he was startled to his feet. A flash of ice, a flash of fire, a bursting gush of blood, went over him, and then he stood transfixed and thrilling. A step mounted the stair slowly and steadily, and presently a hand was laid upon the knob, and the lock clicked, and the door opened.

Fear held Markheim in a vice. What to expect he knew not, whether the dead man walking, or the official ministers of human justice, or some chance witness blindly stumbling in to consign him to the gallows. But when a face was thrust into the aperture, glanced round the room, looked at him, nodded and smiled as if in friendly recognition, and then withdrew again, and the door closed behind it, his fear broke loose from his control in a hoarse cry. At the sound of this the visitant returned.

"Did you call me?" he asked, pleasantly, and with that he entered the room and closed the door behind him.

Markheim stood and gazed at him with all his eyes. Perhaps there was a film upon his sight, but the outlines of the new comer seemed to change and waver like those of the idols in the wavering candlelight of the shop; and at times he thought he knew him; and at times he thought he bore a likeness to himself; and always, like a lump of living terror, there lay in his bosom the conviction that this thing was not of the earth and not of God.

And yet the creature had a strange air of the commonplace, as he stood looking on Markheim with a smile; and when he added: "You are looking for the money, I believe?" it was in the tones of everyday politeness.

Markheim made no answer.

"I should warn you," resumed the other, "that the maid has left her sweetheart earlier than usual and will soon be here. If Mr. Markheim be found in this house, I need not describe to him the consequences."

"You know me?" cried the murderer.

The visitor smiled. "You have long been a favourite of mine," he said; "and I have long observed and often sought to help you."

"What are you?" cried Markheim: "the devil?"

"What I may be," returned the other, "cannot affect the service I propose to render you."

"It can," cried Markheim; "it does! Be helped by you? No, never; not by you! You do not know me yet; thank God, you do not know me!"

"I know you," replied the visitant, with a sort of kind severity or rather firmness. "I know you to the soul."

"Know me!" cried Markheim. "Who can do so? My life is but a travesty and slander on myself. I have lived to belie my nature. All men do; all men are better than this disguise that grows about and stifles them. You see each dragged away by life, like one whom bravos[4] have seized and muffled in a cloak. If they had their own control—if you could see their faces, they would be altogether different, they would shine out for heroes and saints! I am worse than most; myself is more overlaid; my excuse is known to me and God. But, had I the time, I could disclose myself."

"To me?" inquired the visitant.

"To you before all," returned the murderer. "I supposed you were intelligent. I thought—since you exist—you would prove a reader of the heart. And yet you would propose to judge me by my acts! Think of it; my acts! I was born and I have lived in a land of giants; giants have dragged me by the wrists since I was born out of my mother— the giants of circumstance. And you would judge me by my acts! But can you not look within? Can you not understand that evil is hateful to me? Can you not see within me the clear writing of conscience, never blurred by any wilful sophistry, although too often disregarded? Can you not read me for a thing that surely must be common as humanity—the unwilling sinner?"

"All this is very feelingly expressed," was the reply, "but it regards me not. These points of consistency are beyond my province, and I care not in the least by what compulsion you may have been dragged away, so as you are but carried in the right direction. But time flies; the servant delays, looking in the faces of the crowd and at the pictures on the hoardings,[5] but still she keeps moving nearer; and remember, it is as if the gallows itself was striding towards you through the Christmas streets! Shall I help you; I, who know all? Shall I tell you where to find the money?"

"For what price?" asked Markheim.

"I offer you the service for a Christmas gift," returned the other.

Markheim could not refrain from smiling with a kind of bitter triumph. "No," said he, "I will take nothing at your hands; if I were dying of thirst, and it was your hand that put the pitcher to my lips, I should find the courage to refuse. It may be credulous,[6] but I will do nothing to commit myself to evil."

---

4. Desperadoes or hired assassins.
5. Temporary fences used for posting bills and advertisements.
6. I.e., it may be naïve or gullible of me.

"I have no objection to a death-bed repentance," observed the visitant.

"Because you disbelieve their efficacy!" Markheim cried.

"I do not say so," returned the other; "but I look on these things from a different side, and when the life is done my interest falls. The man has lived to serve me, to spread black looks under colour of religion, or to sow tares in the wheat-field,[7] as you do, in a course of weak compliance with desire. Now that he draws so near to his deliverance, he can add but one act of service—to repent, to die smiling, and thus to build up in confidence and hope the more timorous of my surviving followers. I am not so hard a master. Try me. Accept my help. Please yourself in life as you have done hitherto; please yourself more amply, spread your elbows at the board;[8] and when the night begins to fall and the curtains to be drawn, I tell you, for your greater comfort, that you will find it even easy to compound your quarrel with your conscience, and to make a truckling[9] peace with God. I came but now from such a deathbed, and the room was full of sincere mourners, listening to the man's last words: and when I looked into that face, which had been set as a flint against mercy, I found it smiling with hope."

"And do you, then, suppose me such a creature?" asked Markheim. "Do you think I have no more generous aspirations than to sin, and sin, and sin, and, at the last, sneak into heaven? My heart rises at the thought. Is this, then, your experience of mankind? or is it because you find me with red hands that you presume such baseness? and is this crime of murder indeed so impious as to dry up the very springs of good?"

"Murder is to me no special category," replied the other. "All sins are murder, even as all life is war. I behold your race, like starving mariners on a raft, plucking crusts out of the hands of famine and feeding on each other's lives. I follow sins beyond the moment of their acting; I find in all that the last consequence is death; and to my eyes, the pretty maid who thwarts her mother with such taking graces on a question of a ball, drips no less visibly with human gore than such a murderer as yourself. Do I say that I follow sins? I follow virtues also; they differ not by the thickness of a nail, they are both scythes for the reaping angel of Death. Evil, for which I live, consists not in action but in character. The bad man is dear to me; not the bad act, whose fruits, if we could follow them far enough down the

---

7. To corrupt or attempt to corrupt good with evil. In *Matthew* 13:24–30, Jesus tells the parable of the man who represents the kingdom of heaven finding his newly seeded field of wheat contaminated with the seeds of tares (an injurious weed) sown by his enemy. The man advises his servants not to rake up good seed with bad, but to let the plants ripen until harvest-time, when they can be easily separated.
8. A table stocked with food.
9. Compound: compose or settle; truckling: servile.

hurtling cataract of the ages, might yet be found more blessed than those of the rarest virtues. And it is not because you have killed a dealer, but because you are Markheim, that I offer to forward your escape."

"I will lay my heart open to you," answered Markheim. "This crime on which you find me is my last. On my way to it I have learned many lessons; itself is a lesson, a momentous lesson. Hitherto I have been driven with revolt to what I would not; I was a bond-slave to poverty, driven and scourged. There are robust virtues that can stand in these temptations; mine was not so: I had a thirst of pleasure. But to-day, and out of this deed, I pluck both warning and riches—both the power and a fresh resolve to be myself. I become in all things a free actor in the world; I begin to see myself all changed, these hands the agents of good, this heart at peace. Something comes over me out of the past; something of what I have dreamed on Sabbath evenings to the sound of the church organ, of what I forecast when I shed tears over noble books, or talked, an innocent child, with my mother. There lies my life; I have wandered a few years, but now I see once more my city of destination."

"You are to use this money on the Stock Exchange, I think?" remarked the visitor; "and there, if I mistake not, you have already lost some thousands?"

"Ah," said Markheim, "but this time I have a sure thing."

"This time, again, you will lose," replied the visitor quietly.

"Ah, but I keep back the half!" cried Markheim.

"That also you will lose," said the other.

The sweat started upon Markheim's brow. "Well, then, what matter?" he exclaimed. "Say it be lost, say I am plunged again in poverty, shall one part of me, and that the worse, continue until the end to override the better? Evil and good run strong in me, haling me both ways. I do not love the one thing, I love all. I can conceive great deeds, renunciations, martyrdoms; and though I be fallen to such a crime as murder, pity is no stranger to my thoughts. I pity the poor; who knows their trials better than myself? I pity and help them; I prize love, I love honest laughter; there is no good thing nor true thing on earth but I love it from my heart. And are my vices only to direct my life, and my virtues to lie without effect, like some passive lumber of the mind? Not so; good, also, is a spring of acts."

But the visitant raised his finger. "For six-and-thirty years that you have been in this world," said he, "through many changes of fortune and varieties of humour, I have watched you steadily fall. Fifteen years ago you would have started[1] at a theft. Three years back you would have blenched at the name of murder. Is there any crime, is

---

1. I.e., been startled.

there any cruelty or meanness, from which you still recoil?—five years from now I shall detect you in the fact! Downward, downward, lies your way; nor can anything but death avail to stop you."

"It is true," Markheim said huskily, "I have in some degree complied with evil. But it is so with all: the very saints, in the mere exercise of living, grow less dainty, and take on the tone of their surroundings."

"I will propound to you one simple question," said the other; "and as you answer, I shall read to you your moral horoscope. You have grown in many things more lax; possibly you do right to be so; and at any account, it is the same with all men. But granting that, are you in any one particular, however trifling, more difficult to please with your own conduct, or do you go in all things with a looser rein?"

"In any one?" repeated Markheim, with an anguish of consideration. "No," he added, with despair, "in none! I have gone down in all."

"Then," said the visitor, "content yourself with what you are, for you will never change; and the words of your part on this stage are irrevocably written down."

Markheim stood for a long while silent, and indeed it was the visitor who first broke the silence. "That being so," he said, "shall I show you the money?"

"And grace?" cried Markheim.

"Have you not tried it?" returned the other. "Two or three years ago, did I not see you on the platform of revival meetings, and was not your voice the loudest in the hymn?"

"It is true," said Markheim; "and I see clearly what remains for me by way of duty. I thank you for these lessons from my soul; my eyes are opened, and I behold myself at last for what I am."

At this moment, the sharp note of the door-bell rang through the house; and the visitant, as though this were some concerted signal for which he had been waiting, changed at once in his demeanour.

"The maid!" he cried. "She has returned, as I forewarned you, and there is now before you one more difficult passage. Her master, you must say, is ill; you must let her in, with an assured but rather serious countenance—no smiles, no overacting, and I promise you success! Once the girl within, and the door closed, the same dexterity that has already rid you of the dealer will relieve you of this last danger in your path. Thenceforward you have the whole evening—the whole night, if needful—to ransack the treasures of the house and to make good your safety. This is help that comes to you with the mask of danger. Up!" he cried; "up, friend; your life hangs trembling in the scales: up, and act!"

Markheim steadily regarded his counsellor. "If I be condemned to evil acts," he said, "there is still one door of freedom open—I can cease from action. If my life be an ill thing, I can lay it down. Though I be, as you say truly, at the beck of every small temptation, I can yet, by one decisive gesture, place myself beyond the reach of all. My love of good is damned to barrenness; it may, and let it be! But I have still my hatred of evil; and from that, to your galling disappointment, you shall see that I can draw both energy and courage."

The features of the visitor began to undergo a wonderful and lovely change: they brightened and softened with a tender triumph, and, even as they brightened, faded and dislimned.[2] But Markheim did not pause to watch or understand the transformation. He opened the door and went downstairs very slowly, thinking to himself. His past went soberly before him; he beheld it as it was, ugly and strenuous like a dream, random as chance-medley[3]—a scene of defeat. Life, as he thus reviewed it, tempted him no longer; but on the further side he perceived a quiet haven for his bark.[4] He paused in the passage, and looked into the shop, where the candle still burned by the dead body. It was strangely silent. Thoughts of the dealer swarmed into his mind, as he stood gazing. And then the bell once more broke out into impatient clamour.

He confronted the maid upon the threshold with something like a smile.

"You had better go for the police," said he: "I have killed your master."

---

2. Lost their outlines.
3. Haphazard action; as a legal term, "chance-medley" refers especially to manslaughter performed through a combination of fault and misfortune.
4. A small boat.

CHRISTMAS EXTRA.

EARLY in December there will appear a PALL MALL GAZETTE CHRISTMAS "EXTRA," embodying all the features of the successful CHRISTMAS "EXTRA" of last year, together with many attractive and seasonable novelties.

In the first place Mr. ROBERT LOUIS STEVENSON, one of the most powerful imaginative writers of the day, whose vivid picture of the "Suicide Club" has frozen the heart's blood, whose "Treasure Island," written for boys, has fascinated a Prime Minister, and become a classic, has consented to write for us a vivid GHOST STORY, and when ghosts are walking Mr. Stevenson is at his weirdest.

The "EXTRA" will be a guide through the mazes of Christmas-land, where every bush is alive with thorns, eager to catch the heedless explorer. Under its guidance the reader will know where to go, what to buy, and how much to pay. The Literature of Christmas is voluminous. Those brilliant volumes known in the trade as CHRISTMAS BOOKS are often but as Dead Sea Fruit—bloom without, ashes within. To change the metaphor, it will be our function to sift the chaff from the wheat.

As for the SHOPS and the NOVELTIES. If there is anything new under the sun it appears at Christmas. So Christmas cards, Christmas toys, Christmas games, and Christmas presents will all receive respectful, but critical, attention.

Lastly, we offer a sum of TWENTY GUINEAS for an entirely new and characteristic Historico-Political Prophecy, the particulars of which will shortly be announced.

"PALL MALL GAZETTE" OFFICE, 2, NORTHUMBERLAND STREET, STRAND, LONDON, W.C.

Pall Mall Gazette advertisement, November 22, 1884. Reprinted by permission of The British Library. Sensationalistic tales of crime, mystery, and horror commanded a healthy share of the literary market throughout the Victorian era. This advertisement for a forthcoming story by Stevenson in the *Pall Mall Gazette's* Christmas 1884 supplement (the commission for which Stevenson wrote "Markheim," though he ended up substituting "The Body Snatcher") illustrates the particular place held in the sensation fiction market for the Christmas ghost story—or, as Stevenson's friend Sidney Colvin put it, "a 'crawler,' or Christmas story of the blood-curdling kind."[1] *Strange Case of Dr. Jekyll and Mr. Hyde*, published at the end of the holiday season the following year, can itself be seen as a candidate for this category in the book trade: an 1888 *British Weekly* critic reviewing Stevenson's work to date was to suggest that 'Jekyll and Hyde' is the greatest triumph extant in Christmas literature of the morbid kind."[2]

1. Headnote to Stevenson's letter of November 15, 1884, to Edmund Gosse, in Colvin's 1899 edition of Stevenson's letters to family and friends.
2. Gavin Ogilvy, Robert Louis Stevenson, *The British Weekly*, (November 2, 1888); contained in Monterey Stevenson Museum Scrapbook 2, p. 87.

THE NEXT SENSATIONAL LITERARY ADVERTISEMENT; OR, THINGS OF BEAUTY IN OUR STREETS.

Punch cartoon, December 27, 1884: "The Next Sensational Literary Advertisement." Reprinted by permission of The British Library. This cartoon may include among its targets the *Pall Mall Gazette*'s method of advertising Stevenson's "The Body Snatcher" on the streets of London shortly before Christmas 1884: Sidney Colvin reports that the tale was publicized "by sandwich men carrying posters so horrific that they were suppressed, if I remember aright, by the police." Yale *Letters* editor Ernest Mehew adds that "the advertising included a procession of corpses with coffin lids."[1]

1. Colvin in 1899 headnote to Stevenson's letter of November 15, 1884, to Edmund Gosse (Edinburgh Edition *Letters* 1:339); Mehew in Yale *Letters* 5:35, n.1.

ROBERT LOUIS STEVENSON

[How I Came to Be Such a Student of Our Penny Press]†

* * *

How I came to be such a student of our penny press,[1] demands perhaps some explanation. I was brought up on *Cassell's Family Paper*; but the lady who was kind enough to read the tales aloud to me[2] was subject to sharp attacks of conscience. She took the *Family Paper* on confidence; the tales it contained being Family Tales, not novels. But every now and then, something would occur to alarm her finer sense; she would express a well-grounded fear that the current fiction was "going to turn out a Regular Novel;"[3] and the family paper, with my pious approval, would be dropped. Yet neither she nor I were wholly stoical; and when Saturday came round, we would study the windows of the stationer and try to fish out of subsequent woodcuts and their legends the further adventures of our favorites. Many points are here suggested for the casuist; definitions of the Regular Novel and the Family Tale are to be desired; and quite a paper might be written on the relative merit of reading a fiction outright and lusting after it at the stationer's window. The experience at least had a great effect upon my childhood. This inexpensive pleasure mastered me. Each new Saturday I would go from one newsvender's window to another's, till I was master of the weekly gallery and had thoroughly digested "The Baronet Unmasked," "So and so approaching the Mysterious House," "The Discovery of the Dead Body in the Blue Marl Pit," "Dr. Vargas Removing the Senseless Body of Fair Lilias," and whatever other snatch of unknown story and glimpse of unknown characters that gallery afforded. I do not know that I ever enjoyed fiction more; those books that we have (in such a way) avoided reading, are all so excellently written! And in early years, we take a book for its material, and act as our own artists, keenly realizing that which pleases us, leaving the rest aside. I never supposed that a book was to command me until, one disastrous day of storm, the heaven full of turbulent vapors, the streets full of the squalling of the gale, the windows resounding under bucketfuls of rain, my mother read aloud to me *Macbeth*. I cannot say I thought the experience agreeable; I far preferred the ditch-water stories that

† From "Popular Authors," *Scribner's Magazine*, 4 (July, 1888): 125.
1. Broadly popular, often luridly sensationalistic fiction published serially in a penny-paper format.
2. Alison Cunningham, Stevenson's beloved childhood nurse in Edinburgh.
3. I.e., fiction conducive to moral corruption.

a child could dip and skip and doze over, stealing at times materials for play; it was something new and shocking to be thus ravished by a giant, and I shrank under the brutal grasp. But the spot in memory is still sensitive; nor do I ever read that tragedy but I hear the gale howling up the valley of the Leith.

*   *   *

Literary Contexts: Doubles, Devils, and Monsters

Literary genres which critics have proposed as a framework for viewing *Strange Case of Dr. Jekyll and Mr. Hyde* include religious allegory, social exposé, fable, detective story, sensation fiction, science fiction, literature of the *Doppelgänger*, Scottish devil tales, and Gothic novel. The following selections deal with the last three of those genres.

KARL MILLER

[The Modern Double]†

* * *

The story of the modern double starts with the magical science of the eighteenth century in Europe, when Mesmerists or Animal Magnetists went in for an experimental separation of the second self,[1] and romantic writers went in for its cultural exploitation. Jean Paul Richter invented the term *doppelgänger*, and studied the notion of fellowship, of the friend as alter ego * * *; Hoffman identified the double with a part of the personality, with an element of internal threat, and portrayed himself in a character on whom he conferred a "ghostly *Doppelgänger*, born of the heart's blood of his lacerated breast."[2] "Romantic multiple man" had taken the stage * * *. A craze for duality spread from Germany to the rest of Europe. The Gothic strain in the literature of nineteenth-century Scotland and England was to accommodate the lore and idiom of magic, and of the new pseudo-sciences, Magnetism and Phrenology.[3] * * *

† From *Doubles: Studies in Literary History* (Oxford: Oxford University Press, 1985), pp. 49–50, 130, 209, and 416. Reprinted by permission of Karl Miller. Footnotes are by the editor of this Norton Critical Edition.
1. Conceived as a latent visionary consciousness that could be activated through hypnosis.
2. Jean Paul Richter: German writer (1763–1825); *doppelgänger*: i.e., the double; (literally, "double-goer"); Hoffmann: German writer Ernst Theodor Hoffmann (1776–1822).
3. Magnetism posited a manipulable, spiritually powerful fluid magnetic force connecting animate with astronomical bodies. Phrenology held that character could be read from the external configuration of the skull.

124

In the writer's closet, romantic multiple man created a theatre of the self, pored over the enigma of his own inconsistency, and nursed the sense that the mind could be a strange compound of this or that contending power. * * *

* * *

* * * Dualistic productions were becoming an established genre, indeed a mine of activity, in the literatures of Scotland, England and France, and in that of Russia, where the ores were especially rich, with Edinburgh and St. Petersburg the twin capital cities of the subject—the axis of international duality. They are the source and setting of two of its most impressive works: Hogg's novel[4] and Dostoevsky's novel of 1846, *The Double*. * * *

* * *

During the [1880s and 1890s] duality underwent a revival which carried the subject, together with its predicated psychic state, into the century that followed. During these years, which are sometimes mistaken for the inaugural years of the subject, a hunger for pseudonyms, masks, new identities, new conceptions of human nature, declared itself. Men became women. Women became men. Gender and country were put in doubt: the single life was found to harbour two sexes and two nations. Femaleness and the female writer broke free; the New Woman, and the Old, adventured into fiction, and might be found to hold hands there, as sisters. James's tale of 1894, "The Death of the Lion," describes an age in which there seemed to be three sexes, an age tormented by genders and pronouns and pennames, by the identity of authors, by the "he" and the "she" and the "who" of it all. Proteus stole down the back streets of the Late Victorian Babylon, and his portrait came to life. Anglo-America, and well beyond, rang to the cry of Robert Louis Stevenson's Dr Jekyll: "This, too, was myself."[5]

* * *

There can be no satisfying short description of what doubles are, or of what they have become in shedding some part of their supernatural origins, as harbingers of evil and death, and growing into an element of individual psychology and a domestic feature. But * * *

4. Scotsman James Hogg's *The Private Memoirs and Confessions of a Justified Sinner*, the tale of Calvinist youth Robert Wringham who, as Miller puts it, "wishes to be a saint, to rise above the responsibilities of the human condition, and whose delusions of grandeur are turned, with the advent of a diabolical double, into the actions of a common criminal" (Miller, 1). As mentioned on p. 49, n.6 of this edition, Hogg's novel is sometimes cited as an influence on *Strange Case of Dr. Jekyll and Mr. Hyde*. For Stevenson's recollections of how the novel affected him when he read it around 1881, see *Letters* 7: 125–26.

5. *Dr Jekyll and Mr Hyde, and Other Tales* (Everyman; reprinted 1974), p. 51 [Miller's note]. [NCE, p. 51.]

they have often been about running away, and revenge * * *. One self does what the other self can't. One self is meek while the other is fierce. One self stays while the other runs away. These are meanings which can be discovered as we patrol the secret passages of the literature of duality, and they can also be discovered in folklore. Doubles may appear to come from outside, as a form of possession, or from inside, as a form of projection. Doubles are both, and we see them as both * * *.

JENNI CALDER

[Stevenson's Scottish Devil Tales]†

*   *   *

* * * ["Thrawn Janet"] was [Stevenson's] first piece of Scottish fiction, in maturity at least, a story that uses the fears and prejudices of a devil-conscious national imagination with great effect.¹ * * *

Louis had had a longstanding interest in witchcraft and the supernatural. He had been brought up on stories of the devil, he had soaked himself in aspects of Scottish history in which superstition was a powerful element, and he was well aware of the close relationship between the satanic and the romantic. That there were aspects of humanity that somehow only the existence of the devil could explain was a thought that had entered his mind in primitive fashion in earliest childhood. It was to emerge in his writing in several ways. But here was Satan's first entry on the scene of Stevenson's writing. He had written before of the corruptibility of human nature * * * but he was now to write of the susceptibility to the devil as inherent in human nature itself. Two more stories in similar vein followed "Thrawn Janet," though one "The Body Snatchers,"² was not completed that summer. It has a lighter note than either "Thrawn

† From *Robert Louis Stevenson: A Life Study* (New York: Oxford University Press, 1980), pp. 165–66 and 221–22. Copyright © 1980 by Jenni Calder. Reprinted by permission of Oxford University Press, Inc. and PFD on behalf of Jenni Calder. Notes have been edited.
1. "Thrawn Janet" (1881), set in a Scottish moorland parish in the early eighteenth century, gives the local elders' account of a minister who naively attempted to help a palsied old woman ostracized as a witch, only to fall prey to a life-long spiritual terror in the shock of discovering her to be an animated corpse inhabited body and soul by "the black man" (as Stevenson in a footnote explains the devil is often represented in Scotland) [*Editor*].
2. Retitled as "The Body Snatcher" when Stevenson published it in 1884, this tale tells the story of an Edinburgh medical student who becomes an uneasy accomplice in the criminal procurement of dead bodies for anatomical dissection. He meets his nemesis when a female corpse that he and his corrupt older colleague have dug up in the dark of the night metamorphoses into the recomposed body of the dark, sinister, strangely powerful little man the colleague had some time ago murdered and sold to the medical school for dissection [*Editor*].

Janet" or "The Merry Men,"[3] the third and the most striking of the three stories * * *.

* * *

For the first time Stevenson was using the traditions he had absorbed as a child. There was nothing second-hand about such writing, as there is in his earlier fiction, the French short stories which so patently owe their existence to Victor Hugo and Balzac.[4] Now he was handling more intimate material. That the emblematic nature of the stories he now began to produce chimes most closely with those of Nathaniel Hawthorne, who also wrote about a deeply superstitious and high principled society,[5] who also admitted the devil on to his stage, does not detract from their effect. Stevenson had read Hawthorne. Their similarities owe more to recognition than imitation. * * *

* * *

* * * "Markheim" came out just before *Jekyll and Hyde*; the dreaming of the latter clearly reflected current preoccupations. Louis's own uneasiness as resident of Skerryvore may have drawn to the surface again his preoccupation with the double life.[6] "Markheim" concerns the committing of a bloody and pointless murder by a man who is possessed overpoweringly by the need to kill. It is a brief, intense little story with a cathartic quality, drawn out by the murderer's relief when he is able to admit his crime and give himself into the sheltering power of the Devil. It is the acknowledgment that evil has won, and that giving oneself up to it is comforting. The theme is enlarged in *Jekyll and Hyde,* the theme that Louis spoke of, in a subsequent letter to J. A. Symonds, as "that damned old business of the war in the members."[7] It is the Calvinist view that man must maintain a constant struggle with evil, that the slightest lapse in vigilance will allow the Devil to triumph. The reality of evil, its ambivalence, its attractions, had always possessed Louis. The ambivalent characterisation of Long John Silver, so easily the most attractive character in *Treasure Island*, reflects this. Louis's impatience with

3. In "The Merry Men" (1882), the demonically treacherous tides, winds, and underwater snares that wreck a ship off the coast of a desolate Scottish island also cast up a ghostly, black-skinned survivor who sends the narrator's feisty old uncle into a tailspin of madness [Editor].
4. Victor Hugo (1802–1885) and Honoré de Balzac (1799–1850) [Editor].
5. Most famously in *The Scarlet Letter* (1850) [Editor].
6. Homeownership of Skerryvore, the house in Bournemouth Stevenson's father purchased for Stevenson and his wife early in 1885, left the Bohemian Stevenson torn between pleasure in the middle-class comfort he now enjoyed and guilty unease in living so well-cushioned and bourgeois an existence [Editor].
7. RLS to J. A. Symonds [*Letters* 5: 220].

his father's anguished guilt,[8] his condemnation of Calvinist negativism, and his absorption of the devil-ridden folklore of Scotland were all operating in *Jekyll and Hyde.* * * *

JUDITH HALBERSTAM

An Introduction to Gothic Monstrosity†

* * *

Gothic fiction is a technology of subjectivity, one which produces the deviant subjectivities[1] opposite which the normal, the healthy, and the pure can be known. Gothic, within my analysis, may be loosely defined as the rhetorical style and narrative structure designed to produce fear and desire within the reader. The production of fear in a literary text (as opposed to a cinematic text) emanates from a vertiginous excess of meaning. Gothic, in a way, refers to an ornamental excess (think of Gothic architecture—gargoyles and crazy loops and spirals), a rhetorical extravagance that produces, quite simply, too much. Within Gothic novels, I argue, multiple interpretations are embedded in the text and part of the experience of horror comes from the realization that meaning itself runs riot. Gothic novels produce a symbol for this interpretive mayhem in the body of the monster. The monster always becomes a primary focus of interpretation and its monstrosity seems available for any number of meanings. * * *

* * *

Within the nineteenth-century Gothic, authors mixed and matched a wide variety of signifiers of difference to fabricate the deviant body—Dracula, Jekyll/Hyde, and even Frankenstein's monster before them are lumpen bodies, bodies pieced together out of the fabric of race, class, gender, and sexuality. In the modern period and with the advent of cinematic body horror, the shift from the literary Gothic to the visual Gothic was accompanied by a narrowing rather than a broadening of the scope of horror. One might expect to find that cinema multiplies the possibilities for monstrosity but in fact, the visual register quickly reaches a limit of visibility. In *Frank-*

---

8. Through excess of religious conscience. ("My father used to envy the pigs," Stevenson quipped after his father's death, "because as they were always asleep they kept clear of so much sin" [*Letters* 6:110]) [*Editor*].
† From "Parasites and Perverts: An Introduction to Gothic Monstrosity," *Skin Shows: Gothic Horror and the Technology of Monsters*, pp. 2–3, 18–21. Copyright 1995, Duke University Press. All rights reserved. Reprinted with permission. Notes have been edited.
1. I.e., senses of selfhood which are culturally constructed as deviant [*Editor*].

enstein the reader can only imagine the dreadful spectacle of the monster and so its monstrosity is limited only by the reader's imagination; in the horror film, the monster must always fail to be monstrous enough and horror therefore depends upon the explicit violation of female bodies as opposed to simply the sight of the monster.

* * *

* * * To understand the way monster may be equated with Jew or foreigner or non-English national, we need to historicize Gothic metaphors like vampire and parasite. We also have to read the effacement of the connection between monster and foreigner alongside the articulation of monster as a sexual category.

* * *

In an introduction to *Studies on Hysteria* written in 1893, Freud identifies the repressed itself as a foreign body. Noting that hysterical symptoms replay some original trauma in response to an accident, Freud explains that the memory of trauma "acts like a foreign body which, long after its entry, must continue to be regarded as an agent that is still at work."[2] In other words, until an original site of trauma reveals itself in therapy, it remains foreign to body and mind but active in both. The repressed, then, figures as a sexual secret that the body keeps from itself and it figures as foreign because what disturbs the body goes unrecognized by the mind.

The fiction that Freud tells about the foreign body as the repressed connects remarkably with the fiction Gothic tells about monsters as foreigners. Texts, like bodies, store up memories of past fears, of distant traumas. "Hysterics," writes Freud, "suffer mainly from reminiscences" (7). History, personal and social, haunts hysterics and the repressed always takes on an uncanny life of its own. Freud here has described the landscape of his own science—foreignness is repressed into the depths of an unconscious, a kind of cesspool of forgotten memories, and it rises to the surface as a sexual disturbance. Psychoanalysis gothicizes sexuality; that is to say, it creates a body haunted by a monstrous sexuality and forced into repressing its Gothic secrets. Psychoanalysis, in the Freudian scenario, is a sexual science able to account for and perhaps cure Gothic sexualities. Gothicization in this formula, then, is the identification of bodies in terms of what they are not. A Gothic other stabilizes sameness, a gothicized body is one that disrupts the surface-depth relationship between the body and the mind. It is the body that must be spoken, identified, or eliminated.

2. Sigmund Freud and Josef Brauer, *Studies on Hysteria* (1893; reprint, trans. and ed. James Strachey, New York: Basic, 1987) p. 6.

Eve Sedgwick has advanced a reading of Gothic as the return of the repressed. She reads fear in the Gothic in terms of the trope of "live burial" and finds in Gothic "a carceral sublime of representation, of the body, and potentially of politics and history as well."[3] Live burial as a trope is, of course, standard fare in the Gothic, particularly in eighteenth-century Gothic like Matthew Lewis's *The Monk* and Ann Radcliffe's *The Mysteries of Udolpho*. Live burial also works nicely as a metaphor for a repressed thing that threatens to return. Sedgwick's example of the repressed in Gothic is homosexuality. * * *

But Sedgwick's reading tells only half the story. The sexual outsider in Gothic, I am suggesting, is always also a racial pariah, a national outcast, a class outlaw. The "carceral sublime of representation" that, for Sedgwick, marks the role of textuality or language in the production of fear does not only symbolize that Gothic language buries fear alive. Live burial is certainly a major and standard trope of Gothic but I want to read it alongside the trope of parasitism. Parasitism, I think, adds an economic dimension to live burial that reveals the entanglement of capital, nation, and the body in the fictions of otherness sanctified and popularized by any given culture. If live burial, for Sedgwick, reveals a "queerness of meaning," an essential doubleness within language that plays itself out through homoerotic doubles within the text, the carceral in my reading hinges upon a more clearly metonymic structure.[4] Live burial as parasitism, then, becomes a tooth buried in an exposed neck for the explicit purpose of blood sucking or a monstrous Hyde hidden within the very flesh of a respectable Jekyll. Live burial is the entanglement of self and other within monstrosity and the parasitical relationship between the two. The one is always buried in the other.

The form of the Gothic novel, again as Sedgwick remarks, reflects further upon the parasitical monstrosity it creates. The story buried within a story buried within a story that Shelley's *Frankenstein* popularizes evolves into the narrative with one story but many different tellers. This form is really established by Wilkie Collins's *The Woman in White* (1860). In this novel, Collins uses a series of narrators so that almost every character in the novel tells his or her side of the story. Such a narrative device gives the effect of completion and operates according to a kind of judicial model of narration where all witnesses step forward to give an account. Within this narrative system, the author professes to be no more than a collector of documents, a compiler of the facts of the case. The reader, of course, is

---

3. Eve Kosofsky Sedgwick, *The Coherence of Gothic Conventions* (New York and London: Methuen, 1986), p. vi. ["Carceral" means "of or belonging to a prison" (*Editor*).]
4. I.e., a structure more clearly expressive of transferred meaning (in this case, the transferred meaning of parasitism attaching to imagery of live burial) [*Editor*].

the judge and jury, the courtroom audience, and often, a kind of prosecuting presence expected to know truth, recognize guilt, and penalize monstrosity.

In *Dracula* Bram Stoker directly copies Collins's style. Stevenson also uses Collins's narrative technique in *Dr. Jekyll and Mr. Hyde* but he frames his story in a more overtly legal setting so that our main narrator is a lawyer, the central document is the last will and testament of Dr. Jekyll, and all other accounts contribute to the "strange case." All Gothic novels employing this narrative device share an almost obsessive concern with documentation and they all exhibit a sinister mistrust of the not-said, the unspoken, the hidden, and the silent. Furthermore, most Gothic novels lack the point of view of the monster. * * *

* * *

* * * The monster's body, indeed, is a machine that, in its Gothic mode, produces meaning and can represent any horrible trait that the reader feeds into the narrative. The monster functions as monster, in other words, when it is able to condense as many fear-producing traits as possible into one body. Hence the sense that Frankenstein's monster is bursting out of his skin—he is indeed filled to bursting point with flesh and meaning both. Dracula, at the other end of the nineteenth century, is a body that consumes to excess—the vampiric body in its ideal state is a bloated body, sated with the blood of its victims.

Monsters are meaning machines. * * *

Scientific Contexts: Concepts of the Divided Self

Various behaviors proposed as real-life analogues for the repressed element in Jekyll, such as drug or alcohol addiction, homosexuality, multiple personality disorder, and regressive animality, were being examined by scientists in the closing decades of the nineteenth century in the framework of post-Darwinian interest in biological influences on human conduct. Meanwhile, however, the Evangelical mainstream of Victorian society continued to stigmatize such behaviors as shameful acts of madness or morally contaminating acts of sin. The first three excerpts below (one by a modern historian of science, the other two by Victorian writers) focus on emerging medical approaches to criminality, split personality, and addiction. The final excerpt is drawn from the posthumously published memoirs of an eminent Victorian intellectual anguished by what he terms "perpetual discord between spontaneous appetite and acquired respect for social law" in his closeted life as a homosexual.

STEPHEN JAY GOULD

[Post-Darwinian Theories of the Ape Within]†

The concept of evolution transformed human thought during the nineteenth century. Nearly every question in the life sciences was reformulated in its light. No idea was ever more widely used, or misused ("social Darwinism" as an evolutionary rationale for the inevitability of poverty, for example). Both creationists (Agassiz and Morton) and evolutionists (Broca and Galton) could exploit the data of brain size to make their invalid and invidious distinctions among groups. But other quantitative arguments arose as more direct spinoffs from evolutionary theory. * * * [They include] a specific evolutionary hypothesis for the biological nature of human criminal behavior—Lombroso's criminal anthropology. [It] relied upon [a]

---

† From *The Mismeasure of Man* (New York and London: W. W. Norton, 1981; rev. ed. 1996), pp. 142, 152–53. Reprinted by permission of W. W. Norton. Notes have been edited.

132

quantitative and supposedly evolutionary method—the search for signs of apish morphology in groups deemed undesirable.

*   *   *

* * * Cesare Lombroso's theory of *l'uomo delinquente*—the criminal man—[was] probably the most influential doctrine ever to emerge from the anthropometric tradition.[1] Lombroso, an Italian physician, described the insight that led to his theory of innate criminality and to the profession he established—criminal anthropology. He had, in 1870, been trying to discover anatomical differences between criminals and insane men "without succeeding very well." Then, "the morning of a gloomy day in December," he examined the skull of the famous brigand Vihella, and had that flash of joyous insight that marks both brilliant discovery and crackpot invention. For he saw in that skull a series of atavistic features recalling an apish past rather than a human present:

> This was not merely an idea, but a flash of inspiration. At the sight of that skull, I seemed to see all of a sudden, lighted up as a vast plain under a flaming sky, the problem of the nature of the criminal—an atavistic being who reproduces in his person the ferocious instincts of primitive humanity and the inferior animals. Thus were explained anatomically the enormous jaws, high cheek bones, prominent superciliary arches, solitary lines in the palms, extreme size of the orbits, handle-shaped ears found in criminals, savages and apes, insensibility to pain, extremely acute sight, tattooing, excessive idleness, love of orgies, and the irresponsible craving of evil for its own sake, the desire not only to extinguish life in the victim, but to mutilate the corpse, tear its flesh and drink its blood.[2]

Lombroso's theory was not just a vague proclamation that crime is hereditary—such claims were common enough in his time—but a specific *evolutionary* theory based upon anthropometric data. Criminals are evolutionary throwbacks in our midst. Germs of an ancestral past lie dormant in our heredity. In some unfortunate individuals, the past comes to life again. These people are innately driven to act as a normal ape or savage would, but such behavior is deemed criminal in our civilized society. Fortunately, we may identify born criminals because they bear anatomical signs of their apishness. Their atavism is both physical and mental, but the physical signs, or stigmata as Lombroso called them, are decisive. Criminal *behavior* can also arise in normal men, but we know the "born criminal" by

1. The tradition of analyzing human traits on the basis of quantified measurements of anatomy, especially the brain [*Editor*].
2. As quoted in Ian Taylor, Paul Walton, and Jock Young, *The New Criminology* (London: Routledge and Kegan Paul, 1973), p. 41.

his anatomy. Anatomy, indeed, is destiny, and born criminals cannot escape their inherited taint: "We are governed by silent laws which never cease to operate and which rule society with more authority than the laws inscribed on our statute books. Crime . . . appears to be a natural phenomenon."[3]

FREDERIC W. H. MYERS

Multiplex Personality[†]

* * * My theme is the multiplex and mutable character of that which we know as the Personality of man * * *.

I began, then, with one or two examples of the pitch to which the dissociation of memories, faculties, sensibilities may be carried, without resulting in mere insane chaos, mere demented oblivion. These cases as yet are few in number. It is only of late years—and it is mainly in France—that *savants* have recorded with due care those psychical lessons, deeper than any art of our own can teach us, which natural anomalies and aberrant instances afford.

*　*　*

Louis V. began life (in 1863) as the neglected child of a turbulent mother. He was sent to a reformatory at ten years old, and there showed himself, as he has always done when his organisation has given him a chance, quiet, well-behaved, and obedient. Then at fourteen years old he had a great fright from a viper—a fright which threw him off his balance and started the series of psychical oscillations on which he has been tossed ever since. At first the symptoms were only physical, epilepsy and hysterical paralysis of the legs; and at the asylum of Bonneval, whither he was next sent, he worked at tailoring steadily for a couple of months. Then suddenly he had a hystero-epileptic attack—fifty hours of convulsions and ecstasy— and when he awoke from it he was no longer paralysed, no longer acquainted with tailoring, and no longer virtuous. His memory was set back, so to say, to the moment of the viper's appearance, and he

---

3. Translated from Cesare Lombroso, *L'homme criminel* (1887 French translation; Paris: F. Alcan), p. 667.

† From "Multiplex Personality," *Proceedings of the Society for Psychical Research,* 4 (1886–87): 496–97, 499–500, 503–4. The author of this article is the same F. W. H. Myers whose letter to Stevenson about *Strange Case of Dr. Jekyll and Mr. Hyde* is contained in the "reception" materials in this edition. The Society for Psychical Research was an association founded in London in 1882 for the investigation of psychic phenomena, a subject of growing public interest at the time. Stevenson joined the society from Samoa; his name appears on the membership lists for the years 1892 and 1893–4. Footnotes are by the editor of this Norton Critical Edition.

could remember nothing since. His character had become violent, greedy, and quarrelsome, and his tastes were radically changed. * * *

* * *

* * * Inhibit his left brain[1] (and right side) and he becomes, as one may say, not only left-handed but *sinister*; he manifests himself through nervous arrangements which have reached a lower degree of evolution. And he can represent in memory those periods only when his personality had assumed the same attitude, when he had crystallised about the same point.

Inhibit his right brain, and the higher qualities of character remain, like the power of speech, intact. There is self-control; there is modesty; there is the sense of duty—the qualities which man has developed as he has risen from the savage level. But nevertheless he is only half himself. Besides the hemiplegia,[2] which is a matter of course, memory is truncated too, and he can summon up only such fragments of the past as chance to have been linked with this one abnormal state, leaving unrecalled not only the period of sinister inward ascendancy, but the normal period of childhood, before his *Wesen*[3] was thus cloven in twain.[4] * * *

* * *

* * * Let us picture the human brain as a vast manufactory, in which thousands of looms, of complex and differing patterns, are habitually at work. These looms are used in varying combinations; but the main driving-bands which connect them severally or collectively with the motive power, remain for the most part unaltered.

Now, how do I come to have my looms and driving-gear arranged in this particular way? Not, certainly, through any deliberate choice of my own. My ancestor the ascidian,[5] in fact, inherited the business when it consisted of little more than a single spindle. Since his day my nearer ancestors have added loom after loom. Some of their looms have fallen to pieces unheeded; others have been kept in repair because they suited the style of order which the firm had at that time

---

1. "Inhibiting" the left or right brain refers to what appeared to be the effect of depressing the action of one of the two brain hemispheres by activating one or the other side of the body through the magnets, metal conductors, and electrical stimulants which Louis V.'s doctors experimentally applied to different parts of his anatomy.
2. Paralysis of one side of the body.
3. *Wesen*: being.
4. In 1893, Stevenson told a New Zealand newspaper reporter that the history of Louis V. had been brought to his attention (by Myers himself) only after *Strange Case of Dr. Jekyll and Mr. Hyde* was published, and that he had not heard of any actual cases of double personality before he wrote the tale. According to the reporter, Stevenson also spoke of his conviction, however—current at least at the time of this interview—that "there are many consciousnesses in a man" (Monterey Stevenson Museum Scrapbook 3, p. 237).
5. A mollusk considered by Victorian evolutionists to constitute a link in the development of the vertebrates.

to meet. But the class of orders received has changed very rapidly during the last few hundred years. I have now to try to turn out altruistic emotions and intelligent reasoning with machinery adapted to self-preserving fierceness or manual toil. And in my efforts to readjust and reorganise I am hindered not only by the old-fashioned type of the looms, but by the inconvenient disposition of the driving-gear. * * * In this perplexity I watch what happens in certain factories— * * *—where the hidden part of the machinery is subject to certain dangerous jerks or dislocations, after which the gearings shift of themselves and whole groups of looms are connected and disconnected in a novel manner.

* * *

NORMAN KERR

[Abject Slaves to the Narcotic]†

* * *

* * * Men and women of the highest culture, the purest life, the most exalted aims, have become reckless drunkards. The clearest minds, the keenest intellects, the most acute reasoners, have been subdued by alcohol. The warmest hearts, the kindest souls, the most unselfish spirits, have been transformed under the syren influence of "the tricksy spirit," into the coldest, most unkind, and most selfish votaries at the shrine of Bacchus.

Why have these, and a great company of such, fallen so low? Not from a desire to fall, not from wicked and vain imaginings, not from a determination to become drunken, not from any innate love of the inebriating agent, but from a want of power to resist the overwhelming weight of a well-nigh irresistible impulse within them, which, especially when awakened to action on the contact of a narcotic with the nervous system, hurled them away in spite of their vain efforts at escape in a whirlwind of excessive indulgence.

Is drunkenness never the effect of disease? How anyone who has witnessed the career of a confirmed drunkard ever had any doubt on the subject is beyond my comprehension. Yet some deny that intemperance is ever a disease, or the effect of disease, and insist that it is only a moral vice.

† From *Inebriety, Its Etiology, Pathology, Treatment and Jurisprudence* (1882), 2nd ed. (London, H. K. Lewis: 1889), pp. 4, 14–15, 21, 30–31. Kerr, a doctor, was a key figure in the British temperance movement before he began working professionally to direct medical attention to the causes and effects of drug and alcohol addiction. Footnotes are by the editor of this Norton Critical Edition.

*   *   *

Inebriety being a disease, to what group should we assign it? There can be but one answer: inebriety belongs to the group of "diseases of the nervous system," and its nearest ally is "insanity."

* * * Let me not be misunderstood. I am a firm believer in the principles of the Christian faith, and in responsibility to the Judge of all for the proper use of every faculty with which we have been endowed. Therefore I freely concede that there is a moral and religious aspect of intemperance; that if there is inebriety the disease, there is drunkenness the vice and the sin.

But sorrowful experience has shown me that there are many inebriates who are more sinned against than sinning (as there are many lunatics who have lost their senses through no fault of their own), who are so constituted that to drink in what is called "moderation" is beyond their power. * * *

*   *   *

Look at the periodical inebriate. Though almost as clear-headed and as well-disposed as his abstaining brethren in the intervals between the attacks, during each outbreak he is guilty of freaks, and acts of stupidity or violence, which may truly be said to be the acts of a maniac.

*   *   *

* * * The inherited neuropathic predisposition may be transmitted, transformed into a variety of neurotic forms, the special form of insanity, inebriety, paralysis, epilepsy, hysteria, spasmodic asthma, hay fever, or allied nerve inheritance being determined by a concurrence of conditions including the individual environment, and stretching back for generations.

If we employ a restricted definition of insanity, we find it consists in an exaltation or derangement of the nervous faculties, rendering the insane person unable—in some points, though not necessarily in all—to use his reason, exert his will, and control his actions.

Distinguished alienists[1] adopt a wider description, but I prefer this restricted definition in order to apply as crucial a test as possible to the classifying of inebriety almost alongside of insanity. The wider the definition, of course the more will the justness of my contention be confirmed.

In intoxication there is usually an exaltation, short lived it may be, of the faculties of the mind. To secure this exaltation, which occurs even in cases of pronounced alcoholic melancholia, the inebriate will

---

1. Doctors specializing in alienation of the mind, i.e., madness [*Editor*].

often lie, cheat, steal, crawl—at any cost, temporal or eternal—and for any agent which will ensure the fleeting gratification. Alcohol is the exaltant generally resorted to in this country, because it is in common use; but indulgence in opium, chloral, ether, or other narcotic agent, is steadily spreading, and by women frequently in addition to or alternating with alcohol. Even when the exaltation is not apparent—and I have seen cases presenting this feature—there is in inebriety derangement of the mental faculties, so that consciousness, perception, reasoning power, and conscience are impaired. The will being paralyzed (this is most complete in habitual inebriety), though in an interval of abstinence the periodic inebriate seems to be in the full possession of all his normal powers, how often do we see a renewal of the predisposing cause, or a fresh exciting cause, disclose the eclipse of his reason, the deadening of his conscience, and the enfeeblement of his will-power.

JOHN ADDINGTON SYMONDS

[This Aberrant Inclination in Myself]†

It was my primary object when I began these autobiographical notes to describe as accurately and candidly as I was able a type of character, which I do not at all believe to be exceptional, but which for various intelligible reasons has never yet been properly analysed. I wanted to supply material for the ethical psychologist and the student of mental pathology, by portraying a man of no mean talents, of no abnormal depravity, whose life has been perplexed from first to last by passion—natural, instinctive, healthy in his own particular case—but morbid and abominable from the point of view of the society in which he lives—persistent passion for the male sex.[1]

† From *The Memoirs of John Addington Symonds*, ed. Phyllis Grosskurth (New York: Random House, 1984), pp. 182–83, 283. Copyright © 1984 by the London Library. Introduction copyright © 1984 by Phyllis Grosskurth. Reprinted by permission of Random House, Inc. Footnotes are by the editor of this Norton Critical Edition. These autobiographical memoirs were written in secrecy in 1889 by Stevenson's friend and fellow-writer, J. A. Symonds (for whose response to *Strange Case of Dr. Jekyll and Mr. Hyde*, see "reception" materials in this edition.) The memoirs were not released for publication until many years after Symonds' death, however, in accordance with the instructions Symonds had given to the literary executor of his estate.

1. In the margin of Symonds' manuscript at this point, editor Phyllis Grosskurth reports, appears a paragraph which reads: "December 1891: This was written by me at Venice in May 1889. I had not then studied the cases of sexual inversion recorded by Casper-Liman, Ulrichs and Krafft-Ebing. Had I done so, I should not perhaps have dealt with my personal experience so diffusely as I have done in this chapter. What I wrote, I now leave as it stands. It forms a more direct contribution to the psychology of sexual abnormality than if I were to mix it up with the discussion of theories unknown to me at the time of writing."

* * *

This was my primary object. It seemed to me, being a man of letters, possessing the pen of a ready writer and the practised impartiality of a critic accustomed to weigh evidence, that it was my duty to put on record the facts and phases of this aberrant inclination in myself—so that fellow-sufferers from the like malady, men innocent as I have been, yet haunted as I have been by a sense of guilt and dread of punishment,[2] men injured in their character and health by the debasing influences of a furtive and lawless love, men deprived of the best pleasures which reciprocated passion yields to mortals, men driven in upon ungratified desires and degraded by humiliating outbursts of ungovernable appetite, should feel that they are not alone, and should discover at the same time how a career of some distinction, of considerable energy and perseverance, may be pursued by one who bends and sweats beneath a burden heavy enough to drag him down to pariahdom. * * *

* * *

Few situations in life are more painful than this: that a man, gifted with strong intellectual capacity, and exercised in all the sleights of criticism, should sit down soberly to contemplate his own besetting vice. In pleasant moments, when instinct prevails over reason, when the broadway of sensual indulgence invites his footing, the man plucks primroses of frank untutored inclination. They have for him, then, only the fragrance of wayside flowers, blossoms upon the path of exquisite experience. But, when he comes to frigid reason's self again, when he tallies last night's deeds with today's knowledge of fact and moral ordinance, he awakes to the reality of a perpetual discord between spontaneous appetite and acquired respect for social law. By the light of his clear brain he condemns the natural action of his appetite; and what in moments of self-abandonment to impulse appeared a beauteous angel, stands revealed before him as a devil abhorred by the society he clings to. The agony of this struggle between self-yielding to desire and love, and self-scourging by a trained discipline of analytic reflection, breaks his nerve. The only exit for a soul thus plagued is suicide. Two factors, equally uncon-

---

2. The sixteenth-century British law against "buggery" (sexual intercourse with a person of the same sex or with an animal) was replaced in 1885 by a criminal law measure known as the Labouchère amendment, which defined "acts of gross indecency" between two men, whether in public or private, as "misdemeanours," punishable by up to two years of hard labor. While the sentence was milder than the death sentence originally allowed for buggery, the Labouchère amendment carried new weight through both the extension of criminal activity to the private sphere and a social context of active concern about male homosexuality.

querable, flesh and the reason, animal joy in living and mental perception that life is a duty, war in the wretched victim of their equipoise. While he obeys the flesh, he is conscious of no wrongdoing. When he awakes from the hypnotism of the flesh, he sees his own misdoing not in the glass of truth to his nature, but in the mirror of convention. He would fain[3] have less of sense or less of intellect.

* * *

3. Gladly, willingly.

Sociohistorical Contexts: Political Disunity and Moral Conformity

Jekyll's sense of self-division has been viewed by some critics as analogous to, or fostered by, schisms existing within British society. The first piece in this section profiles 1880s London as a site of economic divisions and political tensions. The second item is an 1888 British cartoon using the figures of Jekyll and Hyde in conjunction with a current aspect of Anglo-Irish tension. The third excerpt examines disjunctions between practice and preaching in Victorian society as a frequent result of pressures to conform to middle-class norms of propriety and Evangelical standards of virtue.

JUDITH R. WALKOWITZ

[London in the 1880s]†

By the 1880s, most of the salient features of London's imaginary landscape, which writers like Dickens, Mayhew, and Greenwood had helped to construct,[1] had formalized into a conception of London as an immense world-city, culturally and economically important, yet socially and geographically divided and politically incoherent. Social and political developments of the mid- and late-Victorian period materially reinforced this complex image. London was the largest city in the world, totalling four million inhabitants in the 1880s. Since the first half of the nineteenth century, it had reclaimed its status as the cultural and nerve center of the nation and empire, over-

---

† From *City of Dreadful Delight* (Chicago: University of Chicago Press, 1992), pp. 24–27. © 1992 by Judith R. Walkowitz. Reprinted by permission of the University of Chicago Press. Notes have been edited.
1. I.e., through their writings (Charles Dickens primarily as a novelist; Henry Mayhew and James Greenwood as journalists) [*Editor*].

shadowing Manchester and Liverpool as the embodiment of the "modern city."[2]

In the second half of the century, the West End of Mayfair and St. James had undergone considerable renovation; from a wealthy residential area it had been transformed and diversified into the bureaucratic center of empire, the hub of communications, transportation, commercial display, entertainment, and finance. In the process, a modern landscape had been constructed—of office buildings, shops, department stores, museums, opera, concert halls, music halls, restaurants, and hotels—to service not only the traditional rich of Mayfair but a new middle class of civil servants and clerks * * *.

Yet, in the 1880s, these commercial and institutional developments were imaginatively overshadowed by representations of urban pathology and decline. As the capital city, London epitomized the power of the empire but also its vulnerability. The disquieting effects of the Great Depression,[3] the erosion of mid-Victorian prosperity, the decline of London's traditional industries, and international competition from the United States and Germany for industrial and military supremacy, all contributed to a sense of malaise and decline. This anxious mood was communicated through representations of London itself, particularly those involving political disorder, urban pathology, and physical degeneration.[4]

Despite its economic and social centrality, London lacked a clear political identity. "In London, there is no effective unity," complained John Morley, "interests are too varied and diverse." This great world-city lacked a unified or systematic water, sanitation, and public-health system, and it suffered from periodic plagues of typhus and typhoid. Until 1888, when the London County Council was established, it had no city government other than a Metropolitan Board of Works, dozens of little vestries and parishes, and forty-eight boards of guardians. In addition, there was no local control over the police force (the metropolitan police would remain under the control of the Home Office even after the establishment of the LCC). Debates over centralization at the time certainly intensified public consciousness that the capital of the Empire was "the worst governed city of the Empire."[5]

One apparent symptom of political disorder was London's vulnerability to international terrorism. In the mid-80s, middle-class Lon-

2. Asa Briggs, *Victorian Cities* (New York and Evanston: Harper and Row, 1963), chap. 8.
3. A lengthy economic depression (1873–96) which made many luxury goods unaffordable for the middle class [*Editor*].
4. Gareth Stedman Jones, *Outcast London* (Oxford: Clarendon Press, 1971), pp. 12–16; chaps. 6, 16.
5. John Morley, quoted in P. J. Waller, *Town, City, and Nation: England, 1850–1914* (Oxford: Oxford University Press, 1983), p. 58; *Daily News*, 1911, quoted in ibid., p. 53.

doners were gripped by fears that assassination on the part of Continental anarchists and Irish Fenians was spreading as a political strategy. London was, in fact, a prime target of terrorist attacks. In March 1883 the Local Government Board Offices were blown up, and an unsuccessful attempt was made to blow up the offices of *The Times*. In October 1883, two underground railways were dynamited; in February 1884 a portion of Victoria Station was blown up; in May 1884 the offices of Scotland Yard were attacked.[6] Writing to a friend in January 1885, Henry James was appalled at the "gloomy, anxious" state of London:

> Westminster Hall and the Tower were half blown up two days ago by Irish Dynamiters, there is a catastrophe to the little British force in the Soudan in the air . . . and a general sense of rocks ahead in the foreign relations of the country. . . . The possible malheurs—reverses, dangers, embarrassments, the "decline," in a word, of old England, go to my heart. . . .[7]

Accompanying this political malaise were equally striking social divisions and residential segregation. Slum clearance in the mid-Victorian period had successfully destroyed many of the "plague spots" and rookeries that had previously darkened the glittering landscape of the West End. In his tour of the wilds of London, Greenwood could rejoice that only one "West End Cholera Stronghold" remained after "hideous slums that once disfigured the district between Westminster and Pimlico had been routed and destroyed." Wide new roads cut through the slums, observes historian Jerry White, "letting in air, light and police, and, most important of all, disturbing the inhabitants from their old haunts." The effect of this demolition was to destroy some of the "fever strongholds" and to force the unrespectable poor into the few remaining rough areas, but overall to enforce a stricter residential segregation according to class.[8]

The opposition of East and West increasingly took on imperial and racial dimensions, as the two parts of London imaginatively doubled for England and its Empire. The West End, with its national mon-

---

6. Derek Brewer, Introduction to Henry James, *The Princess Cassamassima* (Harmondsworth, Middlesex: Penguin, 1986), p. 25.
7. James, quoted in ibid., p. 24. Domestic unrest was thus regarded from an imperial perspective; the Home Office and Scotland Yard were rigidly intolerant of lawless political activities, "because imperial responsibilities immediately lent overseas significance to domestic unrest." Colin Ford and Brian Harrison, eds., *One Hundred Years Ago* (Cambridge: Harvard University Press, 1983), p. 178.
8. James Greenwood *The Wilds of London*, London: Chatto and Windus, 1874; reprint, New York: Garland, 1985), p. 350; Jerry White, *The Rothschild Buildings: Life in a Tenement Block, 1887–1920* (London: Routledge and Kegan Paul, 1980), pp. 10, 131; John Davis, "Radical Clubs and London Politics," in *Metropolis London: Histories and Representations since 1800*, ed. David Feldman and Gareth Stedman Jones (London and New York: Routledge, 1989), pp. 113–14.

uments and government offices, served as a site for imperial spectacle: during her golden jubilee in 1887, Queen Victoria, elevated above politics as the mother of the nation, was carted around the major thoroughfares, escorted by an Indian cavalry troop. Meanwhile, another kind of imperial spectacle was staged in the East End. The docks and railway termini of the East End were international entrepôts for succeeding waves of immigrants, most recently poor Jews fleeing the pogroms of Eastern Europe. Gravitating to the central districts, the declining inner industrial rim, the "foreign element" had to compete with the indigenous laboring poor for housing and resources.[9]

In the last decades of the nineteenth century, journalistic exposés highlighted this geographic segregation, impressing on Londoners the perception that they lived in a city of contrasts, a class and geographically divided metropolis of hovels and palaces. A string of highly publicized events and scandals, between 1883 and 1888, sustained the problem of poverty as a subject of concern for the educated reading public. Startling revelations of "Outcast London"[1] familiarized middle-class readers with the sordid and depressing living conditions of the poor and reminded them again, as had the literature of the 1840s, of the dangerous social proximity between vast numbers of casual laborers and a professional criminal class. In the established tradition of urban exploration, George Sims introduced his exposé of London slum housing, *How the Poor Live* (1883), as a "book of travel," a venture through "a dark continent that is within easy walking distance of the General Post Office." * * *

9. David Cannadine, "The Context, Performance, and Meaning of Ritual: The British Monarchy and the Invention of Tradition, c. 1820–1977," in *The Invention of Tradition*, ed. Eric Hobsbawm and Terence Ranger (Cambridge: Cambridge University Press, 1983), pp. 101–65; Thomas Richards, "The Image of Victoria in the Year of Jubilee," *Victorian Studies*, 30, no. 4 (Autumn 1987): 7–32; White, *Rothschild Buildings*, pp. 133–37.
1. An exposé of the living conditions of the London poor published in 1883 under the title, *The Bitter Cry of Outcast London* [Editor].

DR. M'JEKYLL AND MR. O'HYDE.

Punch cartoon, August 18, 1888: "Dr. M'Jekyll and Mr. O'Hyde." Courtesy of The British Library. An example of the political uses to which Stevenson's tale was put, this cartoon reflects British suspicions that Irish Home Rule representatives in the British Parliament, especially the National League land reform activist Charles Stewart Parnell, secretly supported the Irish Fenian terrorist activities which Judith Walkowitz mentions (preceding excerpt) as a source of anxiety for middle-class Londoners in the 1880s. The immediate reference for the cartoon is Parliament's August 13, 1888, establishing of a special investigatory commission on "Parnellism and Crime," a legislative action which followed a series of articles in the London *Times* implicating Parnell and his followers in various Fenian crimes, including the 1882 murder of two British officials in Dublin which Parnell had publicly condemned.

WALTER HOUGHTON

[Hypocrisy]†

* * *

Of all the criticisms brought against them by the Lytton Stracheys of the twentieth century,[1] the Victorians would have pleaded guilty to only one. They would have defended or excused their optimism, their dogmatism, their appeal to force, their strait-laced morality, but they would have confessed to an unfortunate strain of hypocrisy. To understand the charge, it must be broken down into three specific counts. One, they concealed or suppressed their true convictions and their natural tastes. They said the "right" thing or did the "right" thing: they sacrificed sincerity to propriety. Second, and worse, they pretended to be better than they were. They passed themselves off as being incredibly pious and moral; they talked noble sentiments and lived—quite otherwise. Finally, they refused to look at life candidly. They shut their eyes to whatever was ugly or unpleasant and pretended it didn't exist. Conformity, moral pretension, and evasion—those are the hallmarks of Victorian hypocrisy.

Now the leading Victorians, as I said, would have agreed to this bill of particulars, but they would have challenged the wholesale implications of duplicity and cowardice. For they recognized, as modern critics have not, that the circumstances were often extenuating and the motivation by no means always culpable. For one thing, hypocrisy might not be conscious and calculated (for the sake of personal gain). It might very well be unconscious or half-conscious: a conforming to the conventions out of sheer habit, or an understandable piece of self-deception. Furthermore, even when the deception was deliberate, it might be practiced for disinterested reasons, because one honestly believed that candor would do more harm than good; or from pardonable self-protection, because otherwise one might not be able to hold his job or support his family. And as for evasion, one might refuse to look at certain facts from sheer terror quite as much as from selfish prudence. In short, if we are to charge the Victorians with hypocrisy, the term must not carry its usual connotations of guilt. It should be used as they themselves used it for the most part, as a synonym for insincerity. It should be written "hypocrisy."

---

† From *The Victorian Frame of Mind* (New Haven and London: Yale University Press, 1957), pp. 394–95, 397, 404–8, 413, 419. © 1957, by Yale University Press. Reprinted by permission of the publisher. Notes have been edited.

1. I.e., debunkers of Victorian pomposity, in the tradition of Lytton Strachey in his 1918 book, *Eminent Victorians* [Editor].

1. Conformity

In any society which is ambitious and at the same time unsure of itself because it is new, conventions assume enormous force. For his part, the individual himself is only too eager to find something to rely on, and to avoid any ideas or behavior which by distinguishing him from his class—or the class just above—might make him look like an outsider or an upstart. * * *

* * *

The proper thing to do is not only what the individual *wants* to do in order to belong to good society, or what he *does* do out of ingrained habit; it is also what he *must* do if he is to avoid social stigma. Mill's analysis began: "In our times, from the highest class of society down to the lowest, every one lives as under the eye of a hostile and dreaded censorship."[2] The censorship is bourgeois public opinion demanding that the proprieties be observed—or else! Bagehot described its despotism:

> You may talk of the tyranny of Nero and Tiberius; but the real tyranny is the tyranny of your next-door neighbor. . . . Public opinion is a permeating influence, and it exacts obedience to itself; it requires us to think other men's thoughts, to speak other men's words, to follow other men's habits. Of course, if we do not, no formal ban issues; no corporeal pain, no coarse penalty of a barbarous society is inflicted on the offender: but we are called "eccentric"; there is a gentle murmur of "most unfortunate ideas," "singular young man," "well-intentioned, I dare say; but unsafe, sir, quite unsafe."[3]

* * *

2. Moral Pretension

Although everyone at times pretends to be better than he is, even to himself, the Victorians were more given to this type of deception than we are. They lived in a period of much higher standards of conduct—too high for human nature. As men were required to support Christianity by church attendance and active charity, and to accept the moral ideals of earnestness, enthusiasm, and sexual purity, the gap between profession and practice, or between profession and the genuine character, widened to an unusual extent. But here again we encounter various kinds and degrees of insincerity. * * *

2. John Stuart Mill, *On Liberty* (1859) in *Utilitarianism, Liberty, and Representative Government* (New York and London: Everyman's Library, 1950), p. 159.
3. Walter Bagehot, "The Character of Sir Robert Peel," *Works*, ed. Forrest Morgan, 5 vols. (Hartford, Conn.: 1891), vol. 3, pp. 4–5.

*   *   *

No doubt the situation bred its quota of outright hypocrites, like those in Clough's acid poem who repeat the ten commandments with cynical qualifications:

> Thou shalt not steal; an empty feat,
> When it's so lucrative to cheat;

and so with the other nine.[4] But the representative servant of God and Mammon, as Kingsley[5] suggests, was a Pharisee. He imagined, sincerely enough, that although he was sometimes a sinner (like everyone else), he was a true servant of God. * * *

*   *   *

The commercial spirit was not responsible, however, for the most odious forms of moral pretension: the unctuous mouthing of pious sentiments and a sanctimonious prudery. Both must be traced mainly to Puritanism. For when the saintly character became the ideal of religious life, those who could give a reasonable facsimile thereof possessed a ready means of gaining enormous respect or of masking a worldly or vicious career. * * *

3. Evasion

Strictly speaking * * * all forms of self-deception involve evasion. The intense desire to cling to Christianity or to be a model Christian, with the correlative fears of finding doubt in the mind or evil in the heart, and the general pressure to adopt noble attitudes, made clear-eyed self-examination rare and difficult. Whatever threatened needs so great or social requirements so strong was shut out from consciousness. But this is not what we mean by charging the Victorians with evasion. We mean a process of deliberately ignoring whatever was unpleasant, and pretending it did not exist; which led in turn to the further insincerity of pretending that the happy view of things was the whole truth. In a word, they conveniently looked the other way. The charge was made most sharply by Ruskin in 1856. Any effort to attain a real knowledge of ourselves or the existing state of things was being thwarted, he said, by "a fear of disagreeable facts and conscious shrinking from clearness of light which . . . increase gradually into a species of instinctive terror at all truth, and love of glosses, veils, and decorative lies of every sort."[6] * * *

4. Arthur Hugh Clough, "The Latest Decalogue" in *Poems*, ed. H. F. Lowry, A. L. P. Norrington, and F. L. Mulhauser (Oxford: 1951) pp. 60–61.
5. Charles Kingsley (1819–75), English clergyman and novelist [*Editor*].
6. John Ruskin, *Modern Painters*, 3 (1856), Pt. IV, chap. 4, sec. 3, in *Works*, ed. E. T. Cook and A. D. O. Wedderburn, 39 vols. (London: 1902–12), 5:71.

*   *   *

One particular element in human nature that was notoriously ignored was, of course, the sexual passion, for there shame, fear, and the proprieties united to draw a veil of silence or a gloss of euphemism over the facts of life. So far as the motive was not virtue but the appearance of virtue, and what was condemned was not sin but open sin, the evasion was patently hypocritical. *   *   *

Performance Adaptations

Strange Case of Dr. Jekyll and Mr. Hyde began its march toward popular culture icon status within months after the novel's January 1886 publication. The story was picked up first for literary parody in the February 6, 1886, issue of Victorian England's favorite humor magazine, *Punch*, and then for stage parody in a May 1886 London production entitled *The Strange Case of a Hyde and a Seekyl*. Performance adaptations quickly multiplied. A burlesque version called *Dr. Freckle and Mr. Snide* appeared in New York in October 1887, while the most important theater event of these early years occurred when the first serious stage adaptation opened in Boston on May 9, 1887, under the title *Dr. Jekyll and Mr. Hyde*. It was a four-act melodrama collaboratively produced by playwright T. R. Sullivan and the play's leading actor, Richard Mansfield, with quotation permission from Stevenson. The long-running Sullivan-Mansfield version overshadowed competing serious stage adaptations in the years that followed, becoming a central influence on the many silent film versions created in the early twentieth century, including the great 1920 Famous Players-Lasky production starring John Barrymore. By the early 1920s, silent film version of *Jekyll and Hyde* had been produced in the United States, England, Germany, and Denmark, and the phrase "Jekyll and Hyde" had begun to stand on its own as a term descriptive of a personality split between a good and evil side.

The story's familiarity took a further leap in the era of sound films, as *Jekyll and Hyde* joined the Hollywood monster hit parade alongside *Frankenstein* and *Dracula*. The compelling 1931 *Jekyll and Hyde* version directed by Rouben Mamoulian and starring Frederic March, along with the heavily Freudianized 1941 version starring Spencer Tracy, helped make Stevenson's story so deeply entrenched in American popular culture that elements of the plot or of the tale's most famous film renderings had by the 1940s and 1950s begun spilling over into splinter versions and campy allusions in comedies, cartoons, and the occasional TV science fiction episode. The appeal has hardly been confined to English-speaking countries; post-WWII film versions of the tale emerged from Mexico, Italy, Argentina, France, Spain, and the former Soviet Republic. However, the United States foremost, and Great Britain second, have remained the most active sites for performance versions of all sorts. The 1990s alone, for example, saw a British *Jekyll and Hyde* film starring Michael Caine; and in the United States, the movie *Mary Reilly* with John Malkovich; the Eddie Murphy remake of *The Nutty Professor*; a pornographic *Dr. Jeckel and Ms. Hyde*; a gender-switching comedy entitled *Dr. Jekyll and Ms. Hyde*; the Broadway opening of *Jekyll and Hyde: The Musical*; and a Warner Brothers animation segment for TV about a potion-drinking mouse in the series *Pinky and the Brain*.

In this welter of adaptations, inversions, and spin-offs, a mainstream tradition has emerged among serious film and TV horror versions. It is a tradition that draws as much from the 1887 Sullivan-Mansfield stage melodrama as from Stevenson's novel, for it perpetuates many of the melodrama's alterations of plot and character. One huge change is that Jekyll is repeatedly given a love involvement, in conjunction with which he is typically made relatively youthful and heroically high-minded, pursuing his research out of altruistic or visionary motives. (Little indication is given of a pre-existing pattern of dissolute behavior which it might be Jekyll's need or desire to disguise.) As Jekyll shifts character from Stevenson's paunchy, fifty-year-old socially isolated hypocrite to a largely likeable young victim of ambition, the focus of villainy comes to rest increasingly strongly on Hyde. The shock effect of that villainy is amplified by the need to create a striking visual presence on stage or screen for what in the story remains Hyde's physically elusive aura of evil. Further sensationalism results from personalizing Hyde's relationship to his murder victim and making him the agent of deeply painful female suffering. Small wonder that Stevenson complained, speaking of the stage adaptations of his day which were the forerunners to this trend: "Dr. Jekyll should be the central figure and not Mr. Hyde, but on the stage the first character is made subservient to the second, which was not my idea at all."[1]

A range of questions may be raised by the phenomenal success *Jekyll and Hyde* has enjoyed in film history and popular culture. For example, what forms of evil has Hyde been made to stand for, and how do the variations speak for differences in directorial interpretation or changing social concepts of the nature of wickedness? Does the involvement of sex that we find in most versions do damage to Stevenson's intentions or bring to the surface an aspect of the story Stevenson was forced to mute in deference to Victorian propriety? What is lost or gained with the usual refashioning of Jekyll as younger and nobler than Stevenson's original? What have critics found especially interesting or effective about the most famous versions? What does the enormous range of adaptations as a whole tell us about the sources of deepest fascination in Stevenson's tale?

The critical excerpts contained in this section touch on these questions from a variety of angles, some grounded in a broad comparative approach, others in close-up study of individual adaptations. The section concludes with a checklist profiling major stage and film renderings of *Jekyll and Hyde* and offering information on channels of commercial availability.

---

1. As quoted in a June 8, 1888, *San Francisco Examiner* interview article contained in Monterey Stevenson Museum Scrapbook 2, p. 64.

C. ALEX PINKSTON, JR.

The Stage Premiere of Dr. Jekyll and Mr. Hyde†

* * *

The most significant treatments of Stevenson's story are probably the three excellent film versions which appeared in the twentieth century: John Robertson's 1920 film starring John Barrymore; Rouben Mamoulian's 1931 version starring Fredric March; and Victor Fleming's 1941 treatment starring Spencer Tracy. But these three films, and most other film and theatrical treatments of the novel must pay homage to the first professional theatrical adaptation developed in 1887 by Thomas R. Sullivan and the American star actor Richard Mansfield.

Mansfield was one of the thousands of Americans held captive by Stevenson's story, and he was the first actor-manager to see in it the germ of a possible dramatic script. Throughout his career the actor maintained a concern for the psychology of character. Stevenson's novel * * * was precisely the vehicle Mansfield sought at this early stage of his career. While he was aware of the difficulties involved in developing a play from the novel, Mansfield believed the role of Jekyll and Hyde might demonstrate in one production his versatility as an actor and add to his repertoire a character of tragic depth. He foresaw an extraordinary triumph for himself in the dual role if he might visualize to an audience, as his imagination brought to his mind, the contrast between Dr. Jekyll and Mr. Hyde, the weird transformations of the man into the fiend and back again, and the gradual absorption of the good nature by the evil nature as seen by the increasing difficulty of controlling the reversion from Hyde to Jekyll. Moreover, he believed the story contained a noble moral worthy of dramatization.[1]

The actor was playing in Boston when he contracted with Stevenson for production rights, and he urged young Boston writer Thomas Sullivan to adapt the novel for the stage.[2] Sullivan believed it would be tremendously difficult to present on stage the duality of the hero, and he complained the novel lacked the conventionally prescribed love interest and comic relief found in contemporary successes. According to Mansfield's biographer, Paul Wilstach, Mansfield immediately suggested to Sullivan a scenario which his imagination

† From Nineteenth Century Theatre Research, 14 (1986): 21–43. Reprinted by permission of C. Alex Pinkston, Jr. Notes have been edited.
1. Paul Wilstach, Richard Mansfield: The Man and the Actor (New York, 1908), p. 144.
2. The Yale Letters, published subsequent to this article, indicate that the initial request to Stevenson for permission to dramatize was made by Sullivan, rather than Mansfield. See Letters 5:263–64 [Editor].

had already conjured up, repeated a few of Hyde's passages from the novel with ghastly gutturals and in a demonic posture that frightened the writer out of several nights' sleep, and urged him to read the book again, stating that if he did not dramatize it, someone else would. Sullivan accepted the commission (Wilstach, p. 144).

* * *

* * * The play[3] * * * was performed for the first time at the Boston Museum, 9 May 1887. Mansfield withdrew the play on 14 May then opened in New York on 12 September at the Madison Square Theatre (Wilstach, p. 145 * * *). In both cities the critics were unanimous in their praise of the play's staging and Mansfield's performance of Edward Hyde; however, they were divided in their response to Sullivan's adaptation of Stevenson's novel and the actor's interpretation of Henry Jekyll. * * *

* * *

Act I, titled "Slave and Master," establishes the Victorian context for the play's events, provides necessary exposition, and presents the event which incites the play's action: Edward Hyde's murder of Sir Danvers Carew. Retired General and widower Sir Danvers is playing chess with Utterson, a lawyer; Agnes and her Aunt, Mrs. Lanyon,[4] are taking tea. Agnes voices her concern that her fiancé Dr. Henry Jekyll might be in some danger since he did not come to dinner as he promised. Dr. Lanyon arrives to explain that Henry remained at the hospital to treat a patient. On the ladies' departure, Lanyon shares with Danvers and Utterson a story he has heard about a man named Edward Hyde who trampled a young girl underfoot in the street. Knowing Jekyll has befriended Hyde, Utterson determines, after the other men exit, to warn Henry about Hyde's cruelty. Immediately thereafter, Mansfield as Jekyll appears at the French doors; in soliloquy he speaks of a danger threatening him and determines to break his engagement to Agnes in order to save her from tragedy. Utterson greets Jekyll and immediately protests the large bequest to Edward Hyde in Jekyll's will. Jekyll describes Hyde as a "strange case," but assures Utterson that he can be rid of Edward at any

3. I have discovered the promptbook of Mansfield's production among materials located in a costume collection donated to the Smithsonian Museum by Mrs. Mansfield several years after her husband's death. This version contains setting descriptions, blocking, and sound and lighting notations, and so is rich in information regarding Mansfield's staging. Of equal significance, however, is the text itself, for it provides a detailed narrative for the production which, before, could only be gathered from critics' scenarios. Accordingly, it is now possible to determine in what ways and to what extent Sullivan's text differs from Stevenson's novel.

4. Agnes: Agnes Carew, daughter to Sir Danvers and fiancée to Jekyll; Mrs. Lanyon: wife to Dr. Lanyon. In the process of pitting Hyde against the forces of family and domesticity, Sullivan made Carew and Lanyon brothers-in-law [*Editor*].

moment. Somewhat relieved, Utterson promises to carry out the statements in the will and exits. Left alone, Jekyll laments that he is "doomed to eternal wretchedness, the possessor of a secret [he dares] not even whisper" (Act I, p. 13).[5] Keenly aware of the atmospheric potential of stage lighting, Mansfield delivered this soliloquy before the red glow of the fireplace, presumably to suggest Jekyll's Faustian preoccupation with unknown and demonic forces.

Agnes re-enters, and Jekyll attempts to break their engagement, hinting of a dark secret which might end in his ruin. Agnes declares her unalterable devotion, and after a renewal of vows, the lovers exit into the garden. During this Jekyll-Agnes encounter, the lights dimmed, and warm-colored calciums slowly gave way to blues, suggesting a setting sun (Act I, p. 16f). Sir Danvers returns and, seeing the lovers walking in the twilight, sits in his chair by the fire to dwell on the memory of his late wife. Agnes returns alone, and Danvers requests that she play on the piano an old Indian air which reminds him of Agnes' mother. As Agnes played, green calcium lights overwhelmed the warmer lights, casting a green gloom across the room, and the sinister figure of Hyde emerged through the moonlit doors (Act I, p. 19f). Sir Danvers sends Agnes away, and when Hyde demands Sir Danvers call her back, the General attempts to drive Hyde from the house. Hyde leaps on Sir Danvers, chokes and mauls him to death, then disappears through the French doors. Agnes rushes in to find her father dead and to catch sight of the fleeing murderer. Act I concluded with a tableau curtain call: Agnes bending over her father, Hyde posed at the French doors (Act I, p. 20).

*   *   *

Act II, "Hide and Seek," presents three scenes which portray the search for Edward Hyde by Utterson and the authorities. Mansfield contrasted the warm Act I interior with Act II, Scene 1, "Hyde's Lodgings in Soho," * * * a room furnished with "profuse, disorderly luxury—not that of taste, but that of exuberant sensuality."[6] Thus, the play's subject of human duality was apparent not only in the contrast of personalities in Jekyll and Hyde, but in Mansfield's juxtaposition of settings with contrasting atmospheres. * * *

*   *   *

Act III, "Two and the Same," which takes place in Dr. Lanyon's consulting room in Cavendish Square, * * * presents the famous

---

5. Thomas R. Sullivan, *Dr. Jekyll and Mr. Hyde*, promptbook for the Mansfield production (Mansfield Costume Collection, Smithsonian Institution, Washington, D.C.), to which subsequent citations refer. Page numbers followed by an "f" (e.g., p. 1f) indicate that material was taken from the page facing the numbered page cited.
6. William Winter, *New York Daily Tribune* (13 September 1887): 4.

transformation from Hyde to Jekyll in the presence of Lanyon; the dialogue for the scene is Stevenson's own. * * *

* * * A point of contention among the critics was whether Mansfield used any change in make-up for this scene. * * *

Mansfield claimed he used only his natural body. It is possible that those who believed they saw a change in make-up were actually responding to a change in lighting. Recall that all Hyde's appearances were lit with green calciums. When Jekyll appeared at the rear door of his laboratory in Act II, and when Hyde underwent a change to Jekyll in Act III, a special warm light was made to fall on Mansfield as Jekyll. Such a lighting change would certainly cause a contrast on the actor's face.[7]

Whether or not he employed make-up in the changes, Mansfield's greatest triumph in the character transformation was that it came from within. According to Winter (*Tribune*, p. 4), the transformation was especially effective in its portrayal of the simultaneous possession of the body by both Jekyll and Hyde. More important than the changes in physical bearing and facial expression was the change made by Mansfield in his emotional state, in his "radiation of an interior spirit." The *Boston Post* critic * * * agreed: "It is in every way a psychological transformation . . . as powerful, as significant, as impressive as it is free from mere contortion and grimace."[8]

Act IV, "The Last Night," revealed Jekyll in his cabinet * * * on the verge of involuntary transformation to Hyde. * * *

In this act, Mansfield's most challenging, the actor held the stage alone for twenty minutes with only one interruption. Jekyll has worked for many days in his laboratory to duplicate the transforming drug, but has failed. His last hope is that Lanyon may find the original supply of the transforming powder; his fear is that the original supply contained an impurity which can never again be isolated. Mansfield incorporated haunting sound effects and lighting changes to suggest that Jekyll's life was nearing an end. For example, early in

---

7. Wilstach, *Man and the Actor*, p. 147. Despite Winter's, Wilstach's and Mansfield's claims, the critics continued to look for stage tricks. According to Wilstach, Mansfield was accused of using "acids, phosphorus, all manner of chemicals. The mystery spread to London, where someone declared it was 'all perfectly simple. He uses a rubber suit which he inflates and exhausts at pleasure' " (Wilstach, p. 147). Wilstach (pp. 154–55) also records a story told by the comic actor De Wolf Hopper which gives credence to Mansfield's claim that he used only his natural body in the transformations. Hopper was dining with Mansfield one evening and asked the actor the secret to his on-stage change. "There was a single heavily hooded green lamp over the table at an angle which lighted our faces and threw the rest of the spacious chambers into cavernous shadows . . ." said Hopper. "There was even a bell in a neighboring tower. . . . And then and there, only four feet away, under the green light, as that booming clock struck the hour—he did it—changed to Hyde before my very eyes—and I remember that I, startled to pieces, jumped up and cried that I'd ring the bell if he didn't stop!" Mansfield's impromptu transformation frightened Hopper out of his wits, and on stage in New York this moment compelled the audience to such applause that Mansfield was recalled four times before the curtain.

8. *Boston Post* (10 May 1887): 4.

the scene Jekyll hears the clock tower toll six o'clock; then he speaks his despair, his fear of the reversion to bestial Hyde, and his determination to take poison rather than die as Hyde. The lighting fades from late afternoon to twilight as Jekyll says farewell to beauty, goodness and life, gathers into his hands a few flowers from the vase, and tenderly gives them a parting caress.[9] Then he stands before the mirror, "dreading to remove his hands for fear of the demon's face" they might reveal, and gives "a cry of joy" as he discovers the change has not yet come (Wilstach, p. 147). He begins to drink the poison, but stops as a very ill Lanyon enters and delivers the sad news that the original supply of the drug has been exhausted. Lanyon entreats Jekyll to escape to safety; the police, he says, believe Jekyll to be Hyde's accomplice and are on their way to arrest him. Jekyll says it is too late to think of escape, but he beseeches Lanyon to bring Agnes beneath his window so he may look at her one last time. Lanyon exits, and Jekyll sits at his desk to write his final will and confession. The involuntary transformation begins, the green lighting returns, and Jekyll struggles to reach the window and see Agnes passing below. Then he approaches the mirror and cries out in terror when he sees the face of Hyde. He cowers as he hears the footsteps and voices of the authorities and the heavy blows on the door. Utterson calls Jekyll's name, and Hyde responds with a plea of mercy; then Utterson and the police knock down the door, and Hyde takes the poison just as Lanyon, Utterson, Poole and the police enter. Agnes rushes in and asks where Jekyll is. She looks at the body on the floor and asks, "What is there?" Poole pathetically answers, "This is my master."

* * *

The reviewers' major reservation regarding Mansfield's performance was not a criticism of his acting; rather, it was a disagreement with his interpretation of the role of Jekyll. The *Boston Post* reviewer (17 January 1888, p. 4) called Mansfield's Jekyll "too tame, conventional and spiritless"; the awful awareness of his dual personality was "too palpably carried about with him." * * * [I]n a letter to Mansfield, responding to the actor's London performance, Winter commented: "There is a little too much of Jekyll's misery—and misery never was popular, on the stage,—or off! . . . You ought to make Jekyll a more picturesque fellow,—more 'talking,'—even at a sacrifice of strict correctness" (*Life and Art*, I, 99).

* * * For Mansfield, Jekyll was a dreamer and a visionary; and when, at the opening of the play, he knows he is in danger of losing himself to the monster he has created, he becomes "an unhappy and most wretched man." The very fact of his goodness makes the knowl-

9. William Winter, *The Life and Art of Richard Mansfield*, 2 vols. (New York, 1910), II, 44–45.

edge of his badness overwhelming. The terrific strain upon his once powerful system takes its toll, and he finds himself generally less and less able to withstand, both physically and mentally, the encroachment of evil. He is struck with remorse at the thought of the monster he has conjured up, a monster who has come between him and the woman he loves. He feels responsible for the crimes he has committed in his other form, and he finds too late that the good in him must suffer for the indulgence of the evil in him.[1] Accordingly, Mansfield did not attempt to present the Jekyll of Stevenson's novel; he did not bring to the stage a middle-aged, convivial sort who was capable of forgetting his life as Edward Hyde. For Mansfield, Hyde always haunted Jekyll, because Jekyll was a man of morals.

While Mansfield's Jekyll received some negative criticism, his Hyde gained almost overwhelming praise. * * * But the critics' and audience's preference for Mansfield's Hyde suggests that the melodramatic aspects of the production did overwhelm the subtler, more naturalistic aspects. Moreover, the critics' complaints that Hyde's murder of Sir Danvers occurred too quickly and without sufficient motivation, and that the production sacrificed naturalism for theatricality, suggest that Sullivan's adaptation was not a completely successful dramatic translation of Stevenson's novel. * * * But Sullivan's scenario and Mansfield's interpretation of Jekyll laid the foundation for subsequent dramatic treatments; and even Mansfield's and Sullivan's mild failures revealed problems whose solutions would be sought in later versions.

*   *   *

CHARLES KING

[Themes and Variations]†

Since its original publication in 1886, Robert Louis Stevenson's *The Strange Case of Dr. Jekyll and Mr. Hyde* has maintained a remarkable and never-wavering popularity. The story has achieved such a high

1. Richard Mansfield, *New York Sun* (1 January 1888): 13.
† From *"Dr. Jekyll and Mr. Hyde*: A Filmography," *The Journal of Popular Film and Television*, 25:1 (Spring 1997), pp. 9–12. Published by Heldref Publications, 1319 Eighteenth St., NW, Washington, DC 20036–1802. Copyright ©1997. Reprinted with permission of the Helen Dwight Reid Educational Foundation. The text has been changed according to the author's revisions for this Norton Critical Edition publication. Editorial notes in this excerpt provide supplementary information on a number of film citations which King gives in abbreviated form, since in his original article those citations could be linked to the filmography he appends. Where no such editorial note appears in the following selection, it is because the film is one for which information is available in the "Checklist of Major Performance Adaptations" found on pp. 171–74 of this book. Notes have been edited.

level of name recognition that most Americans and Europeans who
have never read the original story could summarize its plot, or at
least explain its central premise. Particularly in the United States,
the story has frequently been adapted for film. Although the film
versions could be claimed with equal authority by the horror and
science fiction genres, they are now numerous enough to constitute
a subgenre. There have been at least 88 film and television adaptations, including shorts and some less-traditional variations. Since
1908, there has not been a period of longer than five years without
a version of the story, and multiple versions in the same year are not
uncommon. Most scholarship on film adaptations of *Dr. Jekyll and
Mr. Hyde* has focused on only a handful of the films, most frequently
Rouben Mamoulian's 1931 version. This article is intended to be an
introduction to the study of the broader subgenre. * * *

* * *

Some Jekyll and Hyde films retain a large part of Stevenson's story,
and others retain only the central premise of a transformation that
separates someone's personality into independent components. The
popularity of Dr. Jekyll and Mr. Hyde may rest less in the specifics
of Stevenson's story—excellent though it is—than on the basic
appeal of the idea of segregating one component of a person from
the whole and giving it a separate physical form. Different filmmakers have treated this premise in a variety of ways, producing everything from grim cautionary tales to slapstick comedy, from
puritanism to pornography. Major themes of the films include the
fear (or celebration) of a loss of self-control, concerns about the
potential of science to violate a natural order, the seductions and
dangers of addiction, and the potential consequences (negative or
positive) of reversing standard social or sexual conventions.

One theme that is found in many of the films, and which derives
from Stevenson's story, is the fear of the "beast within," the idea that
a segment of the personality that is evil or devoted to amoral self-
gratification could be segregated or selectively unleashed. Variations
of this idea can be found in a number of works of nineteenth-century
fiction, including such notable examples as Edgar Allan Poe's *William Wilson* (1839) and Oscar Wilde's *The Picture of Dorian Gray*
(1890). * * *

Probably all of such stories should be seen as manifestations of a
much older folkloric tradition about people who are unable to control
an aspect of their persona that can transform into a fierce beast. The
differences between a werewolf story and a Jekyll and Hyde story are
often not great, as both frequently exploit a fear that the main character (with whom the audience identifies) will be unable to avoid
hurting his or her closest friends, relatives, or lover. * * *

* * * Hyde represents the human potential for violence, both in his casual attacks on strangers and in his destructive personal relationships. Several film versions of the story show the character forming a long-term abusive relationship with a dance-hall girl, spending his days in socially acceptable activities as Jekyll, and then changing to Hyde for evenings spent terrorizing, beating, and sexually abusing his girlfriend. In a time when there is more open discussion of domestic abuse, it is now possible to say in films what Rouben Mamoulian (1931) and Victor Fleming (1941) were probably reluctant to say in theirs, that Hyde's abusive relationship with his mistress is not so different from abusive relationships that actually exist in our society. Part of the continual fascination with Hyde is that the character is only a slight exaggeration of the negative aspects of our culture, and most variations of the story (except for some of the comedies) play on the audience's suspicion that the capacity to become Hyde might be lurking inside of anyone.

One interesting difference between the films and Stevenson's original story is that Stevenson's story lacks any female characters or sexual content.[1] The films tend to emphasize sexual repression as the major force underlying Jekyll's transformation and present the unleashing of sexual desire as the main manifestation of the "beast within." To introduce the sexual elements, the films frequently use one or both of two devices. One is to introduce a lower-class woman (usually a dance-hall girl) whom Jekyll finds attractive but whom he cannot approach because of their difference in status. The other is to give Jekyll a fiancée or girlfriend with whom he cannot have sex because of Victorian prohibitions and because her father is trying to stop or delay their marriage.[2] Several versions, including those of John S. Robertson (1920), Mamoulian (1931), and Fleming (1941), combine the two ideas, making the engagement yet another reason why Jekyll cannot act on his attraction to the dance-hall girl. In *Mary Reilly* (1996) Stephen Frears seems to be trying to combine elements of both in a single person. Mary Reilly is a lower-class, live-in maid who is in love with Jekyll, but who also forms a relationship with Hyde. Other films involve only the dance-hall girl (Reisner, 1955; Jarrott, 1968) or only the fiancée/girlfriend (Borowczyk, 1981;

---

1. For discussions of the original story and its contemporary context, see Martin Tropp, *Images of Fear: How Horror Stories Helped Shape Modern Culture (1818–1918)* (Jefferson, NC: McFarland, 1990) pp. 90–132; the essays collected by William Veeder and Gordon Hirsch in *Dr Jekyll and Mr Hyde after One Hundred Years* (Chicago: University of Chicago Press, 1988); and Harry M. Geduld's anthology, *The Definitive Dr. Jekyll and Mr. Hyde Companion* (New York: Garland, 1983).
2. The fiancée was part of the tradition prior to the first movie, first appearing in T. Russell Sullivan's play *Dr. Jekyll and Mr. Hyde* (1887). The dance-hall girl is almost certainly a borrowing from Wilde's *The Picture of Dorian Gray* (1890). See David J. Skal, *The Monster Show: A Cultural History of Horror* (New York: Norton, 1993) 139–41, and Paul M. Jensen, "Dr. Jekylls and Mr. Hydes: The Silent Years," *Video Watchdog*, 17 (May–June 1993): 42–59.

Wickes, 1990).[3] When Jekyll transforms, Hyde acts (or at least attempts to act) on the desires that Jekyll repressed, but always in the ugliest possible way. Hyde's relationship with the lower-class woman is abusive, and he threatens Jekyll's fiancée/girlfriend with rape. Hyde's attempt to assault Jekyll's girlfriend can be found in versions as early as that of Henderson[4] (1912). In *Jekyll & Hyde* (Wickes, 1990), he succeeds in raping her.

It is perhaps a tribute to the versatility of Dr. Jekyll and Mr. Hyde that filmmakers have taken the same plot elements and presented fundamentally incompatible interpretations. One reading is as a strict cautionary tale against unleashing destructive desires against loved ones. The fear of such an unleashing may be a common element in traditional werewolf lore, but Stevenson's story is better suited to advocating specifically sexual restraint, for Jekyll is changing into Hyde voluntarily, and that is a self-indulgence he could avoid. Because of the destructive potential in any relationship in which one of the parties is only interested in self-gratification, the story of Hyde can be used to argue that restraint is good, and that society requires it to survive.

Some of the films go so far in advocating sexual restraint that they suggest that sexual desire in general is a danger that should be suppressed. In Robertson's version (1920), when Jekyll simply looks at a dancer and finds her attractive, a silent title card reads, "For the first time in his life, Jekyll had wakened to a sense of his baser nature." In Jarrott's version (1968), the dancer makes a pass at Jekyll saying, "What does it feel like, doing something you want for a change?" Jekyll's response is to change involuntarily into Hyde and attack her. In these films (particularly Robertson's), Hyde's eventual destruction of Jekyll's life seems to be a punishment for Jekyll's failure to maintain his self-control.

Other films take a different tack. Mamoulian's *Dr. Jekyll and Mr. Hyde* (1931) and Wickes's *Jekyll & Hyde* (1990) both emphasize a contrast between the positive relationship Jekyll has with his fiancée/girlfriend and the abusive relationships of Hyde.[5] Although the films are still cautionary tales against violence and sexual excesses, the blame shifts subtly from individual lust to society's restrictions. If Jekyll could pursue his love affair without the barriers erected by social convention and the woman's father, he would not

3. Allen Reisner, 1955, USA: *Dr. Jekyll and Mr. Hyde*, starring Michael Rennie. An episode in the CBS television series, *Climax*, with screenplay by Gore Vidal. For Borowczyk, 1981, see n. 6 [*Editor*].

4. Lucius Henderson, 1912, USA: *Dr. Jekyll and Mr. Hyde*, starring James Cruze. A brief silent-film version. Thanhouser [*Editor*].

5. In *Jekyll & Hyde*, the woman is not Jekyll's fiancée, but the sister of his dead wife. She and Jekyll are in love, but their relationship is blocked because she is trapped in a loveless marriage to a husband who is away in the navy and because her father unfairly blames Jekyll for her sister's death from pneumonia.

have been tempted to transform himself into Hyde. Moderate sexual desire and moderate sexual fulfillment are therefore affirmed as virtues: their restriction doomed Jekyll and might doom others.

Far more radical is Walerian Borowczyk's 1981 version,[6] which rejects any moral restraints, on sex or anything else. Borowczyk's Hyde sexually assaults most of the film's characters, both male and female, and only those who have freed themselves of social restraints and are themselves in some way subverting bourgeois conventions survive his attack. In Borowczyk's film, unleashing the beast within is preferable to enduring the endless banalities of bourgeois society, and, as the film progresses, Borowczyk presents Hyde's victims with less and less sympathy. At the end of the film, Jekyll's fiancée Fanny Osbourne[7] voluntarily transforms herself into a Hydelike female, helps Hyde slaughter her family, and then elopes with him. The final scene shows the pair of them inside a carriage, licking blood from each other's nude bodies in an orgy of anarchic triumph.

Like Robertson's film, Borowczyk's has several supporting characters and plot elements that are still recognizable as being drawn from Stevenson's story, but it reflects a moral and political perspective as different from that of Robertson as any story could be. What is remarkable about Stevenson's central plot premise is that it allows any number of variant themes to be constructed on its basic framework, even within a specific motif like the beast within. *Dr. Black, Mr. Hyde* (Crain, 1975)[8] shifts gears (at least partially) from sex to race and suggests that the beast within a black man who wants to heal is a white man who wants to kill.

In addition to concerns about sexual repression and the beast within, other themes in Jekyll and Hyde films derive from the idea of a transformation that is scientifically and deliberately enacted (at least at first). One issue is the question of when science goes too far. Should men attempt to alter "God's plan" for the universe? In his book Per Schelde perhaps exaggerates when he presents "not playing god" as the primary (indeed, sole) theme of the Dr. Jekyll and Mr. Hyde story,[9] but the theme is certainly present in several film versions. In the films of Mamoulian (1931), Fleming (1941), Jarrott

6. Walerian Borowczyk, 1981, France: *Le cas étrange du Dr. Jekyll et Miss Osbourne*, aka *Bloodlust*, aka *Dr. Jekyll et les femmes*, starring Udo Kier and Gérard Zalcberg. Whodunit / Allegro / Multimedia [*Editor*].
7. The name is that of Robert Louis Stevenson's real-life wife, a curious touch by the film-maker.
8. William Crain, 1975, USA: *Dr. Black, Mr. Hyde* aka *The Watts Monster*, starring Bernie Casie. Dimensions Pictures / Hyde Productions [*Editor*].
9. Per Schelde, *Androids, Humanoids, and Other Science Fiction Monsters* (New York: New York University Press, 1993) pp. 47–50. Schelde is a good example of an author who only discusses Mamoulian's 1931 version. He defends this focus by saying that the other films are "only minimal variations" (12). Is a film really just a "minimal variation" when it endorses the crimes of Hyde (as in Borowczyk's film) or when Jekyll and Hyde are supporting characters, as in *Mary Reilly*?

(1968), and Wickes (1990), Jekyll's experiments are described as "blasphemy," and the negative outcome of the experiment confirms the point. Even in *The Nutty Professor* (1963), Jerry Lewis makes a speech about how science can go too far.

Another major theme in the films is addiction. In the beginning, Jekyll controls his use of the drug, but in the end the drug controls him. In Allen Reisner's television version (1955), Jekyll tells his lawyer that he enjoys the release that the drug gives him, but in the end he cannot control the transformations. *Mary Reilly* (1996) uses the title character's alcoholic father as an overt comparison to Jekyll and his transformations, a metaphor both for the way a drug can alter personality and for Jekyll's compulsive need for it.

One of the more unusual slants on the drug theme is in *Edge of Sanity* (Kikoine, 1988),[1] in which Hyde smokes his formula from what looks like an opium pipe. What is odd is that he repeatedly shares the drug with other people who merely become intoxicated. In other words, the drug is nothing but a simple narcotic that removes inhibitions, and there is no transformation outside of Jekyll's mind. If "Hyde" kills people under the drug's influence, it is because Jekyll is already insane. This Jekyll, too, is addicted to his drug-induced freedom, and given a choice between the drug and the life of his wife, he chooses the former.

Comic versions tend to concentrate on the humorous potential of transformations in unexpected forms, at unexpected times, or in ways which reverse the expected status quo. In Steno's *Dottor Jekyll e gentile signora* (1979),[2] the aging Mr. Hyde offers his formula to his grandson, an ambitious industrialist, telling him that it will improve his business by transforming him into a completely ruthless business competitor. Instead, the formula changes the grandson into a benevolent humanitarian. In the cartoon version *Hyde and Go Tweet* (Freling, 1960),[3] the seemingly helpless Tweety Bird suddenly becomes more than a match for his larger pursuer Sylvester the Cat, to the cat's total bewilderment (and the audience's satisfaction). In both versions of *The Nutty Professor* (Lewis, 1963; Shadyac, 1996),[4] an unattractive professor transforms himself into a handsome ladies' man, only to switch back at inconvenient moments as his two personas battle for control of his body. Both personas pursue the same woman, who eventually chooses the doctor's original form.

The comedies often drift far from Stevenson's book, but they nev-

---

1. Gerard Kikoine, 1988, UK/Hungary: *Edge of Sanity*, starring Anthony Perkins. Allied Vision/Hungarofilm [*Editor*].
2. Steno, aka Stefana Vazino, 1979, Italy: *Dottor Jekyll e gentile signora*, starring Paolo Villagio. Medusa [*Editor*].
3. Fritz Freling, 1960, USA: *Hyde and Go Tweet*. Warner Brothers [*Editor*].
4. Tom Shadyac, 1996, USA: *The Nutty Professor*, starring Eddie Murphy. Universal. A remake of the 1963 Jerry Lewis version by the same title [*Editor*].

ertheless form an interesting flip side to the more serious adaptations, in that they are basically wish-fulfillment fantasies. It is perhaps worth remembering that when people fantasize about changing to a different persona, it is more likely to be a pleasant "what if" fantasy than a cautionary tragedy. The hero of both versions of *The Nutty Professor* is able to find out what his life would be like if he were handsome and self-confident, but he also finds love in his original form: two fantasies for the price of one.

One final subgroup of wish-fulfillment versions should be noted: movies in which a male Jekyll changes into a female Hyde. There are now four such films, which demonstrates the popularity of the idea. As a group they are extremely lightweight, usually aiming for cheap laughs (as in *Dr. Jekyll and Ms. Hyde*; Price, 1995)[5] or the potential for sexual titillation inherent in a temporary change in gender. *Dr. Jeckel and Ms. Hyde* (Craig, 1990) is a hardcore pornographic film, and *The Adult Version of Jekyll and Hide* (Raymond and Elliot, 1971)[6] was X-rated by the standards of its day. Only *Dr. Jekyll and Sister Hyde* (Baker, 1971) makes more than the most token effort to be a horror movie. The flimsiness of these movies suggests that although the idea of temporarily changing genders might have some appeal as a male sex fantasy, it is not a fantasy that the male filmmakers want to look at too rigorously. * * *

SCOTT ALLEN NOLLEN

Dr. Jekyll and Mr. Hyde (Paramount, 1931)†

* * *

The creators of Paramount's 1931 *Dr. Jekyll and Mr. Hyde* drew as much of their inspiration from previous screenplays as they did from Stevenson, but this adaptation captures the very mood and philosophical essence of the novella. Combining an outstanding array of technical achievements with powerful acting and a brilliant script, this film is one of the classic American cinema's true masterpieces * * *.

* * *

5. David Price, 1995, USA: *Dr. Jekyll and Ms. Hyde*, starring Tim Daly and Sean Young. Savoy Pictures [*Editor*].
6. Michael Craig, 1990, USA: *Dr. Jeckel and Ms. Hyde*, starring Mike Horner and Ashlyn Gere. Las Vegas Video. Lee Raymond and Ron Elliot, 1971, USA: *The Adult Version of Jekyll and Hide*, starring Jack Buddliner. Entertainment Ventures [*Editor*].
† From *Robert Louis Stevenson: Life, Literature and the Silver Screen* (Jefferson, NC: McFarland, 1994), pp. 179, 181–83, 195–97, 199. © Scott Allen Nollen. Reprinted by permission of McFarland & Company, Inc. Notes have been edited.

A Paramount star director and one of Hollywood's few intellectual filmmakers, Mamoulian was born in Tiflis, Georgia, Russia, in 1898, and later studied criminology at the University of Moscow and Stanislavskian dramatic technique at the Moscow Art Theatre. In 1918 he developed his own drama studio and two years later toured England with the Russian Repertory Theatre. In 1922 he studied drama at the University of London and directed his first play. According to film historian Ephraim Katz, Mamoulian's initial attempt favored "the traditional Russian naturalistic style but from then on disavowed realism in favor of a stylized, rhythmic, lyrical impressionism."[1]

*   *   *

When Paramount selected *Dr. Jekyll and Mr. Hyde* for Mamoulian's third film project, the studio planned to cast Irving Pichel in the leading role. Mamoulian recalled:

> I thought the idea was atrocious, and I said that I wouldn't be interested in doing the film with him. They said that he would make such a wonderful Hyde. "I'm not worried about Hyde," I said. "I'm worried about Jekyll. I want Jekyll to be young and handsome, and Mr. Pichel can't play that." I wanted to use Freddie March who was at that time a light comedian. He had just done a film called *Laughter*. They said, "You're crazy. How can March play this part?" I told them that if I couldn't use Freddie March, I wouldn't do the film. I'd never even met March, I'd just seen him on the screen. Finally the studio gave in, and March won an Academy Award for his performance.[2]

Mamoulian's vision of a "young and handsome" Jekyll is indicative of his overall approach to the character. He borrowed Stevenson's ideas of the dual personality and the scientist's exploration of the evil self, incorporated the earlier film depiction of the philanthropic doctor, and tied all three elements together with his own personal interpretation. Again Stevenson's mystery structure was abandoned in favor of encouraging viewer identification with Jekyll (an element emphasized by Samuel Hoffenstein and Percy Heath's screenplay and Karl Struss's subjective camera technique, which places the viewer inside Jekyll's head in the opening scene and at various other points).

Mamoulian erred in thinking that the novella includes a sexual component, but he carefully elaborated upon his rationale:

1. Ephraim Katz, *The Film Encyclopedia* (New York: Thomas Y. Crowell, 1979), p. 786.
2. All quotations from Mamoulian can be found in Thomas R. Atkins, "An Interview with Rouben Mamoulian," *The Film Journal*, 2:2 (Jan–Mar 1973): 36–44 [*Editor*].

In Stevenson's original work, which might be called a horror story, Dr. Jekyll is a florid man of 55—a big, plump guy who is irked by the restrictions of morality. I wouldn't even say Victorian morality—just morality. He'd like to indulge in all sorts of sexual excess and debauchery but can't do it as Dr. Jekyll, without losing face. His aim is to separate the two parts of his nature so he can have one hell of a good time and still keep up his hypocritical virtuous facade. I thought this interpretation was not interesting enough and not pertinent enough to the spectators who were going to see the film. I thought that a more interesting dilemma would be not that of good versus evil or moral versus immoral but that of the spiritual versus the animalistic which are present in all of us. That is our common dilemma. God knows we struggle and battle constantly with ourselves about which instinct to follow.

Therefore, as a prototype for Hyde, I didn't take a monster but our common ancestor, the Neanderthal man. Mr. Hyde is a replica of the Neanderthal man. He is not a monster or animal of another species but primeval man—closest to the earth, the soil. When the first transformation takes place, Jekyll turns into Hyde who is the animal in him. Not the evil but the animal. Animals know no evil; they're completely innocent and much better morally than we are. Animals never kill except to eat. They don't torture each other. The first Hyde is this young animal released from the stifling manners and conventions of the Victorian period. He is like a kitten, a pup, full of vim and energy. He knows no evil, he simply gives vent to all his instincts. . . .

But, of course, he's not only an animal. He's partly a human being, and a human being—let's face it—is a very perverse creature. So because he is part human and possesses a human brain, which on the one hand reaches heaven and on the other wallows in depravity, he begins to refine his unorthodox pleasures—cruelty, sadism, and murder. Gradually Hyde changes from an innocent animal into a vicious—I won't say beast because beasts are not vicious—human monster, a monster that is part of us but which we usually keep under control. Throughout the film you see Hyde getting worse, both physically and psychologically; and you also see Jekyll, instead of becoming liberated as he had hoped, deteriorating with Hyde. It's a sad story.

Although Mamoulian's claim that "beasts are not vicious" is no longer a valid generalization about nonhuman animals (recent studies have proved that chimpanzees, the closest human relative, are often brutal and murderous), his approach to the Hyde character remains fascinating and innovative.

The inclusion of two morally opposite female characters again parallels the spiritual and animalistic sides of the Jekyll character.

Muriel Carew (Rose Hobart), daughter of Brigadier General Carew (Halliwell Hobbes) and fiancée of Jekyll, represents the unattainable good woman whose desirable attributes are kept at a distance by her father. Jekyll wishes to be married as soon as possible but is prevented by Carew's rigid conservatism. On the other hand, Ivy Pierson (Miriam Hopkins), dance-hall singer and prostitute, represents the sensual urges that plague Jekyll and are enjoyed by Hyde.

In an early scene Jekyll delivers a lecture at St. Simon's Hospital. Prior to his address, the tone of the film is established by four spectators:

> *Student One*: I hope Jekyll's in form today.
> *Student Two*: He's always in form. The old codgers are in for another joke.
> *Older Professor*: Obviously our friend has something up his sleeve again, Dr. Lanyon.
> *Dr. Lanyon*: Jekyll is always sensational, always indulging in spectacular theories.

Within a few seconds the division between Victorian conservatism (the old-guard professoriate) and progressive liberalism (the younger generation of students) is suggested. As Jekyll begins to speak, this dichotomy is established:

> Gentlemen, London is so full of fog that it has penetrated our minds, set boundaries on our vision. As men of science we should be curious and bold enough to peer beyond it into the many wonders it conceals. I shall not dwell today on the secrets of the human body, in sickness and in health. Today I want to talk to you of a greater marvel, the soul of man. My analysis of the soul, the human psyche, leads me to believe man is not truly one, but truly two. One of him strives for nobility. This we call the good self. The other self seeks an expression of impulses that binds him to some dim animal relation with the earth. This we may call the bad. These two carry on an eternal struggle in the nature of man, yet they are chained together and that chain spells repression to the evil, remorse to the good. Now, if these two selves could be separated from each other, how much freer the good in us would be. What heights it might scale, and the so called evil, once liberated, would fulfill itself and trouble us no more. I believe the day is not far off when this separation will be possible. In my experiments I have found that certain chemicals have the power . . .

At the outset Mamoulian, Hoffenstein, and Heath emphasize the conflict between the individual thinker and society at large and set the stage for Jekyll's (and soon Hyde's) attempts to combat stifling conservative pressures. Unlike Stevenson's Jekyll, Mamoulian's character is the ultimate idealist (even more of a utopianist than those depicted in earlier film versions) who wishes to eradicate the bad self from the human psyche. When he fails to obtain support from the establishment (particularly represented by Lanyon and Carew), Jekyll assumes the role of lone scientist and experiments upon himself (and, in turn, Hyde obtains the sexual gratification that Jekyll has been unable to get from Muriel). Jekyll wants to be "clean in his thoughts and desires," but it is these sentiments that separate him from the upright, stilted world which surrounds him.

* * *

Jekyll's first Hyde experience lasts only a few minutes. Alone in the laboratory, he mixes the final combination of chemicals, glances over at a nearby skeleton (the camera pans over to it and back again), and writes a short note:

> My darling Muriel,
>   If I die—it is in the cause of science. I shall love you always—through eternity.
>
>   Harry

Raising the flask to eye level, he peers into it (a tight close-up registers his point of view and then focuses on a mirror in front of him) before downing the contents. He grimaces, grabs his throat (first with one hand, then with both), gropes about, and falls to the floor. The scene depicts the first (unedited) stages of the transformation before cutting to a surrealistic hallucination sequence, in which Jekyll sees whirling images of Muriel and himself in the garden, the mocking faces of Lanyon and General Carew, and Ivy sitting on her bed. Sounds of his heartbeat are interspersed with Carew's "positively indecent. . . . It isn't done, it isn't done," and Lanyon's "Your conduct is disgusting. . . . You're mad, mad!" The hallucination concludes when Ivy seductively offers, "Come back soon, won't you, come back, come back, come back."

As the scene focuses on a pot in the fireplace (still Jekyll's point of view), the camera pans and tracks back over to the mirror, where Hyde soon appears. "Free! Free at last!" he shouts. "Ah! Mad—eh, Lanyon? Eh, Carew! Ah, you hypocrites, deniers of life. If you could see me now, what would you think?" He stretches, laughs, walks around in apish fashion, and ties on a cape before a knock at the door interrupts his pleasure. The scene cuts outside to Poole as the door opens and Jekyll appears. Assuring the butler that his friend, "Mr. Hyde," has left through the back entrance, Jekyll checks his appearance in the mirror and returns to the lab table as the scene fades out.

Mamoulian revealed some of the techniques used to create Jekyll's subconscious state:

> That transformation scene was a breakthrough in terms of sound. Here you have a totally unrealistic event. Well, pictorially I knew how to do it. To capture the feeling of Jekyll's vertigo, I had the camera revolve around on its axis 360 degrees, the first time this was done on the screen. One cameraman had to sit on the floor, and the man holding the focus—luckily a very small guy who looked like a jockey—was tied with ropes on top of the camera box, so that he could control it from the top. Because the camera revolved, the whole set had to be lighted which was a real tough job.
>
> With such a fantastic transformation what sound do you use? Do you put music in here? God, it's coming out of your ears, the scoring. I thought the only way to match the event and create this incredible reality would be to concoct a melange of sounds that do not exist in nature, that a human ear cannot hear. I said, "Let's photograph light." We photographed the light of a candle in various frequencies of intensity directly transforming light into sound. Then I said, "Let's record the beat of a gong, cut off the impact, run it backwards." And we recorded other things like that. But when we ran it, the whole thing lacked rhythm. I'm a great believer in the importance of rhythm. I said, "We need some kind of a beat." So they brought in all sorts of drums, a bass drum, a snare drum, a Hawaiian drum, Indian tom-toms. But no matter what we used, it always sounded like what it was—a drum. Finally in exasperation I got this wonderful idea. I ran up and down the stairway for a few minutes, and then I put a microphone to my heart and said, "Record it." And that's what is used as the basic rhythm in the scene—the thumping noise which is like no drum on earth because it's the heart beat, my own heartbeat. So when I say my heart is in *Dr. Jekyll and Mr. Hyde*, I mean it literally.

After a brief scene in which the libidinous Jekyll asks Muriel to elope, the action again shifts to the laboratory. Poole now notices that his master is a bit nervous, so he suggests that Jekyll go out and amuse himself at one of London's gentlemanly attractions. "Gentlemen like me have to be very careful about what they do and say," Jekyll replies. When Poole leaves, Jekyll's sexual tension is punctuated by a series of close-ups which show his fingers drumming on the table, his foot tapping on the hardwood floor, and the fireplace kettle blowing its lid! Surrendering to temptation, he drinks a second dose of potion. This time the full metamorphosis is shown in what appears to be a continuous take, with the camera panning back and forth between March's face and hands as he sits in a chair. However, close inspection reveals two edits that piece the sequence together (the cuts occur as the camera moves from hand to face). The early stages again are shown in close-up, with the filtering process revealing darker skin and harsher facial features, but the heavier makeup appears in two successive takes (when the camera pans from the left hand to the face, and again from the right hand to the face). Although it is not the marvel of technology hailed by past historians, the sequence is rendered superbly by Struss's mobile camera and William Shea's near-seamless editing.

Back in his primitive state, Hyde displays simian movements, dons his cape, and exits through the back door. Outside, he raises his face to the pouring rain and drinks, grinning happily, before heading toward Ivy Pierson's apartment.

* * *

Released on December 26, 1931, *Dr. Jekyll and Mr. Hyde* benefited from the current horror vogue. *Frankenstein*, which had been drawing record crowds for three weeks, was seen as competition in some areas of the United States, but the film quickly became a major attraction in most large cities. When it opened in Detroit, a local critic remarked that *Frankenstein* was "a comedy" by comparison.[3] * * *

3. *Variety*, (December 29, 1931): 8.

A Checklist of Major Performance Adaptations†

Sullivan, Thomas Russell. *Dr. Jekyll and Mr. Hyde* (stage play). Opened in Boston on May 9, 1887, before touring in the United States and Great Britain. This first serious theatrical rendering of *Strange Case of Dr. Jekyll and Mr. Hyde* capitalized on both the outstanding popularity of Stevenson's novel and the interest of actor Richard Mansfield's virtuoso on-stage transformations between the two title roles. The long stage life of this melodrama (Mansfield starred in revivals until 1907) helps explain why Sullivan's reworking of the plot to center around a domestically entangled love interest left its mark on stage and film adaptations for decades to come. Unpublished; undated typescript in the Theatre Collection, New York Public Library, Lincoln Center Branch (microfilm copy at the Ohio State University Theatre Research Institute); variant version undated typescript in the Smithsonian Institution, National Museum of American History, Mansfield Costume Collection, accession number 62906, Catalog 19526.

Dr. Jekyll and Mr. Hyde (U.S.A., 1920). Directed by John S. Robertson; screenplay by Clara Beranger; Famous Players-Lasky Corporation (Paramount); John Barrymore as Jekyll/Hyde. The most famous of the early silent film versions. Plot follows the Sullivan model with an admixture of motifs borrowed from Oscar Wilde's 1890 novel, *The Picture of Dorian Gray*. A virtuous, idealistic, sexually naïve Jekyll experiments with the transforming potion only after being led into a taste for debauchery by the worldly, self-indulgent father of his sweetheart, Millicent Carew. Moral responsibility nonetheless accrues to Jekyll himself in this rendering, the opening title card for which proclaims: "In each of us two natures are at war— the good and the evil. . . . But in our own hands lies the power to choose." There are ample visual pleasures to be found in this version, including the creepy appearance of the spiderlike Hyde who emerges from Barrymore's athletic paroxysms of transformation. Kino International.

Dr. Jekyll and Mr. Hyde (U.S.A., 1931). Directed by Rouben Mamoulian; screenplay by Samuel Hoffenstein and Percy Heath; Paramount Pictures; Frederic March as Jekyll/Hyde; Rose Hobart as fiancée

---

† I offer here a chronological listing only of what I take to be particularly aesthetically and culturally significant English-language stage, film, and television adaptations, working within the range of retrievable versions fairly closely oriented towards Stevenson's text. For more comprehensive and reasonably up-to-date listings of performance adaptations, see the works by Charles King, Scott Nollen, and Brian Rose cited in the Bibliography.

Muriel Carew and Miriam Hopkins as the prostitute Ivy Pierson. Widely viewed as the classic film version, memorable for its combination of fine acting (March landed an Academy Award), powerful visual symbolism, and innovative special effects. Follows the Sullivan plot pattern but makes Jekyll a charming, brilliant, dedicated doctor stifled by repressive Victorian propriety. His first dose of the potion turns him into a youthfully exuberant, amoral animal (Mamoulian claimed Neanderthal man as his model; some subsequent critics see an additional dimension of racialized blackness), but over the course of successive transformations, we see this apish figure degenerate into a haggard, driven sadist who tortures and strangles his prostitute paramour before murdering the father of Jekyll's fiancée. MGM/UA Home Video.

Dr. Jekyll and Mr. Hyde (U.S.A., 1941). Directed by Victor Fleming; screenplay by John Lee Mahin; MGM; Spencer Tracy as Jekyll/Hyde; Lana Turner as fiancée Beatrix Emery; and Ingrid Bergman as prostitute Ivy Peterson. Widely available and frequently shown on television, this is largely a heavy-handed imitation of Mamoulian's 1931 Paramount version (to which MGM bought rights and which it for several decades suppressed). A certain interest resides nonetheless in the against-the-grain female casting, the period-piece Freudian sexual imagery (as in Jekyll's split-second fantasy of Beatrix and Ivy as a pair of horses plunging under his lash), and the restrained make-up changes used to suggest that Hyde is just under the surface of this version's over-reaching Jekyll. MGM/UA Home Video.

The Two Faces of Dr. Jekyll (U.K., 1960), released in the United States as *The House of Fright*. Directed by Terence Fisher; screenplay by Wolf Mankowitz; Hammer Films, U.K.; Paul Massie as Jekyll/Hyde. A lurid extravaganza with a brashly enterprising conceptual twist. Jekyll is here a married man whose self-absorbed workaholism has helped push his wife into an affair with his best friend. All three members of the love triangle have a stake in the theme Jekyll expounds at the beginning about man's being torn between a vision of his most perfect self and a pull towards his most hedonistic self. The plot moves into high gear as this version's handsome, macho young Hyde pursues freedom, pleasure, and revenge against a backdrop of music hall chorus lines, deadly snakes, opium dens, rape, murder, and bodies crashing through glass roofs. However, the final focus is, as in Stevenson's text, on the cunning battle Hyde wages against Jekyll himself for rights of bodily survivorship. Columbia Tristar Home Video.

The Nutty Professor (U.S., 1963). Directed by Jerry Lewis; screenplay by Jerry Lewis and Bill Richmond; Paramount Pictures; Jerry Lewis as Julius Kelp/Buddy Love and Stella Stevens as Stella Purdy. A screwball comedy set on an American college campus in the 1960s, *The Nutty Professor* retains only a thin plot connection to Stevenson's story around the premise of the experimental chemist who concocts his own transformational drug. However, its enduring popularity has given it a significant role in the cultural visibility of the Jekyll and Hyde motif (further perpetuated by the 1996 Eddie Murphy remake of this movie), not least because Jerry Lewis interestingly reworks the Victorian polarized identity theme around a mid-twentieth-century American framing of the dilemma of masculinity. Julius Kelp, chemistry professor, has brains and sensitivity but is a paralyzingly shy, duck-voiced bumbler barely able to speak to the curvaceous, level-headed blond coed he fancies. The "monster" he unlocks through the drug—until the embarrassing moments when its effects begin to wear off—is the boorishly arrogant, self-infatuated hipster Buddy Love whose vocal abilities and smart talk quickly make him king of the student social hangout. The dichotomy takes a deeper turn when shy Kelp suggests that the aggressive Love might be keeping "the inner man locked up so nobody steps on him." Lewis' high-energy comic talent issues in a steady stream of enjoyable punch lines, sight gags, and plot hijinks, as well as a fine version of the split personality role. Paramount Video.

"Robert Louis Stevenson's *The Strange Case of Dr. Jekyll and Mr. Hyde*" (U.S.A./Canada, 1968). Directed by Charles Jarrott; screenplay by Ian MacLellan Hunter; Jack Palance as Jekyll/Hyde. A two-part video drama presented in Canada on CBC television and in America on ABC. This Jekyll is a nervous, shy, middle-aged bachelor who despite his stated goal of liberating the purely virtuous self, is in fact charmed when his Hyde comes out—initially—as a flamboyant ladykiller who makes an instant conquest of a pretty prostitute. Unrepressed sexual instinct quickly gives way to unrepressed aggression, however, and a thriller element is mounted in this well-known story through a heavy dose of stalk and slash suspense as we wait to see where and how Hyde will strike next. After a string of murders, Hyde is finally shot to death by his next intended victim, the lawyer Devlin (as Utterson is here re-named). This TV drama was nominated for several Emmy awards; certainly one attraction is Palance's transformation from the self-effacing professor to a menacing, manic whirlwind of a man, sporting a wolfishly thick head of hair, bushy black eyebrows, and the jittery, taunting laugh of the psychopath. MPI Home Video.

Dr. Jekyll and Sister Hyde (U.K., 1971). Directed by Roy Ward Baker; screenplay by Brian Clemens; Hammer Productions; Ralph Bates as Dr. Jekyll and Martine Beswick as Sister Hyde. The earliest and most interestingly rendered version of the Jekyll-to-Hyde transformation as a sex change, despite the cooked-up sensationalism of a plot which creates double sibling love affairs, imports bodysnatchers Burke and Hare from the 1820s, and casts Jekyll as the 1888 murderer Jack the Ripper. This Jekyll, a thirty-year-old bachelor researcher, needs a steady supply of female sex organs to develop a hormone-based life-lengthening potion so he can complete his research on the prevention of infectious diseases. His ingestion of the potion turns him into a sexy, self-possessed knockout of a woman, with dark hair and high cheekbones nicely matching his, whom he passes off to his respectable upstairs girlfriend and her keenly interested brother as his widowed sister, Mrs. Hyde. At first Jekyll utilizes Sister Hyde as a convenient disguise in which to carry on the murders of young women to which he has been driven after his supply of bodies from other sources has dried up. He soon discovers that his female avatar has her own ideas about when she will take over his body and whom she will kill. The female element so marginalized in Stevenson's text and so regularly imported for sexual titillation or melodramatic victimization in popular adaptations, is here brought to center stage in all its complexity of cultural value: revered source of the life principle which at the same time yields the horror of a literal *femme fatale*. EMI/Republic Pictures Video.

I, Monster (U.K., 1971). Directed by Steven Weeks; screenplay by Milton Subotsky; Amicus Productions; Christopher Lee as Marlowe/Blake. This adaptation shifts the date to 1906 to support an overtly Freudian framework (albeit with some anachronistic touches). Jekyll, here renamed Marlowe, is a pioneering London psychotherapist who cites the new theories of Dr. Freud of Vienna to explain the variable effects of the anti-repressant drug he has begun to try on a few of his more intractable talk-cure patients. The viewer in time learns of Marlowe's history of childhood beatings at the hand of a cane-wielding father, and is left to deduce why the Jekyll-figure in this version for once lacks any romantic involvement with a woman, and why his Hyde (here named Blake) uses his cane first to bludgeon a prostitute who has spurned him and then to turn on Jekyll's paternally concerned older friend, Mr. Utterson. The interest of this adaptation lies partly in the energy with which it pursues its Freudian premise, including Christopher Lee's flamboyant acting out of his id-release; and partly in the enterprise with which it at the same time contrives to preserve a significant amount of Stevensonian plot and dialogue surrounding the roles of Utterson, Enfield, and Lanyon. Video Search of Miami.

"Jekyll and Hyde" (U.K., 1990). Directed and written by David Wickes; a production of David Wickes Television, in association with London Weekend Television and King Phoenix Entertainment; Michael Caine as Jekyll/Hyde, Cheryl Ladd as Sarah Lanyon Crawford. Eminent free-thinking scientist Jekyll is a widower, in love with a married lady who is also sister to Jekyll's dead wife and daughter to Jekyll's academic arch-rival, the conservative Dr. Lanyon. After Jekyll's philanthropically motivated experiment spawns a towering, bald-headed ghoul who beats and rapes Sarah (with consequences unto the next generation), the penitent doctor enlists the aid of his nobly generous lady love to banish the "viper"—too late, of course. Despite romantic schmalz, this adaptation interestingly revivifies many features of Stevenson's story, such as a narrative frame via Utterson, Hyde's reverse transformation in front of a horrified Lanyon, and a century-bridging evocation of the Victorian science versus religion debate. Screenwriter Wickes shows a well-informed historical appreciation for the density of the Victorian taboo system (including the bizarre British law that from 1835 to 1907 forbade a man to marry his deceased wife's sister) and for the pressure being brought to bear on that system at the end of the century by a scandal-mongering yellow press. Vidmark Entertainment.

Mary Reilly (U.S.A., 1996). Directed by Stephen Frears; screenplay by Christopher Hampton; based on the 1990 novel, *Mary Reilly*, by Valerie Martin; John Malkovich as Jekyll/Hyde, Julia Roberts as Mary Reilly. The drama unfolds around the perceptions of a character newly created by novelist Martin, a maid in Jekyll's house whose childhood history of abuse at the hands of her alcoholic father fosters both her love for the refined, inhibited Dr. Jekyll and her intuition of psychological complexity in the leering maniac, Hyde. A version full of Gothic gore. Attractions include Malkovich's free-wheeling rendering of the two alter ego roles and colorfully grotesque bit parts for Michael Gambon and Glenn Close. Also interesting is the recreation of much of Utterson's role in Mary, as disturbed dreamer, seeker after Hyde, and moral reference point for Jekyll's psychological escape-act. Tristar Pictures.

Richard Mansfield as Jekyll/Hyde, 1887 stage adaptation. Reproduced by permission of The Library of Congress.

John Barrymore as Hyde, 1920 silent film version. Reproduced by permission of Photofest.

Hyde (John Barrymore) making a pass at Jekyll's fiancée, Millicent Carew (Martha Mansfield), 1920 silent film version. Reproduced by permission of Photofest.

Frederic March as Jekyll/Hyde, 1931 film version. Reproduced by permission of Photofest.

Hyde (Frederic March) facing Dr. Lanyon (Holmes Herbert), 1931 film version. (The portrait over Lanyon's desk is of Queen Victoria.) Reproduced by permission of Photofest.

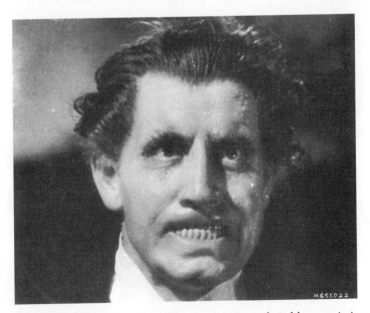

Spencer Tracy as Hyde, 1941 film version. Reproduced by permission of Photofest.

Ralph Bates as Dr. Jekyll and Martine Beswick as Sister Hyde, 1971 film version. Reproduced by permission of Photofest.

CRITICISM

G. K. CHESTERTON

[The Real Stab of the Story]†

* * *

* * * [I]t seems to me that the story of Jekyll and Hyde, which is presumably presented as happening in London, is all the time very unmistakably happening in Edinburgh. More than one of the characters seem to be pure Scots. Mr. Utterson, the lawyer, is a most unmistakably Scottish lawyer, strictly occupied with Scots Law. No modern English lawyer ever read a book of dry divinity in the evening merely because it was Sunday. Mr. Hyde indeed possesses the cosmopolitan charm that unites all nations; but there is something decidedly Caledonian about Dr. Jekyll; and especially something that calls up that quality in Edinburgh that led an unkind observer (probably from Glasgow) to describe it as "an east-windy, west-endy place."¹ The particular tone about his respectability, and the horror of mixing his reputation with mortal frailty, belongs to the upper middle classes in solid Puritan communities. * * * It is the tragedy of a Puritan town, every bit as much as that black legend which Stevenson loved, in which the walking-stick of Major Weir went walking down the street all by itself.² * * *

* * * most of those who mention it do not know the moral, possibly because they have never read the fable. From time to time those anonymous authorities in the newspapers, who dismiss Stevenson with such languid grace, will say that there is something quite cheap and obvious about the idea that one man is really two men and can be divided into the evil and the good.³ Unfortunately for them, that does not happen to be the idea. The real stab of the story is not in the discovery that the one man is two men; but in the discovery that the two men are one man. After all the diverse wandering and war-

---

† From *Robert Louis Stevenson* (London: Hodder and Stoughton, 1927; New York: Dodd, Mead & Co., 1928), pp. 51–54. Reprinted by permission of A. P. Watt Ltd. on behalf of the Royal Literary Fund.
1. "West-endy" borrows on the connotations of London's West End to connote prosperity and snobbish respectability [*Editor*].
2. In his 1878 *Edinburgh Notes*, Stevenson recounts with relish the legend of Major Weir, a citizen of Edinburgh whose reputation for piety crumbled when his neighbors began suspecting that he had turned his house into a brothel. Their way of pillorying his hypocrisy was to let his walking-staff take the blame: town folklore had it that when Major Weir was called to his ungodly business about the city, "the Major's staff went upon his errands, and even ran before him with a lantern on dark nights." Stevenson characterizes this bit of folklore as the "fine flower of a dark and vehement religion" (*Picturesque Notes on Edinburgh* in *The Works of Robert Louis Stevenson*, Edinburgh Edition [Edinburgh, 1894], pp. 30–31) [*Editor*].
3. Stevenson's reputation at the time Chesterton was writing this commentary was under attack from critics whom Chesterton terms "the Post-Victorian mudslingers" (Chesterton, 56) [*Editor*].

ring of those two incompatible beings, there was still one man born and only one man buried. Jekyll and Hyde have become a proverb and a joke; only it is a proverb read backwards and a joke that nobody really sees. But it might have occurred to the languid critics, as a part of the joke, that the tale is a tragedy; and that this is only another way of saying that the experiment was a failure. The point of the story is not that a man *can* cut himself off from his conscience, but that he cannot. The surgical operation is fatal in the story. It is an amputation of which both the parts die. Jekyll, even in dying, declares the conclusion of the matter; that the load of man's moral struggle is bound upon him and cannot be thus escaped. * * *

VLADIMIR NABOKOV

[A Phenomenon of Style]†

* * *

* * * Please completely forget, disremember, obliterate, unlearn, consign to oblivion any notion you may have had that "Jekyll and Hyde" is some kind of a mystery story, a detective story, or movie. It is of course quite true that Stevenson's short novel, written in 1885, is one of the ancestors of the modern mystery story. But today's mystery story is the very negation of style, being, at the best, conventional literature. Frankly, I am not one of those college professors who coyly boasts of enjoying detective stories—they are too badly written for my taste and bore me to death. Whereas Stevenson's story is—God bless his pure soul—lame as a detective story. Neither is it a parable nor an allegory, for it would be tasteless as either. It has, however, its own special enchantment if we regard it as a phenomenon of style. It is not only a good "bogey story," as Stevenson exclaimed when awakening from a dream in which he had visualized it much in the same way I suppose as magic cerebration had granted Coleridge the vision of the most famous of unfinished poems.[1] It is also, and more importantly, "a fable that lies nearer to poetry than

---

† From *Lectures on Literature*, ed. Fredson Bowers (New York: Harcourt Brace Jovanovich, 1980), pp. 179–80, 182–84 and 192–94, 196, 204. Copyright © 1980 by the Estate of Vladimir Nabokov; reprinted by permission of Harcourt, Inc. Bowers edited this collection from lecture notes preserved from Nabokov's teaching of "Masters of European Literature" at Cornell University between 1953 and 1958. Footnotes are by the editor of this Norton Critical Edition. For a response to Nabokov's comments on *Strange Case of Dr. Jekyll and Mr. Hyde*, see Andrew Jefford, "Dr. Jekyll and Professor Nabokov: Reading a Reading" in *Robert Louis Stevenson*, ed. Andrew Noble.

1. "Kubla Khan: A Vision in a Dream," the poetic fragment that Samuel Taylor Coleridge in 1797 recorded upon awaking from an opium dream.

to ordinary prose fiction"[2] and therefore belongs to the same order of art as, for instance, *Madame Bovary* or *Dead Souls*.

There is a delightful winey taste about this book; in fact, a good deal of old mellow wine is drunk in the story: one recalls the wine that Utterson so comfortably sips. This sparkling and comforting draft is very different from the icy pangs caused by the chameleon liquor, the magic reagent that Jekyll brews in his dusty laboratory. Everything is very appetizingly put. Gabriel John Utterson of Gaunt Street mouths his words most roundly; there is an appetizing tang about the chill morning in London, and there is even a certain richness of tone in the description of the horrible sensations Jekyll undergoes during his *hydizations*. Stevenson had to rely on style very much in order to perform the trick, in order to master the two main difficulties confronting him: (1) to make the magic potion a plausible drug based on a chemist's ingredients and (2) to make Jekyll's evil side before and after the hydization a believable evil. * * *

* * *

Three important points are completely obliterated by the popular notions about this seldom read book:

1. Is Jekyll good? No, he is a composite being, a mixture of good and bad, a preparation consisting of a ninety-nine percent solution of Jekyllite and one percent of Hyde * * *. Jekyll's morals are poor from the Victorian point of view. He is a hypocritical creature carefully concealing his little sins. He is vindictive, never forgiving Dr. Lanyon with whom he disagrees in scientific matters. He is foolhardy. Hyde is mingled with him, within him. In this mixture of good and bad in Dr. Jekyll, the bad can be separated as Hyde, who is a precipitate of pure evil, a precipitation in the chemical sense since something of the composite Jekyll remains behind to wonder in horror at Hyde while Hyde is in action.

2. Jekyll is not really transformed into Hyde but projects a concentrate of pure evil that becomes Hyde, who is smaller than Jekyll, a big man, to indicate the larger amount of good that Jekyll possesses.

3. There are really three personalities—Jekyll, Hyde, and a third, the Jekyll residue when Hyde takes over.

* * * [I]f you look closely at Hyde, you will notice that above him floats aghast, but dominating, a residue of Jekyll, a kind of smoke ring, or halo, as if this black concentrated evil had fallen out of the remaining ring of good, but this ring of good still remains: Hyde still wants to change back to Jekyll. This is the significant point. * * * It follows that Jekyll's transformation implies a concentration of evil

---

2. Fredson Bowers here notes that Nabokov stated that critical quotations in this essay are drawn from Stephen Gwynn, *Robert Louis Stevenson* (London: Macmillan, 1939).

that already inhabited him rather than a complete metamorphosis. Jekyll is not pure good, and Hyde (Jekyll's statement to the contrary) is not pure evil, for just as parts of unacceptable Hyde dwell within acceptable Jekyll, so over Hyde hovers a halo of Jekyll, horrified at his worser half's iniquity.

The relations of the two are typified by Jekyll's house, which is half Jekyll and half Hyde. * * *

* * *

Stevenson has set himself a difficult artistic problem, and we wonder very much if he is strong enough to solve it. Let us break it up into the following points:

1. In order to make the fantasy plausible he wishes to have it pass through the minds of matter-of-fact persons, Utterson and Enfield, who even for all their commonplace logic must be affected by something bizarre and nightmarish in Hyde.

2. These two stolid souls must convey to the reader something of the horror of Hyde, but at the same time they, being neither artists nor scientists, unlike Dr. Lanyon, cannot be allowed by the author to notice details.

3. Now if Stevenson makes Enfield and Utterson too commonplace and too plain, they will not be able to express even the vague discomfort Hyde causes them. On the other hand, the reader is curious not only about their reactions but he wishes also to see Hyde's face for himself.

4. But the author himself does not see Hyde's face clearly enough, and could only have it described by Enfield or Utterson in some oblique, imaginative, suggestive way, which, however, would not be a likely manner of expression on the part of these stolid souls.

I suggest that given the situation and the characters, the only way to solve the problem is to have the aspect of Hyde cause in Enfield and Utterson not only a shudder of repulsion but also something else. I suggest that the shock of Hyde's presence brings out the hidden artist in Enfield and the hidden artist in Utterson.* * *

* * *

Critics such as Stephen Gwynn have noticed a curious flaw in the story's so-called familiar and commonplace setting. "There is a certain characteristic avoidance: the tale, as it develops, might almost be one of a community of monks. Mr. Utterson is a bachelor, so is Jekyll himself, so by all indications is Enfield, the younger man who first brings to Utterson a tale of Hyde's brutalities. So, for that matter, is Jekyll's butler, Poole, whose part in the story is not negligible. Excluding two or three vague servant maids, a conventional hag and a faceless little girl running for a doctor, the gentle sex has no part in the action. It has been suggested that Stevenson, 'working as he did under Victorian restrictions,' and not wishing to bring colours into the story alien to its monkish pattern, consciously refrained from placing a painted feminine mask upon the secret pleasures in which Jekyll indulged."

* * *

* * * [T]his Victorian reticence prompts the modern reader to grope for conclusions that perhaps Stevenson never intended to be groped for. For instance, Hyde is called Jekyll's protegé and his benefactor, but one may be puzzled by the implication of another epithet attached to Hyde, that of Henry Jekyll's favorite, which sounds almost like *minion*. The all-male pattern that Gwynn has mentioned may suggest by a twist of thought that Jekyll's secret adventures were homosexual practices so common in London behind the Victorian veil.[3] Utterson's first supposition is that Hyde blackmails the good doctor—and it is hard to imagine what special grounds for blackmailing there would have been in a bachelor's consorting with ladies of light morals. Or do Utterson and Enfield suspect that Hyde is Jekyll's illegitimate son? "Paying for the capers of his youth" is what Enfield suggests. But the difference in age as implied by the difference in their appearance does not seem to be quite sufficient for Hyde to be Jekyll's son. Moreover, in his will Jekyll calls Hyde his "friend and benefactor," a curious choice of words perhaps bitterly ironic but hardly referring to a son.

In any case, the good reader cannot be quite satisfied with the mist surrounding Jekyll's adventures. And this is especially irritating since Hyde's adventures, likewise anonymous, are supposed to be monstrous exaggerations of Jekyll's wayward whims. Now the only thing that we do guess about Hyde's pleasures is that they are sadistic—he enjoys the infliction of pain. * * *

In his essay "A Gossip on Romance" Stevenson has this to say about narrative structure: "The right kind of thing should fall out in the right kind of place; the right kind of thing should follow; and . . . all the circumstances in a tale answer one another like notes in music. The threads of a story come from time to time together and make a picture in the web; the characters fall from time to time into some attitude to each other or to nature, which stamps the story home like an illustration. Crusoe recoiling from the footprint [*Emma smiling under her iridescent sunshade; Anna reading the shop signs along the road to her death*],[4] these are the culminating moments in

---

3. Several subsequent critics have argued for the effectiveness of just such a reading, including Elaine Showalter in her book *Sexual Anarchy: Gender and Culture at the Fin de Siècle* (New York: Viking, 1990).
4. The brackets mark Nabokov's insertion of examples from Gustave Flaubert's *Madame Bovary* (1857) and Leo Tolstoy's *Anna Karenina* (1877).

the legend, and each has been printed on the mind's eye for ever. Other things we may forget; . . . we may forget the author's comment, although perhaps it was ingenious and true; but these epoch-making scenes which put the last mark of [artistic] truth upon a story and fill up, at one blow, our capacity for [artistic] pleasure, we so adopt into the very bosom of our mind that neither time nor tide can efface or weaken the impression. This, then, is [the highest,] the plastic part of literature: to embody character, thought, or emotion in some act or attitude that shall be remarkably striking to the mind's eye."

"Dr. Jekyll and Mr. Hyde," as a phrase, has entered the language for just the reason of its epoch-making scene, the impression of which cannot be effaced. The scene is, of course, the narrative of Jekyll's transformation into Mr. Hyde which, curiously, has the more impact in that it comes as the explanation contained in two letters after the chronological narrative has come to an end * * *.

* * *

I would like to say a few words about Stevenson's last moments. As you know by now, I am not one to go heavily for the human interest stuff when speaking of books. Human interest is not in my line, as Vronski[5] used to say. But books have their destiny, according to the Latin tag, and sometimes the destinies of authors follow those of their books. There is old Tolstoy in 1910 abandoning his family to wander away and die in a station master's room to the rumble of passing trains that had killed Anna Karenin. And there is something in Stevenson's death in 1894 on Samoa, imitating in a curious way the wine theme and the transformation theme of his fantasy. He went down to the cellar to fetch a bottle of his favorite burgundy, uncorked it in the kitchen, and suddenly cried out to his wife: what's the matter with me, what is this strangeness, has my face changed?— and fell on the floor. A blood vessel had burst in his brain and it was all over in a couple of hours.[6]

What, has my face changed? There is a curious thematical link between this last episode in Stevenson's life and the fateful transformations in his most wonderful book.

---

5. A character in *Anna Karenina*.
6. This description of Stevenson's death follows the account given by Stevenson's stepson Lloyd Osbourne to Sidney Colvin. For variations on details, see *Letters* 8: 401–4 and 408–9.

PETER K. GARRETT

[Instabilities of Meaning, Morality, and Narration]†

* * *

As in its thematic oppositions, so again in the narrative form of *Jekyll and Hyde* we encounter a strong conservative strain, a force that marshalls the voices of the tale so that "everything holds together." It is necessary to recognize the strength of this force in order to appreciate the factors that resist it and to realize possibilities of reading that might lead beyond good and evil or toward greater plurality.

* * *

As hermeneutic denouement,[1] Jekyll's "Statement" gathers up the threads of the preceding episodes—the encounter with Enfield, the murder of Carew, the appeal to Lanyon—and joins them in a continuous, intelligible sequence. * * * Yet at the same time that the "Statement" discloses and defines its divided subject, it also reopens the questions it claims to answer. It begins a new narrative: "I was born in the year 18— . . ." (81)[47], presenting the relation of Jekyll and Hyde not as an established fact but as a developing story. This sequence opens in a mood of unqualified identification as Jekyll observes his new form: "I was conscious of no repugnance, rather of a leap of welcome. This too was myself. It seemed natural and human" (84)[51], and it moves toward equally unqualified denial and dissociation: "He, I say—I cannot say I. That child of Hell had nothing human; nothing lived in him but fear and hatred" (94)[59].

These instances show how the drama of shifting relations between Jekyll and Hyde is played out in terms of grammatical and narrative positions, the permutations of "I," "he," and "it." As narrator and author of his "Statement," Jekyll is "I," but as protagonist or object of his narrative he is sometimes "I," sometimes "he" or "Jekyll," while "Hyde" is sometimes replaced by "I." Observe how quickly these positions shift in this summary of the early stages of divided existence:

> The pleasures which I made haste to seek in my disguise were, as I have said, undignified; I would scarce use a harsher term.

---

† From "Cries and Voices: Reading *Jekyll and Hyde*," *Dr Jekyll and Mr Hyde after One Hundred Years*, ed. William Veeder and Gordon Hirsch (Chicago: The University of Chicago Press, 1988), pp. 59–72. © 1988 by the University of Chicago. All rights reserved. Reprinted by permission of the publisher. Garrett's page references to Stevenson's text, which use the Penguin *The Strange Case of Dr Jekyll and Mr Hyde and Other Tales*, ed. Jenni Calder, are followed by page numbers in square brackets to this Norton Critical Edition. Notes have been edited.

1. I.e., as problem-solving final revelation. Garrett alludes to critic Roland Barthes' theory that the endings of texts classically answer questions that earlier parts of the text have raised, and thereby constrain possibilities for interpretation [*Editor*].

But in the hands of Edward Hyde, they soon began to turn toward the monstrous. When I would come back from these excursions, I was often plunged into a kind of wonder at my vicarious depravity. This familiar that I called out of my own soul, and sent forth alone to do his good pleasure, was a being inherently malign and villainous; his every act and thought centered on self; drinking pleasure with bestial avidity from any degree of torture to another; relentless like a man of stone. Henry Jekyll stood at times aghast before the acts of Edward Hyde; but the situation was apart from ordinary laws, and insidiously relaxed the grasp of conscience. It was Hyde, after all, and Hyde alone, that was guilty. Jekyll was no worse; he woke again to his good qualities seemingly unimpaired; he would even make haste, where it was possible, to undo the evil done by Hyde. And thus his conscience slumbered.(86–87)[53]

Tension between the splitting and joining of persons is both represented in the narrative and enacted in the narration of this passage. The "I" who seeks pleasures and wonders at his vicarious depravity is replaced by the formally distanced "Henry Jekyll"; the "I" who judiciously describes Jekyll's pleasures modulates into an unmarked "omniscient" voice that judicially condemns Hyde's and, like a typical Victorian authorial narrator, both ironically represents Jekyll's rationalizations and irresponsibility in indirect discourse and adds a summary moral comment.

Like Jekyll in his role as protagonist, the narrative voice of his "Statement" often refuses identification with Hyde, as in skirting "the details of the infamy at which I thus connived (for even now I can scarcely grant that I committed it)" (87)[53]. But this voice can also merge completely with Hyde, even in the account of his most extreme action, the assault on Carew. "With a transport of glee, I mauled the unresisting body, tasting delight from every blow" (90)[56]. The unnamed narrator who can speak for either Jekyll or Hyde is matched within the story by an indeterminate figure who is neither: "Between these two I now felt I had to choose" (89)[55]. Who is this anonymous agent? Who writes "Henry Jekyll's Statement"? The more we ponder its disclosures, the more mysterious and unstable it becomes.

We may wish to say, like Jekyll, that, strange as the circumstances are, the source of these uncertainties is as old and commonplace as narrative, the doubling of the subject that is always produced by telling one's story. That is already saying a great deal, since it suggests how Stevenson's tale discloses the actual strangeness of the commonplace, including the commonplace notion of human duality. But more is at stake in this multiplication and interweaving of voices. It not only disrupts the projection of a stable subject; it makes speech and writing irresponsible by preventing us from determining their origins. Such undecidability is just what the conservatism of opposite values and final disclosures cannot admit. It is what scandalizes Jekyll when, imagining Hyde as utterly alien, "not only hellish but inorganic," he also senses a force that transgresses fundamental oppositions and subverts responsible utterance. "This was the shocking thing: that the slime of the pit seemed to utter cries and voices" (95)[60].

As his "Statement" nears its end, Jekyll reasserts his separation from Hyde by identifying himself with his narrative, its last words with his death. "Will Hyde die upon the scaffold? or will he find courage to release himself at the last moment? God knows; I am careless; this is my true hour of death, and what is to follow concerns another than myself. Here, as I lay down the pen and proceed to seal up my confession, I bring the life of that unhappy Henry Jekyll to an end" (97)[62]. As the last words of *Jekyll and Hyde*, these produce a poignant effect of narrative reflexivity, in which Jekyll's life is doubled and replaced by "the life of . . . Henry Jekyll," the written account. But we can also reconstruct a different story, with rather different last words, from the narrative that precedes Jekyll's "Statement" and presents the events that follow its writing, a story that reaches its climax as Utterson stands before the door of Jekyll's cabinet and insists on being admitted.

> "Jekyll," cried Utterson, with a loud voice, "I demand to see you." He paused a moment, but there came no reply. "I give you fair warning, our suspicions are aroused, and I must and shall see you," he resumed; "if not by fair means, then by foul—if not of your consent, then by brute force!"
> "Utterson," said the voice, "for God's sake have mercy!"
> "Ah, that's not Jekyll's voice—it's Hyde's!" cried Utterson. "Down with the door, Poole!" (69)[38]

The desperate plea for mercy could well be taken for Jekyll's last words, addressed to his old friend and the man who has replaced Hyde as his heir. But Utterson believes he can identify the true source of these words, and this confident certainty authorizes the violence of foul means and brute force. In place of verbal dialogue, the crash of the axe against the door is answered by "a dismal screech, as of mere animal terror" (69)[38]. The "real stab of the story"[2] may be neither the discovery that one is two nor that two are one but the discovery of the violence entailed in assigning any univocal meaning to these cries and voices.

2. An allusion to the comment by G. K. Chesterton which Garrett earlier quoted: "The real stab of the story is not in the discovery that the one man is two men; but in the discovery that the two men are one man" (see p. 183 in this edition) [*Editor*].

Here we begin to move from the instabilities of Jekyll's "Full State-ment" to those of the fuller narrative context and from the formal aspects of voice and person to the representation of character and action. The tension between splitting and joining reappears here as the basis of Jekyll's scientific project, his sense of the continuous struggle between his "two natures" as a curse, which leads to his dream of "the separation of these elements" as in a process of chem-ical purification (82)[49]. * * *

* * *

Believing he has succeeded in separating and projecting his evil nature, Jekyll describes an asymmetrical relation between his "two characters . . . one was wholly evil and the other was still the old Henry Jekyll, that incongruous compound" (85)[52]. His later account of their attitudes toward each other elaborates this pattern.

> My two natures had memory in common, but all other faculties were most unequally shared between them. Jekyll (who was composite) now with the most sensitive apprehensions, now with a greedy gusto, projected and shared in the pleasures and adventures of Hyde; but Hyde was indifferent to Jekyll, or but remembered him as the mountain bandit remembers the cavern in which he conceals himself from pursuit. Jekyll had more than a father's interest; Hyde had more than a son's indifference. (89)[55]

Here there is no overt attempt at dissociation, but the sense of sep-aration is clear; little of Jekyll but a vague memory remains in Hyde. The action of the story, however, displays a much more complicated relation and a stronger mix of memories, as in the episode of Jekyll's appeal to Lanyon, of which each gives a partial account.
* * * [T]he letter to Lanyon is written by Hyde, but its voice, as we can observe from its transcription in Lanyon's narrative (74–75)[41–43], seems entirely and convincingly Jekyll's. Whether we consider Hyde capable of extraordinary ventriloquism or rather sup-pose that much of Jekyll subsists within him, their relation hardly matches Jekyll's description. It is precisely while telling of Hyde's journey to Lanyon's house that Jekyll's "Statement" pauses to insist on their radical separation—"He, I say—I cannot say I. That child of Hell had nothing human; nothing lived in him but fear and hatred" (94)[59]—precisely at the point where we are best able to sense how much more lives in him.
Lanyon's account of their interview strengthens this sense. Once Hyde's desperation subsides and the potion is ready, he speaks in tones we do not hear elsewhere in the tale, offering a fateful choice between ignorance and "a new province of knowledge and new ave-

nues to fame and power," and then, binding Lanyon by the "vows
. . . of our profession," triumphantly displaying that power. "And
now, you who have so long been bound to the most narrow and
material views, you who have denied the virtue of transcendental
medicine, you who have derided your superiors—behold!" (80)[46–
47]. Not only are these words spoken as if by Jekyll but their melodramatic intensity offers a glimpse of the pride and ambition, as well
as the desire for irresponsible pleasure, that went into the making
of Edward Hyde, and that live in him as well. On the level of character and action as well as on the level of narration, we find neither
unity nor purified duality but a complex weave of voices that resists
conservative simplifications.

A reading that dwells on such tensions and discrepancies does not
simply replace a classic, readerly coherence in which everything
holds together with a writerly plurality in which nothing does. Such
a symmetrical reversal, still governed by a faith in opposites, would
do little to account for the power of *Jekyll and Hyde*, which depends
to a large extent on holding together what both characters and readers try to separate.[3] Jekyll realizes at the end that his supposed success in separating the elements so painfully mixed within him and
in projecting a purified essence of evil depended on a crucial
"unknown impurity" in one of the ingredients of the potion (96)[61].
This ironic discovery applies to the tale as well, which achieves its
most impressive and unsettling effects by compounding an impure,
murderous mixture of motives.

Like Jekyll, several of the other characters try to dissociate themselves from Hyde, but the "instinctive" repulsion they feel toward
him also binds them to him, as Lanyon is held by "a disgustful curiosity" (77)[45]. This fascination is presented most fully in Utterson's
response to Enfield's story.

> Hitherto it had touched him on the intellectual side alone, but
> now his imagination was also engaged, or rather enslaved; and
> as he lay and tossed in the gross darkness of the night and the
> curtained room, Mr. Enfield's tale went before his mind in a
> scroll of lighted pictures. He would be aware of the great field
> of lamps of a nocturnal city; then of the figure of a man walking
> swiftly; then of a child running from the doctor's; and then these
> met and that human Juggernaut trod the child down and passed
> on regardless of her screams. Or else he would see a room in a
> rich house, where his friend lay asleep, dreaming and smiling

3. This is where my concern with reading differs most from other approaches, such as Thomas's [i.e., Ronald R. Thomas's essay, "The Strange Voices in the Strange Case," in *Dr
Jekyll and Mr Hyde after One Hundred Years*, pp. 73–93], which also stress the subversion
of a coherent self or story. The contending impulses that produce and disrupt readerly
coherence also deny the reader any secure position, including that of detached writerly
sophistication.

at his dreams; and then the door of the room would be opened, the curtains of the bed plucked apart, the sleeper recalled, and lo! there would stand by his side a figure to whom power was given, and even at that dead hour, he must rise and do its bidding.(37)[14–15]

The two scenic images of the faceless Hyde are repeated and multiplied obsessively in Utterson's troubled dreams. Enfield has said of the scene he witnessed, "It sounds like nothing to hear, but it was hellish to see" (31)[9]; here the vision is recreated by Utterson's enslaved imagination ("in a scroll of lighted pictures," which prefigures cinematic versions) and complemented by another that we will eventually realize to be literally impossible but an accurate prefiguration of Hyde's ascendance. The images both represent and exercise power, figured in an interplay of accelerating movement and compulsive repetition, as Utterson sees "the figure . . . move the more swiftly, and still the more swiftly, even to dizziness, through wider labyrinths of lamp-lighted city, and at every street corner crush a child and leave her screaming." Utterson's efforts to break the spell that has enslaved his imagination lead him to replace these repeated images with his own purposeful movement, the search for Hyde, but that project also binds them together in complementary roles ("If he be Mr. Hyde . . . I shall be Mr. Seek" (38)[15]). It leads not just to their encounter by the outer door where the tale began but to their final dialogue through the door of Jekyll's cabinet, where it will be Utterson who presses on, "regardless of [the other's] screams." Narrative movement yields in turn to an uncanny repetition of violence and domination as these two exchange places.

The opposition between Hyde and others repeatedly begins to blur as soon as it is posited. In the account of his trampling the child, as in the later account of his attack on Carew, his evil is presented as uniquely gratuitous, violent aggression, which Jekyll amplifies by describing the monstrous turn of Hyde's depravity as "drinking pleasure with bestial avidity from any degree of torture to another" (86)[53]. But from the beginning there is a sense of him not just as an isolated embodiment of rage and cruelty but also as the occasion of them in others. Enfield tells how, after he has captured Hyde, he, the child's family, and even the unemotional doctor become possessed "with desire to kill him. . . . I never saw a circle of such hateful faces" (32)[9–10]. Those who confront and oppose Hyde seem to turn into his doubles.

* * *

Similar effects of contamination can be traced in the motives of the tale itself and the ways they implicate the reader, as the taint of sadistic aggression spreads from Hyde to other, opposed figures and at last to the whole narrative. Wherever we locate the real stab of the story, we should recognize that it really means to stab. It may arouse guilty identification like Utterson's, the sense of a corresponding doubleness ("You are certainly wrong about Hyde being overdrawn," Hopkins wrote to Bridges: "my Hyde is worse."[4]) But even without or apart from such recognition, there is a covert cruel streak in the narrative that also seeks to implicate us. * * *

* * *

It may seem that this violence is contained and redefined within the tale's larger moral purpose, in which the insistence on evil and its inseparability from human existence opposes Jekyll's mistaken project of purification. His own scientific optimism has been harshly refuted: "I have been made to learn that the doom and burthen of our life is bound forever on man's shoulders, and when the attempt is made to cast it off, it but returns upon us with more unfamiliar and more awful pressure" (83)[49]. But the logic of the cautionary tale, with its insistence on the appropriateness of the retribution that overtakes him ("If I am the chief of sinners, I am the chief of sufferers also. I could not think that this earth contained a place for sufferings and terrors so unmanning" (58)[30]), is produced by a punitive impulse that is the respectable double of Hyde's pleasure from torture to another. The tale provides no position, no point of identification, that is not implicated in some form of victimization and violence.[5]

To consider whether any conception of *Jekyll and Hyde*'s moral purpose can contain and stabilize its tensions is to return to our initial question. The possibilities of reading we have been exploring suggest that the tale's greatest power and interest derive less from any high philosophic intention we may ascribe to it than from its fictional irresponsibility, its refusal or failure to offer any secure position for its reader or to establish any fixed relation between its voices. The conservative, ordering force of its moral oppositions and the

4. Paul Maixner, ed., *Robert Louis Stevenson: The Critical Heritage* (London: Routledge and Kegan Paul, 1981), p. 229.
5. Claims have recently been made in feminist film theory that all narrative entails such domination. Laura Mulvey declares that "Sadism demands a story, depends on making something happen, forcing a change in another person, a battle of will and strength, victory/defeat, all occurring in a linear time with a beginning and an end" ("Visual Pleasure and Narrative Cinema," *Screen* 16, no. 3 [Autumn 1975]:14). This equation of narrative and sadism is elaborated in terms of the Oedipal structures of patriarchy in Teresa de Lauretis, *Alice Doesn't: Feminism, Semiotics, Cinema* (Bloomington: Indiana University Press, 1984), pp. 103–57. One need not accept such a comprehensive indictment to recognize how narrative always involves questions of power, or how, in a tale so insistently concerned with the infectious transfer of violence, the effort to impose narrative order itself becomes contaminated. In reading *Jekyll and Hyde*, and many other gothic tales, we are confronted with a troubling representation of our own demand for narrative intelligibility.

constraining coherence of its mystery plot lose their grip on a reading that recognizes the insidious, subversive effects we have traced. We may wonder, however, whether such a reading necessarily loses its own grip on the most obvious and fundamental features of the tale, the elements preserved by the perpetuation of its story as popular myth and its title as byword. A certain estrangement from the obvious and the popular does indeed seem necessary; stage, film, and television versions, as well as commonplace allusions (all the available ways of "knowing" *Jekyll and Hyde* without reading it), tend not only to reproduce but to exaggerate its dualism by making its moral oppositions more symmetrical. To undermine those oppositions is to challenge the common understanding of the tale.

But there is another way in which a subversive or sceptical reading can rejoin and reinterpret the common sense. Like any popular tale of terror, *Jekyll and Hyde* exploits the drama of uncertain control, of mysterious threat, the struggle for mastery, and the spectacle of victimization. As Jekyll's triumphant discovery of "a new province of knowledge and new avenues to fame and power" leads to utter and terrifying loss of control, we recognize an appeal to impulses and anxieties more powerful than the tale's moral framework, to fantasies and fears of releasing desire from social restraints and responsibilities. Gothic fiction depends at least as much on producing such disturbance as on containing it; its characteristic complication of narrative form and multiplication of voices, whether in conflict or complementarity, always express the effort required to establish control of meaning and often suggest its uncertain success. The narrative of *Jekyll and Hyde* advances precisely through a series of such efforts, through Utterson's quest and Enfield's, Lanyon's, and Jekyll's narratives, and through the larger development of the mystery plot that includes them. To observe how the voices and positions of the tale shift and blur is to see how these efforts all fail. Like Jekyll, the tale releases a force that cannot be mastered—not because it simply overwhelms all resistance but because all efforts at resistance or containment themselves become further instances of its cruel logic.

Our own efforts as readers join this series of struggles by the enslaved imaginations of the characters. Our position may be best indicated by the way the account of Utterson is suspended on the threshold of a scene of reading, as he "trudged back to his office to read the two narratives in which this mystery was now to be explained" (73)[41]. That reading, left unrecorded, becomes our own, since we never return to Utterson or learn what he makes of those two narratives. Would he have recognized his own role in the destruction of his friend, the way he had become identified with what he opposed, and the violence produced by his demand for explanation? But we hardly care to be shown Utterson's response to what he has read, any more than we care to reflect on our own complicity. That, perhaps, would be too cruel.

PATRICK BRANTLINGER

[An Unconscious Allegory about the Masses and Mass Literacy]†

* * *

"The wheels of Byles the Butcher drive exceedingly swiftly," Stevenson wrote apologetically to F. W. H. Myers. Therefore, *"Jekyll* was conceived, written, re-written, re-re-written, and printed inside ten weeks" [Yale *Letters* 5: 216]. What Stevenson meant by "Byles the Butcher" was perhaps his "initial monetary impulse."[1] The "white-hot haste" with which he produced the story, Stevenson hoped, would help to excuse some of the solecisms Myers detected in it. Paradoxically it could perhaps also explain or excuse its astonishing popular success. Other stories that Stevenson labored over and considered more serious might never be best-sellers; but popularity and seriousness seemed antithetical to him. Despite lavish praise by Myers and others, Stevenson's own statements about the story tend to be defensively ironic. Instead of a masterpiece that would win the unconditional approval of the most discriminating readers, he had produced a "Gothic gnome," a "fine bogey tale." Through the revision prompted by his wife Fanny, he had converted the tale into a "moral allegory," but the revision had perhaps only given it another source of appeal to the mass readership who, both he and [his publisher] Longmans believed, were the real arbiters of the late-Victorian literary marketplace.

In part because of his deep-rooted ambivalence toward that marketplace, Stevenson responded ambivalently to *Jekyll and Hyde*, at times referring to it as if it were a despised double, or at least the unwanted spawn of the weaker, Hyde-like side of himself, as in the Byles-the-Butcher letter, or in his account of its genesis in "A Chapter on Dreams," according to which his "Brownies" invented Hyde

---

† From *The Reading Lesson: The Threat of Mass Literacy in Nineteenth-Century British Fiction* (Bloomington: Indiana University Press, 1998), ch.8, (pp. 167, 175–80). Reprinted by permission of Indiana University Press. Brantlinger's page references to Stevenson's text, which use the Penguin *The Strange Case of Dr Jekyll and Mr Hyde and Other Tales*, ed. Jenni Calder, are followed by page numbers in square brackets to this Norton Critical Edition. Notes have been edited.
1. Roger Swearingen, *The Prose Writings of Robert Louis Stevenson* (Hamden, Conn.: Archon, 1980), p. 99.

while his waking or rational self supplied the "morality."[2] Such ambivalence suggests that *Jekyll and Hyde* can be read, in part, as a kind of Gothic version of George Gissing's *New Grub Street*.[3] It has always been read as an "allegory" about good and evil, about "the war in the members" and the "double nature" of human nature. But it can also be read as an unconscious "allegory" about the commercialization of literature and the emergence of a mass consumer society in the late-Victorian period.

*   *   *

* * * [I]n 1876, Cesare Lombroso had published his influential study of the hereditary nature of crime and "moral insanity," arguing that much criminal activity could be explained in terms of physical and mental "atavism." Lombroso also argued that, "contrary to general belief, the influence of education on crime is very slight" (149):[4] His chief work, *L'uomo delinquente*, was not translated into English until 1911, but his basic ideas had gained currency by the 1880s through social scientists and evolutionary psychologists such as Stevenson's friend James Sully.[5]

Hyde himself is, of course, an atavistic creature, whose "dwarfish . . . ape-like" appearance reflects the stereotype of the Irish hooligan. As Perry Curtis describes the stereotype, "Paddy" was "childish, emotionally unstable, ignorant . . . primitive . . . dirty, vengeful, and violent" (53).[6] He was also "ape-like" and often stunted in growth or "dwarfish." Curtis quotes a letter by Charles Kingsley describing "white chimpanzees" in Ireland, and in 1845 James Anthony Froude found much of that country's population "more like tribes of squalid apes than human beings."[7] The threat of Fenianism and the Irish Home Rule controversy, which was to split the Liberal party in 1886, form the political context of Stevenson's *The Dynamiter* (1885),[8] and help to explain Hyde's stereotypically Hibernian traits. Though originally belonging to Utterson, the "heavy cane" with which Hyde

---

2. In connection with such ambivalence, Brantlinger interestingly suggests elsewhere in the chapter that conflicts between high art and popularity for Stevenson relate to a pattern in his life of a pull between bourgeois and bohemian values wherein "Stevenson affirms the creative energy or vitality of what he simultaneously regards as the lower less serious or less moral half of the antithesis" (Brantlinger, p. 169) [*Editor*].
3. The 1891 novel in which Gissing depicted the demeaning effects of late Victorian mass literary tastes on authors and authorship [*Editor*].
4. Cesare Lombroso, *Criminal Man* (Montclair, N.J.: Patterson Smith, 1972), p. 149.
5. Ed Block, Jr., "James Sully, Evolutionist Psychology, and Late Victorian Gothic Fiction," *Victorian Studies* 25 (1982): 463.
6. L. P. Curtis, *Anglo-Saxons and Celts: A Study of Anti-Irish Prejudice in Victorian England* (Bridgeport, Conn.: Bridgeport University Press, 1968), p. 53.
7. Curtis, pp. 84–85; see also Howard Malchow, *Gothic Images of Race in Nineteenth-Century Britain* (Stanford: Stanford University Press, 1996), pp. 126–29.
8. *The Dynamiter*, co-authored with Fanny Stevenson, is a comic picaresque novella, inspired initially by news of several botched dynamiting attempts in London; the dedication, however, sounds a serious note, honoring two policemen injured in a bomb attempt made on the House of Commons on January 24, 1885 [*Editor*].

"clubs" Sir Danvers Carew might easily have been a shillelagh, and
the brutal murder of an M.P. in Stevenson's "crawler" must have
caused many readers to recall the 1882 Phoenix Park murders in
Dublin.[9] The theme of the increasingly dangerous "Irish Frankenstein," often employed by English caricaturists, has both Celtic and
Gothic overtones, which Stevenson's portrayal of Hyde also reflects.[1]

Nevertheless, *Jekyll and Hyde* does not deal explicitly with any
contemporary political themes or controversies. The allegorization
prompted by Fanny did not involve making the story more topical
but perhaps the reverse. Hyde is an emanation of Jekyll's "transcendental medicine" or of Stevenson's nightmare, rather than of either
a social class system that spawned criminality or an imperial domination that had shackled Ireland for centuries. Whatever the "moral"
of the story—and at first it had none—it concerns good versus evil
in the abstract, not the politics or the police of late-Victorian society.
The novella's anachronistic style and ahistoricism help it to seem
timeless and universal, while also obscuring the literary sleight of
hand that sneaks Hyde into the heart of the respectable bourgeoisie
(or, better, into the heart of a respectable, bourgeois doctor). Jekyll's
metamorphosis is a matter of certain unbelievable "powders," not of
politics nor even of science. But the mass-cultural format of the first
edition promised topical reality enough to the "populace"—in other
words, to the same readers who would have responded to the newsboys whom Utterson hears "crying themselves hoarse along the footways: 'Special edition. Shocking murder of an M.P.' " (53)[27].

Stevenson as popular author of a "shilling shocker" shares in the
criminal popularity or populace-like nature of Hyde. The statement
"There must be something wrong in me, or I would not be popular"
[see Yale *Letters* 5:171] is itself, in a sense, the formula of *Jekyll and
Hyde*. There is "something wrong in" the story—that is, Hyde—and
this "something" accounts for its popularity. Further, the story was
"wrong" not only because Hyde was "in" it as well as within Jekyll,
but because the germ of it was still the "crawler" that perhaps did
nothing more than pander to the low tastes of "that fatuous rabble
. . . the public" [*Letters* 5:171]. Fanny, after all, told its author that
the first draft was "all wrong"; it needed to be rendered morally
acceptable, even though allegorization did not necessarily move it
closer to the sort of masterpiece by which Stevenson longed to gain
permanent, as opposed to merely popular, recognition. The story was
"wrong" because it was immediately and immensely popular; more
than anything else he had written, *Jekyll and Hyde* made Stevenson's

9. In which the newly appointed British Chief Secretary for Ireland and one of his senior
   officials were assassinated [*Editor*].
1. For the impact of Fenianism on late-Victorian fiction, see Barbara Melchiori, *Terrorism
   in the Late Victorian Novel* (London: Croon Helm, 1985).

fame and fortune. Hyde was thus both a chief cause of his creator's popular success and an ironic, albeit perhaps unconscious, image of that popularity: the "ape-like," atavistic image of "the populace," the mass reading public. For Hyde, after all, is a reader—he is literate, just as Bill Sikes and the other criminals in Oliver Twist are literate— and, even more significantly, he is a writer, an author of sorts.

Despite his degenerate nature, Hyde retains at least one of Jekyll's upper-class traits. Though his hands are smaller, more gnarled, yet stronger than Jekyll's, Hyde's handwriting is identical to Jekyll's; Hyde therefore tries to disguise it by slanting it differently. * * * * * * Further, more often than not the disguise is dropped, as in the Regent's Park episode or in the privacy of Jekyll's laboratory. On these occasions, Hyde writes like Jekyll. And he also makes use of Jekyll's library. In Jekyll's quarters, Hyde apparently entertains himself by reading whatever is available. Given Jekyll's sober, upper-class tastes, however, such reading material is far removed from penny dreadfuls or shilling shockers. "There were several books on a shelf; one lay beside the tea things open, and Utterson was amazed to find it a copy of a pious work for which Jekyll had several times expressed a great esteem, annotated, in his own hand, with startling blasphemies" (71; my italics)[40]. In his narrative, Jekyll speaks of "the ape-like tricks that [Hyde] would play on me, scrawling in my own hand blasphemies on the pages of my books" (96; my italics)[61].

Works of theology are, perhaps, an odd sort of reading for a mad scientist, let alone for his demonic double. Within the terms of the Stevenson romance, however, they perhaps correspond to "moral allegory" as the obverse of "crawler" or "shilling shocker." In any case, Utterson is also in the habit of sitting down by the fire after his solitary, abstemious dinners with "a volume of some dry divinity on his reading-desk" (35)[12]. In the chapter where this is mentioned, however, Utterson neglects such "dry," pious reading for a more intriguing although distressing sort—the "holograph" will that Jekyll has drawn up and entrusted to the lawyer. Or did Hyde draw up the will? In his narrative, Jekyll says, "I next drew up that will to which you [Utterson] so much objected" (86)[52], but the "I" is ambiguous in this context. Because they share the same handwriting, it is impossible to know whether Jekyll or Hyde authored the will. Utterson cannot know, since he "had refused to lend the least assistance in the making of it." Similarly, Utterson can't tell whether Jekyll or Hyde wrote the check for ninety pounds to recompense the trampled girl and her family, though no doubt Hyde was its author because he obtains it so quickly. Enfield thought it might prove to be "a forgery," but on the contrary "the cheque was genuine" (32)[10]. The ambiguous, perhaps double authorship of several pieces of writing within the text mirrors its double nature as "story" and "allegory," shilling shocker and tale with a "conscience," at once criminal and morally improving.

Among the various recommendations by which Myers hoped to help Stevenson turn a near-masterpiece into the genuine article, one concerned the improbability of Hyde's retention of Jekyll's handwriting. "I think you miss a point for want of familiarity with recent psycho-physical discussions," Myers told Stevenson. "Handwriting in cases of double personality . . . *is not* and *cannot be* the same in the two personalities. Hyde's writing might look like Jekyll's done *with the left hand,* or done when partly drunk, or ill; that is the kind of resemblance there might be. Your imagination can make a good point of this."[2] But through the motif of identical penmanship, Stevenson makes a deeper, much more interesting point about cultural authority. Though their values are several worlds, or at least social classes, apart, Jekyll and Hyde share the same ability to express those values, and they do so even in the same "hand" or with the same "signature." Though Jekyll, like all mad scientists, menaces society through his overcultivated, overambitious intellect, Hyde menaces society not just by his criminal violence but by his ability to write checks and letters, draw up wills, and pen blasphemies in books of "divinity." Further, though he apparently does not write his confessions (he leaves that up to Jekyll), let alone a culturally blasphemous shilling shocker, Hyde is nevertheless the hero or antihero of just such a shocker—one that was, perhaps, purely "evil" until allegorized. And this shilling shocker, bearing "Satan's signature" (40)[17] as its central image (Utterson reads that "signature" in Hyde's face), helped to establish Stevenson's literary celebrity and success story. As the Brownies (Stevenson claimed) were the authors of the originary nightmare, so the uncannily literate Edward Hyde was in an important way the author of the Stevenson romance.

When Utterson and Inspector Newcomen enter Hyde's Soho residence, they discover something quite different from its "blackguardly surroundings." The rooms Hyde uses are "furnished with luxury and good taste." They are evidently the rooms of an epicure who takes pleasure in art. "A closet was filled with wine; the plate was silver, the napery elegant; a good picture hung upon the walls, a gift (as Utterson supposed) from Henry Jekyll, who was much of a connoisseur; and the carpets were of many plies and agreeable in colour" (49)[24]. Stevenson seems almost to be illustrating Oscar Wilde's thesis, in "Pen, Pencil, and Poison," that "there is no essential incongruity between crime and culture."[3] Perhaps Hyde retains more of Jekyll's traits than just his handwriting. Or is the evidence

2. Maixner, *Robert Louis Stevenson: The Critical Heritage,* p. 215.
3. Oscar Wilde, "Pen, Pencil, and Poison," in *The Soul of Man Under Socialism and Other Essays,* ed. Philip Rieff (New York: Harper, 1970), p. 98.

of epicureanism pure Hyde, whereas Jekyll, like Utterson, adheres
to a routine of abstinence and "dry divinity"? Whatever the case, the
Soho flat is not some Fagin's roost in the underworld slums,[4] but a
setting that implies sensual enjoyment, perhaps libertinism, of an
apparently upper-class sort. Further, there is more evidence of
Hyde's reading in the apartment—unless it is Jekyll's reading—or
perhaps it is evidence of his/his writing. The rooms, says Utterson,
appeared to have been "recently and hurriedly ransacked," while on
"the hearth there lay a pile of grey ashes, as though many papers had
been burned" (49)[24].

*   *   *

Whatever the burned pages may represent within the context of
the story, within the context of the Stevenson romance the associations between high culture and the furnishings of the Soho apartment and between Hyde's incineration of "papers" and Stevenson's
incineration of his unallegorized first draft point to the buried theme
of cultural authority. If Hyde shares Jekyll's handwriting, he also
shares Stevenson's. He is the shadowy, demonic double of the
author, bent on complete bohemian, artistic license and also on the
desecration of art, for whom the ultimate "temptation" is to live or
at least to write stories "all wrong"—"blasphemies," "forgeries," stories of and about pure evil, though perhaps allegorized to make them
seem respectable—calculated only to thrill the ignorant masses into
granting them a meretricious popularity. Such stories could be purchased as penny numbers in Soho, from newsboys hawking papers
on the streets, from Longmans as shilling shockers, or perhaps even
transmuted into sermons about the duality of human nature. Their
heroes and readers alike might be Edward Hydes, and so also might
their authors, who would write and sign themselves with "Satan's
signature." "This was the shocking thing," Jekyll declares, "that the
slime of the pit seemed to utter cries and voices" (95)[60]. His distress echoes Stevenson's in regard to "the bestiality of the beast
whom we feed. What he likes is the newspaper; and to me the press
is the mouth of a sewer, where lying is professed as from a university
chair" [Yale *Letters* 5:171].

Hyde's writing produces lies or half-lies, forged checks that are
genuine, and blasphemies in Jekyll's "own hand," scrawled in revered
texts. Within the larger context of the Stevenson romance, Hyde
lurks in a shadowy borderland between a criminal literature of the
slums—penny numbers, shilling shockers—and the moral allegory
Fanny urged her husband to write, while the authentic masterpiece
that Stevenson dreamed of writing hovered outside his range like a

4. The squalid lodgings of the thieves' ringleader Fagin in Dickens' *Oliver Twist* (1837)
   [*Editor*].

mirage. What renders Hyde especially menacing in these cultural terms, however, has perhaps less to do with the Stevenson romance than with the late-Victorian politics of education and literacy. Hyde's ability to write in Jekyll's "hand" renders him dangerous in a more insidious way than his violence. "We must educate our masters," as Robert Lowe had argued at the time of the Second Reform Bill.[5] The Third Reform Bill had passed in 1884, but the hope that mass literacy would hold back the barbarous anarchy or the criminal degeneracy that the upper classes had always feared the "lower orders" would visit upon society and culture seemed, perhaps, even less realistic than it had in 1867 or 1832.[6]

Jekyll and Hyde insists on the dualism of human identity, and yet, as Peter Garrett, Jerrold Hogle, and other critics have argued, that insistence may itself conceal a deeper fear of incoherence, anarchy, or dissolution on both a psychological and a political level.[7] Jekyll claims that he has discovered "the thorough and primitive duality of man," but then goes on to confess:

> I say two, because the state of my knowledge does not pass beyond that point. Others will follow, others will outstrip me on the same lines; and I hazard the guess that man will ultimately be known for a mere polity of multifarious, incongruous and independent denizens. (82)[48]

In this passage, the unity and even duality of the self give way to something like Arnold's account of "anarchy": the conflict of classes, and of "ordinary selves" or individuals within those classes, pulling centrifugally, perhaps disastrously, against the unity both of the body politic and of the "Best Self." Certainly Jekyll's political metaphor for the "multifarious, incongruous" disunity of individual identity reinforces my contention that Stevenson's story expresses, at least subliminally, anxiety about the masses and the consequences of mass literacy. From this perspective, Hyde is not so much the symmetrical double of Jekyll as a figure for the "multifarious, incongruous," and dangerous disunity of "the populace," "the lower orders," or "the masses." For Stevenson, Gissing, and many other late-Victorian intellectuals, popular or mass culture and mass literacy themselves

---

5. In the parliamentary debates leading up to passage of the Education Act of 1870, Lowe said in his speech of 15 July 1867, "I believe it will be absolutely necessary that you should prevail on our future masters to learn their letters" (qtd. in John Hurt, *Elementary Schooling and the Working Class*, 21). I have rendered his language as it has been frequently, and dramatically, misquoted: "We must educate our masters."
6. The Reform Bills of 1832, 1867, and 1884 successively enlarged and democratized voting privileges among Britain's adult male population [*Editor*].
7. Garrett in the essay excerpted in this Norton Critical Edition; Hogle in "The Struggle for a Dichotomy: Abjection in Jekyll and His Interpreters" in *Dr Jekyll and Mr Hyde after One Hundred Years* [*Editor*].

threaten a sort of cultural entropy or abjection, the swamps or sewers of mediocrity or vulgarity into which, they feared, excellence—high intelligence; literary and artistic aura—was sinking.[8]

*   *   *

KATHERINE LINEHAN

Sex, Secrecy, and Self-Alienation in *Strange Case of Dr. Jekyll and Mr. Hyde*[†]

At the end of his life, realizing with horror the profundity of the physical bond connecting him to the now-despised alter ego within him, the middle-aged bachelor Henry Jekyll uses a striking phrase to describe that bond. Hyde was "knit" to him, he writes, "closer than a wife, closer than an eye" (61).[1]

Peculiar absences make up much of the stuff of *Strange Case of Dr. Jekyll and Mr. Hyde* and "closer than a wife" waves like a flag over one such absence: the lack of a woman in any visibly important role in the lives of Jekyll-as-Jekyll, Jekyll-as-Hyde, or, for that matter, any of the bachelors who make up the tale's small all-male central cast. For many readers and critics, the non-appearance of women as equals or intimates to the main characters, taken together with the tale's lack of specificity about Jekyll's night-time pleasures, has stood out as a speaking absence in the text, an invitation from an author gagged by Victorian rules of reticence about sexuality to read the shadowy Mr. Hyde as an expression of underground sexual appetite on Jekyll's part. Exactly how that sexuality is to be seen is a matter of some of dispute. Victorian readers F. W. H. Myers and Gerard Manley Hopkins construe Hyde's acts of violence as displaced forms

---

8. For a general account of how late-Victorian intellectuals responded to "the masses" and mass culture, see John Carey, *The Intellectuals and the Masses*. Jerrold Hogle's interpretation of *Jekyll and Hyde* in terms of Julia Kristeva's concept of "abjection" makes perfect sense in psychoanalytic terms; I am suggesting that, as it is usually figured, "the masses" is a sociopolitically "abject" category. See Hogle, "Struggle for a Dichotomy," in Veeder and Hirsch, eds., *Dr Jekyll and Mr Hyde after One Hundred Years*. For that matter, all of the psychoanalytic interpretations of Stevenson's tale in Veeder and Hirsch's anthology make sense, but do not preclude the more historical interpretation I am presenting here. Besides Hogle's essay, see also the essays by Veeder, Peter Garrett, and Ronald Thomas.

† Derived from " 'Closer Than a Wife': The Strange Case of Dr. Jekyll's Significant Other," a paper delivered at the "RLS 2000" conference in Little Rock, Arkansas, November 11, 2000, and included in *Robert Louis Stevenson Reconsidered: New Critical Perspectives*, ed. William B. Jones, Jr. (Jefferson, NC: McFarland & Company, forthcoming 2003). The present article differs substantially from the original on which it is based and is printed with the permission of McFarland & Company, Inc., Publishers.

1. Page numbers are from this Norton Critical Edition.

of heterosexual sadism.[2] Vladimir Nabokov in the 1950s suggested that the "all-male pattern" of the tale evokes notions of "homosexual practices so common in London behind the Victorian veil," whether Stevenson intended it or not; several subsequent critics, including Elaine Showalter, have argued that a study of the repressions engendered by taboos against homosexuality is exactly what Stevenson intended.[3] Still other commentators, such as Stephen Heath, William Veeder, and Janice Doane and Devon Hodges, have variously interpreted Hyde as emblematic of unrecognized male sexual neurosis, unresolved oedipal anger, or an attraction-repulsion response to female emotionality.[4]

Many of these recent readings view meaning in the tale as emanating partly from a realm of semi-conscious creation, in which Stevenson's doubtless complex personal feelings about sexuality interact with attitudes and anxieties embedded in his culture. Without repudiating what can be the value of that approach, I would like to turn the prism of Stevenson's multifaceted little masterpiece to examine the role of what I take to be a particularly conscious component of authorial thought in shaping ideas and imagery in the story around issues of sex, secrecy, and self-alienation. I propose to consider the tale (published in 1886) in light of Stevenson's comments about it in a November 1887 letter to John Paul Bocock, as well as two unfinished commentaries on ethics Stevenson composed between 1879 and 1883, in order to explore the logic of Stevenson's insistence to Bocock that hypocrisy, not sex, was the source of what was harmful in Jekyll's activities as Hyde. That exploration helps us appreciate the way that Stevenson, a rebel against the sexual puritanism of his childhood religion, but inheritor of its concern for moral self-vigilance, saw secrecy and a withdrawal from human bonds as preconditions for a form of self-alienation disastrous to psychological and spiritual well-being. Viewed in this framework, the absence of women from the plot as *sex* objects may be less of a clue to Hyde's violent nature than their absence as *love* objects. Similarly, the particular nature of Jekyll's appetite for pleasure, sexual or otherwise,

2. *The Letters of Gerard Manley Hopkins*, ed. Catherine Phillips (Oxford: Clarendon Press, 1990), p. 243 [see p. 101 in this edition]; F. W. H. Myers to R. L. Stevenson, February 27, 1886, in *Robert Louis Stevenson: The Critical Heritage*, ed. Paul Maixner (Boston: Routledge & Kegan Paul, 1981), p. 215.

3. Vladimir Nabokov, *Lectures on Literature*, ed. Fredson Bowers (New York: Harcourt Brace Jovanovich, 1980), p. 194; Elaine Showalter, *Sexual Anarchy: Gender and Culture at the Fin de Siècle* (New York: Viking, 1990), pp. 105–114.

4. The emphases respectively of Stephen Heath in "Psychopathia sexualis: Stevenson's *Strange Case*," in *Critical Quarterly* 8: 1–2 (1986): 93–108; William Veeder in "Children of the Night," in *Dr Jekyll and Mr Hyde after One Hundred Years*, ed. William Veeder and Gordon Hirsch (Chicago: University of Chicago Press, 1988); and Janice Doane and Devon Hodges in "Demonic Disturbances of Sexual Identity," in *Novel* (Fall 1989): 63–74.

may matter far less than the fact that by living a double life to avoid
moral accountability, he shuts the door of his soul to conscience and
thereby opens another door to the entry of what Stevenson calls "the
diabolic in man."

    The November 1887 letter in which Stevenson addresses issues
of sexuality and hypocrisy in the tale comes as an indignant response
to a report that Bocock, an American journalist, sent him concerning
the acclaim given by New York theater-goers to actor Richard Mansfield's sensationalized stage portrayal of Hyde as a sexual predator
who commits murder in his lecherous desire for access to the newly
created figure of Jekyll's fiancée. In a reply marked "Private," Stevenson vents his exasperation with the Victorian prudery that
equates sexual appetite with evil, and thereby fails to see that Hyde's
cruelty stems not from Hyde's drive for sex, but Jekyll's drive for
concealment:

> Hyde was . . . not, Great Gods! a mere voluptuary. There is no
> harm in a voluptuary; and none, with my hand on my heart and
> in the sight of God, none—no harm whatever—in what prurient
> fools call "immorality." The harm was in Jekyll, because he was
> a hypocrite—not because he was fond of women. . . . The Hyp-
> ocrite let out the beast Hyde—who is no more sexual than
> another, but who is the essence of cruelty and malice, and self-
> ishness and cowardice: and these are the diabolic in man—not
> this poor wish to have a woman, that they make such a cry
> about.[5]

Sexuality is often mistaken for evil, Stevenson adds, because it can
readily become an *arena* for the worst in human behavior: as he puts
it to Bocock, "The sexual field and the business field are perhaps the
two best fitted for the display of cruelty and cowardice and selfishness. That is what people see; and these they confound."
    The proposition that sexual desire carries absolutely no intrinsic
harm appears also in the third chapter of Stevenson's "Lay Morals,"
an essay he began drafting in 1879 in the midst of a passionate
involvement with the American woman he was to marry in 1880,
Fanny Osbourne. Stevenson further proposes in the essay, however,
that sexuality can become a *vehicle* for the good *or* ill of the human
soul, depending upon whether it serves as a force for self-integration
or self-alienation. His argument on this point is worth briefly sum-
marizing, given the implications for *Strange Case of Dr. Jekyll and
Mr. Hyde* of what the essay proposes about both the danger of self-
division and the role of love in promoting self-unification.

5. All quotes in this paragraph are from Stevenson's letter of [? Mid-November 1887] to John
    Paul Bocock, Yale *Letters* 6:56–57, excerpted on pp. 86–87 of this Norton Critical Edition.

Stevenson's central claim in the third chapter of "Lay Morals" is that we live most fully and well when all our faculties, sensual, emotional, and spiritual, are utilized in a way that accords with something he variously calls "conscience," "the central self," "inner self or soul," or "righteousness."[6] This "Something" ("it may well be the love of God; or it may be an inherited . . . instinct") carries a sense of larger purpose and rightness which flashes upon us intermittently; when it does, "the intimacy" with "inner self" is "renewed again with joy." The risk in sexuality, he observes to readers assumed to be male, is that though sexual appetite is merely "a physical need like the want of food or slumber," it is so "imperious" in its demands that "in the satisfaction of this desire, as it first appears, the soul . . . oft unsparingly regrets and disapproves the satisfaction." The likely outcome is a fracturing of the self, a condition of living "alternately with our opposing tendencies in continual see-saw of passion and disgust."

However, division of soul and body such as the demands of sexuality can impose is only a minor version of what the essay goes on to define as that form of more permanent estrangement from the "central self" that makes the worst ill of the human soul. The "one declension which is irretrievable and draws on the rest" Stevenson warns, "is to lose consciousness of oneself." Moments of communion with the inner self or soul are intermittent at best, he suggests; drifting away altogether from the effort of maintaining contact with the soul produces what he apocalyptically characterizes as "temporal damnation, damnation on the spot and without the form of judgment." The darkly religious language here is a clue, I think, to Stevenson's being on the same track of thought involved in his statement to Bocock that "the Hypocrite" in Jekyll "let out" the evil qualities that represent "the diabolic in man." For all his rebellion against puritanical prudery and hypocrisy, and for all his interest in a secularizing reconsideration of Christian theology in light of Victorian science, Stevenson retained from the Scotch Presbyterianism of his Edinburgh childhood a large burden of concern about the way small sins could grow into large ones if left unvisited by the eye of conscience. And surely habitual hypocrisy invites just such a drift from responsiveness to soul and conscience. A public image of sanctity becomes an alibi to the self *from* the self, a shield under which fault can breed and fester undetected.

If such is the danger of alienating body from soul and deed from conscience, Stevenson on the other hand credits maturely committed sexual love with a considerable power of combating such self-alienation. In "Lay Morals," he suggests that the glory of

6. "Lay Morals," published posthumously in the 1896 Edinburgh Edition of *The Works of Robert Louis Stevenson* 4 ("Miscellanies"). These and all subsequent quotes from "Lay Morals" can be found on pp. 342–348 in this edition of the essay.

wholehearted love is that it can educate the senses into harmony with the best impulses of mind and conscience:

> But let the man learn to love a woman as far as he is capable of love; and for this random affection of the body there is substituted a steady determination, a consent of all his powers and faculties, which supersedes, adopts, and commands the other. The desire survives, strengthened, perhaps, but taught obedience, and changed in scope and character. Life is no longer a tale of betrayals and regrets; for the man now lives as a whole; . . . through all the extremes and ups and downs of passion, he remains approvingly conscious of himself.

In "Reflections and Remarks on Human Life," a commentary on ethics begun a year later than "Lay Morals," Stevenson extols the very conditions of matrimony as a source of self-integration. His point, in the paragraph headed "Marriage," is that when two loving, inevitably fallible human beings share life and lodgings, moral self-awareness is invaluably advanced through the resulting increased accountability of deed to conscience. Theological language is invoked in this tribute to marriage on a note of exaltation that contrasts strikingly with the threat of "temporal damnation" associated with estrangement from conscience in "Lay Morals":

> To take home to your hearth that living witness whose blame will most affect you, to eat, to sleep, to live with your most admiring and thence most exacting judge, is not this to domesticate the living God? Each becomes a conscience to the other, legible like a clock upon the chimney-piece. Each offers to his mate a figure of the consequence of human acts. . . . and though I continue to sin, it must now be with open eyes.[7]

The passage's image of a marital partner as a divinely educative mirror makes it a suggestive point of reference for Henry Jekyll, narcissistically infatuated with his own image in the cheval-glass as Hyde, and so unresponsive to the consequences of his acts that "conscience slumbered"(53) while his inner self descended to murderous violence.

Indeed, turning back to the story from the prose writing, it becomes apparent that many of the ideas presented in Stevenson's moral essays about love's capacity to promote psychic self-unification and moral self-awareness are played out in reverse in *Strange Case of Dr. Jekyll and Mr. Hyde*. Or rather, intimations of love's gifts hover in this magnificently suggestive spook story as a kind of ghost presence latent in the all-important motif of bonds, while Hyde stands

---

7. "Reflections and Remarks on Human Life," published posthumously in the 1896 Edinburgh Edition of *The Works of Robert Louis Stevenson*, Appendix, 40.

as a damning commentary on the intensification of psychic self-alienation and moral blindness that come with Jekyll's accelerating breaking of bonds.

The word "bond," taken as a noun or verb, is woven throughout the tale. It is variously used in reference to bonds of affectionately close acquaintance, inner bonds of spirit and flesh, and bonds of social responsibility. Henry Jekyll throughout his adult life has apparently had at best only a limited tolerance for any of them. Tormented by "an almost morbid sense of shame" over his irresistible attraction to pleasures he finds "undignified," as he puts it in the document he leaves for Utterson, he has long held the conviction that "it was the curse of mankind that these incongruous faggots [the "just" and "unjust" selves within him] were thus bound together"(49). He sought to unbind those tendencies in himself even before the creation of Hyde, simply by assigning them separate existences, one of the day and one of the night, left unaccountable to each other or to the world at large. It is unthinkable that a wife or family member should be allowed close enough to know of his secret life. Only the bonds of male friendship remain to Jekyll, and they, along with the bonds of social restraint, will be sacrificed through his creation of Hyde.[8] A decade before the present action of the tale, a quarrel with Lanyon over the theories that will produce Hyde breaks "a bond of common interest" between the two men. The actual emergence of Hyde through a process of chemical transformation is accompanied by a characteristic sensation which Jekyll twice describes as "a solution of the bonds of obligation"(50, 58). As that unnatural freedom from accountability gives license, over time, to the most recklessly willful of impulses, Hyde bludgeons an old man to death in a scene that the maid who witnesses it describes by saying that "Mr. Hyde broke out of all bounds." In the end, with Hyde a hunted murderer and Jekyll ever more subject to involuntary transformations, Jekyll withdraws from all social contacts. The man who broke all bonds and bounds is seen immured in a "house of voluntary bondage"(31) and destined for suicide.

If we consider Jekyll's flight from the "curse" of man's dual nature in light of Stevenson's point in "Lay Morals" that desires of flesh and spirit are likely to *seem* irreconcilable until a man "learn[s] to love a woman as far as he is able," we glimpse a little-considered interpretive possibility: that Jekyll is the victim of a flawed assumption about human nature from beginning to end. The lesson Jekyll concludes he has "been made to learn," that "the doom and burthen of our life

---

8. For an argument that bonds of social connection and social restraint in the tale can be viewed as part of a Victorian debate about the values of autonomy versus community, see Martin Danahay, *A Community of One* (Albany: State University of New York at Albany Press, 1993), pp. 135–45.

is bound forever on man's shoulders"(49) may be right in regard to the inviolability of the bond that connects flesh to spirit within the self, but not, as I am supposing Stevenson would see it, in regard to the belief that this bond constitutes the "doom" of human existence. By this reading, Jekyll gets into trouble—and retains a central element of narrative impercipience—partly as a result of a form of underdevelopment. He never credits and so never discovers sexuality's power to bridge body and soul. Seeing no way of breaking out of his cycle of pleasure and remorse but to give guilt-free license to his desires, he compounds self-alienation and accomplishes the very reverse of developmental maturation, enacting through Hyde a social Darwinist nightmare of regression to the level of the child, the animal, even "the slime of the pit"(60). It is a form of self-sabotage which deserves to be read partly as Stevenson's rueful commentary on the damage that can be done to the psyche by the sexual puritanism rampant in Victorian society.

Such a reading can strengthen the sympathy readers may feel for the sheer, reckless, lust-for-life energy of Jekyll's blind rebellion against an unlivable ideal of goodness. That touch of renegade sympathy is surely precisely the effect Stevenson wants at certain moments in the tale—as for example, the moment of Jekyll's first chemical transformation, which Jekyll in his statement recounts in a sentence constructed so as to turn its second half into a deliciously subversive surprise: "I knew myself, at the first breath of this new life, to be more wicked, tenfold more wicked, sold a slave to my original evil; and the thought, in that moment, braced and delighted me like wine"(50).

At the same time, Stevenson also weaves into the text various indicators of what remains in Jekyll's case a component of reprehensible moral blindness—a blindness that reflects not on the assumptions of his society, but on his own choice of deceit and social isolation to avoid accountability for actions he considers shameful. One measure of Jekyll's personal responsibility for his plight is the point of contrast we are given in Utterson. Utterson has been identified by a number of commentators as a *parallel* to Jekyll: a repressed bachelor given to puritanical self-censorship, wearing an air of professional respectability, and harboring something like vicarious pleasure in other men's high-spirited misdeeds. My own sense is that Stevenson manages to allow such parallels to intensify the atmosphere of slippery surface appearances and risky domestic isolation built up around his all-bachelor cast, but he meanwhile cues us to see that Utterson, quite unlike Jekyll, would never be the man to parade as a paragon of virtue while indulging his desires on the sly. The "dusty, dreary and yet somehow lovable Utterson" is too unprepossessing for that and too excessively, even comically diligent in monitoring himself—

as when after meeting Hyde, he is left "groping in all the corners of memory, lest by chance some Jack-in-the-Box of an old iniquity should leap to light there"(19).

A weightier hint of Jekyll's culpability speaks through the opening line of the poem with which Stevenson dedicates *Strange Case of Dr. Jekyll and Mr. Hyde* to his cousin Katharine de Mattos: "It's ill to loose the bands that God decreed to bind." In its dedicatory context a celebration of a loving kinship tie, the line also doubles as an epigraph for Jekyll's story of bond-breaking. Most importantly, by warning against the breaking of bonds in terms that echo God's own rebuke to human presumption in the Book of Job ("Canst thou bind the sweet influences of Pleiades, or loose the bands of Orion?" [Job 38:31]), the line connects to the tale's use of biblical allusion, imagery of bonds, and devil-associations for Hyde in ways that invite us to consider Jekyll's creation of Hyde as an act of Satanic presumption yielding a Satanic nemesis.

We are brought here to the tale's most powerful intimation of blame against Jekyll, but at the same time its most powerful source of dread on his behalf. True to the story's origins in "a fine bogey tale" of a dream,[9] Stevenson lets us dwell throughout the story in the terrified perception of the characters, Jekyll included, that Hyde is an autonomous being motivated by an inexplicable, repellant force of evil suggestive of the devil himself.[1] Overtones of the supernatural resonate almost as a subliminal effect as those who meet Hyde testify to the chill felt in the very marrow of one's bones, the sinking of the pulse, the "haunting sense of unexpressed deformity"(24) that his presence produces. Enfield resorts to calling Hyde "hellish" and "like some damned Juggernaut"; Utterson concludes after meeting him that he has seen "Satan's signature upon a face"(17). Jekyll himself, recounting the march of events by which the tastes of his biochemically projected alter ego "began to turn towards the monstrous," ends by calling him "my devil," "that child of Hell," and "something not only hellish but inorganic"(56, 59, 60). The sequence of terms reflects Jekyll's increasing sense of persecution at the hands of an invading alien, a thing of darkness he is by no means willing to call his.[2] In this way, Stevenson gets what I suspect he most wants from the devil-associations given to Hyde: a breadth of suggestiveness appropriate to the power, multidimensionality, and unfathomability of evil, or of horror itself; and an effect of nightmare fear in imagining the self occupied, mind and body, by an ever-stronger potential for a seemingly inhuman sabotage of all that we want to call good, sane,

---

9. See p. 77 in this edition.
1. For Jenni Calder's framing of a context for the devil-dimension of Hyde, see the excerpt on pp. 126–28 in this edition.
2. Cf. Prospero's line about Caliban in Shakespeare's *The Tempest* 5.275–76: "This thing of darkness I acknowledge mine."

or civilized. However, Stevenson also insinuates a number of details
into the text indicating that Jekyll, in ways he cannot see but bears
responsibility for, remains every bit as much Hyde's author as he was
in the beginning—and indeed gives signs of it in the way that his
Jekyll-persona is inhabited by the diabolic. Jekyll's "full statement,"
as well as Hyde's letter to Lanyon, echoes Scripture for the purpose
of turning a sacred lesson about human subjection to God's power
into a bid for escaping accountability.³ Jekyll in his "smooth-
faced"(19) duplicity, as well as Hyde in his hell-bent licentiousness,
shows an aspect of the face of evil.⁴

Stevenson leaves entrenched deep within the allegorical framework of the story the logic that refers Hyde's increasing demonism
to the growth of fault made possible by Jekyll's abandonment of
moral accountability. He promotes our empathetic engagement first
with Utterson and then with Jekyll as he plunges us from the bewil-
dered spectator standpoint into the last act of a drama in which Jekyll
is symptomatically embroiled in the demonic consequences of his
own two-facedness. We see Jekyll struggling in anguish to preserve
what he intuitively feels to be the shrinking remains of his soul and
clinging to an awareness of the element of a genuine love of virtue
in himself as a sign that he is no hypocrite; we are little inclined to
dwell on the fact that the self-estranged doctor, poor devil, is shrinking from ownership of the side of his being that flourished in the
licentiousness he himself granted it.

The carefully worked imagery of bonds in the tale remains the
reader's chief vehicle for glimpsing the possibility that the absence
of women as love objects traces back to the same source as the presence of the diabolical: impulses of secrecy and self-alienation likely
open to fly-by-night sexual encounters, but closed to love's lessons
in self-revelation and self-integration. Stevenson does boost the visibility of this embedded motif in the final chapter, however, by weaving grotesque inversions of familial and domestic intimacy into
Jekyll's own description of the final stage of his relationship to Hyde.
Distorted, even murderous inversions of bonds bespeak the nemesis
Jekyll has brought on himself. The "polar twins" he had thought to
liberate from one another have turned to battle with a "hate . . .
equal on each side." The biochemically produced offspring toward
whom he once had "more than a father's interest" has become a

3. Hyde's "my troubles will roll away as a story that is told" subverts the message of Psalms
   90:9: "all our days are passed in thy wrath: we spend our years as a tale that is told."
   Similarly, Jekyll's likening of Hyde to the captives of Philippi gaining release from prison
   glosses over the fact that the captives of Philippi in Acts 16:26 are God's servants, Paul
   and Silas, whom God sets free as a deliverance from religious persecution.
4. Stevenson may be hinting as much when he drops a folk-term for the devil, "Old Harry"
   into the very apostrophe to Jekyll with which the unsuspecting Utterson laments the evil
   he sees on the face of Hyde: "O my poor old Harry Jekyll, if ever I read Satan's signature
   upon a face, it is on that of your new friend."

"child of Hell," an "insurgent horror" who "lay caged in his flesh, where he heard it mutter and felt it struggle to be born"(61), and who, in one of those cycles of birth, vengefully burns the letters and destroys the portrait of Jekyll's own father. The crowning irony inheres in the image of matrimony contained in the phrase with which this essay began. For it is surely the most grimly apt of punishments that Jekyll's flight from the bonds of love and conscience, as well as his attempted escape from the detecting eye of judgment (such as, in "Lay Morals," a spouse can divinely represent), should turn implosively into his appalled awareness of being haunted by a succubus who dwells within him "closer than a wife, closer than an eye."

Robert Louis Stevenson:
A Chronology

1850	Born November 13 in Edinburgh, Scotland, the only child of Thomas Stevenson, member of a famous family of lighthouse and civil engineers, and Margaret Isabella Balfour, daughter of a Church of Scotland (Presbyterian) minister.
1852–67	An imaginative, affectionate, high-strung child who suffers frequent illness. His parents engage as a nurse Alison Cunningham, to whom RLS will later dedicate A *Child's Garden of Verses*. RLS is educated at various private schools, Edinburgh Academy, and by private tutors.
1867	Enrolls at Edinburgh University to study engineering. Through what he later called "an extensive and highly rational system of truancy," RLS reads widely and pursues his chosen task of learning to write.
1871	In April tells his father that he has no interest in engineering and cares for nothing but literature. As a compromise agrees to study law. Builds a circle of close friends. His chief intimate and confidant is his cousin Bob Stevenson. A period of bohemianism in the pubs and brothels of Edinburgh. Continues to write, mostly essays, literary sketches, and stories.
1873	Bitter conflict with his father over religion. A turning point is his meeting with Sidney Colvin (then newly appointed Slade Professor of Fine Art at Cambridge and later Keeper of Prints and Drawings at the British Museum) and Colvin's friend Mrs. Frances Sitwell. Colvin becomes a mentor and lifelong friend. RLS falls in love with Mrs. Sitwell and for the next two years she becomes, through his long diary-letters, his adored confidante. Colvin and Mrs. Sitwell both encourage RLS's ambition to become a writer. Suffering from nervous exhaustion and threatened lung trouble RLS spends the winter of 1873–74 at Menton in the south of France.

1874   Resumes legal studies. Through Colvin's influence his essays begin to be published in leading literary magazines.

1875   Becomes friends with William Ernest Henley, poet and journalist. Pays first visits to the artists' colonies in the Forest of Fontainebleau, France, frequented by his cousin Bob Stevenson, and for next three years spends much time at Barbizon and Grez, as well as in Paris. In July 1875 passes final examination and is admitted to the Scottish Bar. After four routine appearances in court, RLS abandons the pretense of law altogether and returns to writing.

1876   With friend Walter Simpson, takes a canoe trip in Belgium and France. In September at Grez meets and falls in love with his future wife, Fanny Osbourne, an American woman ten years his senior, estranged from her husband but not yet divorced. She is in France with her two surviving children to study art. Isobel (known as Belle) is eighteen; Samuel Lloyd (known then as Sam, later as Lloyd) is eight.

1877   In January joins Fanny in Paris and spends much of the next eighteen months with her and her children in Paris and Grez. Closely involved with Henley in short-lived magazine, *London*. RLS's first published short story appears there anonymously. Other stories soon follow, published in established journals and under his own name.

1878   Fanny and her children return to America in August. RLS goes to France for the walking tour described in *Travels with a Donkey in the Cévennes* (1879). Collaborates with W. E. Henley on a play RLS had first worked on at the age of fourteen about the eighteenth-century Edinburgh figure Deacon Brodie, master craftsman by day and burglar by night. (The play, printed in 1880 as *Deacon Brodie, or, The Double Life*, was produced several times during the 1880s but achieved no commercial success.) First book published: *An Inland Voyage*, an account of the 1876 canoe trip with Simpson. Publication in December (following serial publication earlier in the year) of *Edinburgh: Picturesque Notes*.

1879   In August, in response to a telegram from Fanny, without consulting his parents and in spite of efforts by friends to dissuade him, RLS travels by emigrant ship to New York and by train across America to join her in Monterey, California. Determined to live from his own resources, he badly strains his health as a result of the hardships of the journey and his dearth of funds. Fanny returns home to Oakland and in December obtains an uncontested divorce.

1880   In San Francisco, RLS has a complete physical breakdown and comes very near death following the first of the lung hemorrhages that were to plague him the rest of his life. Fanny nurses him devotedly and they are married in San Francisco in May. RLS and Fanny spend their honeymoon in a bunkhouse at an abandoned silver mining camp on Mount Saint Helena, overlooking the Napa Valley, California. In August, RLS returns to Scotland with his wife and twelve-year-old stepson Lloyd Osbourne. *The Amateur Emigrant,* describing his journey to America, is withdrawn from publication, RLS and his father agreeing that it is too personal and not his best work. (The first part, an account of the voyage, was posthumously published in 1895; the second part, the train journey, appeared in *Longman's Magazine* as "Across the Plains" in 1883.)

1880–82   With RLS suffering from chronic lung disease and at risk of hermorrhages, he and Fanny for two years alternate summers in the Highlands of Scotland with winters in Davos, Switzerland, then favored for treatment of respiratory complaints. RLS becomes friends at Davos with Renaissance historian and man of letters J. A. Symonds. *Treasure Island,* begun as an amusement for Stevenson's stepson, is published serially in *Young Folks* magazine starting in October 1881. (Its real fame was to begin with its publication in book form in 1883.) Publication in 1881 of *Virginibus Puerisque,* a collection of early essays most of which had appeared in the *Cornhill Magazine* and elsewhere from 1876 onwards. Publication in 1882 of *Familiar Studies of Men and Books* (previously published essays on such figures as Victor Hugo, Robert Burns, Walt Whitman, and John Knox) and *New Arabian Nights* (previously published tales, including "The Suicide Club," "The Rajah's Diamond," "Pavilion on the Links" and "Providence and the Guitar.")

1882–84   In a further vain search for health RLS and Fanny spend nearly two years in the south of France, most of it at the winter health resort of Hyères, near Marseilles, later recalled by RLS as the happiest period of his life. He works on new essays, stories, and a novel to be titled *Prince Otto.* *The Silverado Squatters* (based on the journal kept during his honeymoon) is published serially in 1883 and in book form in January 1884. In early 1884, his health takes a particularly bad turn, culminating in a severe hemorrhage in May.

1884   RLS and Fanny move to Bournemouth, on the south coast of England. There over the next three years RLS was to live the life of an invalid, plagued by colds and hemorrhages and often confined to bed. Nevertheless he maintains productivity. Between July and December 1884, collaborates with W. E. Henley on several new plays, publishes "A Humble Remonstrance" in response to Henry James' "The Art of Fiction," and writes "Markheim" to fulfill a commission to the *Pall Mall Gazette* (though he ultimately submits "The Body Snatcher" instead).

1885   Publication in March of *A Child's Garden of Verses*. Publication in April of *More New Arabian Nights: The Dynamiter*, tales co-authored with Fanny. Also in April, RLS and Fanny move into the house in Bournemouth bought as a wedding present for Fanny by Stevenson's father; they give it the name "Skerryvore" in honor of the Scottish lighthouse built by an uncle of Stevenson's. Henry James becomes a frequent visitor and close friend. In August, John Singer Sargent paints the more famous of his two extant portraits of Stevenson: the thin, stalking figure by the open door at Skerryvore. In late September or early October, RLS has the dream that led to the writing of *Strange Case of Dr. Jekyll and Mr. Hyde*; by the end of October, he has submitted the manuscript for publication. In November *Prince Otto*, his first full-length adult novel, comes out in book form after serial publication earlier in the year.

1886   *Strange Case of Dr. Jekyll and Mr. Hyde* is published in January; by April, 16,000 copies have been sold in the United States alone; by July nearly 40,000 copies have been sold in Britain. *Kidnapped* is published that spring, first serially in *Young Folks* and then in book form.

1887   On May 8, RLS's father dies. In August, RLS travels to America with his mother, wife, and stepson. On arrival in New York City, finds himself sought after by reporters eager to interview the author of *Strange Case of Dr. Jekyll and Mr. Hyde*. Spends the winter at Saranac Lake, New York (in the Adirondack Mountains), where Dr. J. L. Trudeau had recently established a sanitarium for tuberculosis. Over the course of this year three books are published: *The Merry Men and Other Tales* (previously published stories, including, besides the title piece, "Markheim," "Thrawn Janet," "Olalla," and "The Treasure of Franchard"); *Underwoods* (poetry); and *Memories and Portraits* (largely previously published essays, including "A Gossip on Romance" and "A Humble Remonstrance," RLS's closest approximations of an artistic credo).

1888   Works on various projects while at Saranac Lake, including twelve essays to be published monthly in *Scribner's Magazine*. They include "A Chapter on Dreams" (giving the genesis of *Strange Case of Dr. Jekyll and Mr. Hyde*) and "A Christmas Sermon" and "Pulvis et Umbra" (presenting his views on religion and ethics). In March, RLS and W. E. Henley quarrel irrevocably after Henley writes to suggest that Fanny has plagiarized a story called "The Nixie" that she has just published in *Scribner's Magazine*. RLS and Fanny decide upon a cruise in the South Seas, hoping that the tropical climate may benefit his health; they are also encouraged by a liberal offer of money from the publisher S. S. McClure for letters written during the voyage. In late June, the family party embarks from San Francisco in the chartered yacht *Casco* and visits the Marquesas and the Paumotu (or Tuamoto) Archipelago before reaching Tahiti at the end of September. RLS convalesces in Tahiti from a serious illness until the end of the year.

1889   The *Casco* cruise ends in Honolulu in January. Fanny's daughter Belle, her husband the painter Joe Strong and young son Austin (who were living in Honolulu) join the family group. During his five months in Honolulu RLS completes his novel *The Master of Ballantrae* (begun at Saranac Lake) and it appears in book form in September, following serial publication. Also completed in Honolulu is *The Wrong Box*, a humorous story begun by Lloyd Osbourne at Saranac Lake, largely rewritten by Stevenson, and published under their joint authorship; it is the first of what is to be a series of literary collaborations between RLS and his stepson. In late June, RLS, Fanny, Lloyd, and Joe Strong (RLS's mother having returned to Scotland) set off on another cruise on the trading schooner, the *Equator*. After voyaging through the Gilbert Islands they reach Samoa in December.

1890   Because of the great improvement in his health RLS decides to settle in Samoa. In January buys an estate, which he calls Vailima, on the island of Upolu in the hills near the port town of Apia (good postal connections). Leaving the land to be cleared he goes to Sydney. Here another serious illness forces him to abandon plans for a visit to Britain and he recuperates by a third Pacific voyage from April to August on a trading steamer, the *Janet Nicoll*.

He returns to Samoa in September and he and Fanny live in a cottage while the "big house" is built.

1891   In April RLS and Fanny move into the new house. The household includes RLS's mother, his stepson Lloyd, his stepdaughter and her husband and son, and a number of Samoan servants. Stevenson is given the Samoan name "Tusitala" (Writer of Tales) and accomplishes a great deal of literary work as well as becoming interested in local politics. The collection of letters describing his voyages (copyrighted in November 1890 as *The South Seas*) is published serially in the New York *Sun*, in *Black and White* (London), and in Australian and New Zealand newspapers.

1892   Book publication of *The Wrecker*, a novel written in collaboration with Lloyd Osbourne. Publication of *A Footnote to History: Eight Years of Trouble in Samoa*.

1893   *David Balfour*, a continuation of *Kidnapped*, is published in book form in England and America; in England the title used is *Catriona*, the name of the heroine. Publication of *Island Nights' Entertainments*, consisting of three South Seas stories already published serially: "The Bottle Imp," "The Isle of Voices," and "The Beach of Falesá."

1894   On December 3, in the late afternoon, Stevenson suffers a cerebral hemorrhage. He dies that evening and the next day is buried, in keeping with his wishes, at the top of nearby Mt. Vaea. The last book published in his lifetime appeared earlier that year following serial publication: *The Ebb-Tide*, a novel sketched and partly drafted with Lloyd Osbourne, but written in final form entirely by RLS.

1895   Posthumous publication in *Longman's Magazine* of a group of fables written by RLS over a twenty-year period.

1896   Posthumous publication of the novel Stevenson was chiefly working on at the time of his death, under the title *Weir of Hermiston: An Unfinished Romance*. Another unfinished novel, *St. Ives*, begins serial publication at the end of this year.

Selected Bibliography

• indicates those works excerpted in this Norton Critical Edition.

BIBLIOGRAPHY, BIOGRAPHY, ESSAYS, LETTERS

• Balfour, Graham. *The Life of Robert Louis Stevenson*. 2 vols. London: Methuen and Co., 1901.
• Booth, Bradford A. and Ernest Mehew, eds. *The Letters of Robert Louis Stevenson*. 8 vols. New Haven and London: Yale University Press, 1994–95.
• Calder, Jenni. *RLS: A Life Study*. New York: Oxford University Press, 1980.
Furnas, J. C. *Voyage to Windward: The Life of Robert Louis Stevenson*. New York: William Sloane Associates, 1951.
Norquay, Glenda, ed. *R. L. Stevenson on Fiction: An Anthology of Literary and Critical Essays*. Edinburgh: Edinburgh University Press, 1999.
Swearingen, Roger. *The Prose Writings of Robert Louis Stevenson: A Guide*. Hamden, Conn.: Archon Books, 1980.

TEXTUAL CRITICISM

Arata, Stephen. *Fictions of Loss in the Victorian Fin de Siècle*. Cambridge: Cambridge University Press, 1996.
Block, Ed. Jr. "James Sully, Evolutionist Psychology, and Late Victorian Gothic Fiction." *Victorian Studies*, 25:4 (Summer 1982): 443–67.
• Brantlinger, Patrick. *The Reading Lesson: The Threat of Mass Literacy in Nineteenth-Century British Fiction*. Bloomington: Indiana University Press, 1998.
• Chesterton, G. K. *Robert Louis Stevenson*. New York: Dodd, Mead & Company, 1928.
Clunas, Alex. "Comely External Utterance: Reading Space in *The Strange Case of Dr Jekyll and Mr Hyde*." *The Journal of Narrative Technique*, 24:3 (Fall 1994): 173–89.
Danahay, Martin. *A Community of One: Masculine Autobiography and Autonomy in Nineteenth-Century Britain*. Albany: State University of New York Press, 1993.
Dury, Richard. "Introduction." *The Annotated Dr Jekyll and Mr Hyde*. Milan: Guerini Studio, 1993, pp. 15–81.
Eigner, Edwin M. *Robert Louis Stevenson and Romantic Tradition*. Princeton: Princeton University Press, 1966.
Fraustino, Daniel V. "*Dr. Jekyll and Mr. Hyde*: Anatomy of Misperception." *Arizona Quarterly*, 38:3 (1982): 235–40.
• Garrett, Peter K. "Cries and Voices: Reading *Jekyll and Hyde*." In *Dr Jekyll and Mr Hyde after One Hundred Years*, ed. William Veeder and Gordon Hirsch. Chicago: University of Chicago Press, 1988, pp. 59–72.
• Halberstam, Judith. *Skin Shows: Gothic Horror and the Technology of Monsters*. Durham and London: Duke University Press, 1995.
Hirsch, Gordon. "*Frankenstein*, Detective Fiction, and *Jekyll and Hyde*." In *Dr Jekyll and Mr Hyde after One Hundred Years*, ed. William Veeder and Gordon Hirsch. Chicago: University of Chicago Press, 1988, pp. 223–46.
Heath, Stephen. "Psychopathia sexualis: Stevenson's *Strange Case*." *Critical Quarterly*, 28:1–2 (Spring–Summer 1986): 93–108.
Hogle, Jerrold E. "The Struggle for a Dichotomy: Abjection in Jekyll and His Interpreters." In *Dr Jekyll and Mr Hyde after One Hundred Years*, ed. William Veeder and Gordon Hirsch. Chicago: University of Chicago Press, 1988, pp. 161–207.

Jefford, Andrew. "Dr. Jekyll and Professor Nabokov: Reading a Reading." In *Robert Louis Stevenson*, ed. Andrew Noble. Totowa: Barnes & Noble, 1983, pp. 47–72.

Lawler, Donald. "Reframing *Jekyll and Hyde*: Robert Louis Stevenson and the Strange Case of Gothic Science Fiction." In *Dr Jekyll and Mr Hyde after One Hundred Years*, ed. William Veeder and Gordon Hirsch. Chicago: University of Chicago Press, 1988, pp. 247–61.

Maixner, Paul. *Robert Louis Stevenson: The Critical Heritage*. Boston: Routledge & Kegan Paul, 1981.

Mighall, Robert. *A Geography of Victorian Gothic Fiction: Mapping History's Nightmares*. Oxford: Oxford University Press, 1999.

• Miller, Karl. *Doubles: Studies in Literary History*. Oxford: Oxford University Press, 1985.

• Nabokov, Vladimir. *Lectures on Literature*, ed. Fredson Bowers. New York: Harcourt Brace Jovanovich, 1980.

Persak, Christine. "Spencer's Doctrines and Mr. Hyde: Moral Evolution in Stevenson's 'Strange Case.'" *The Victorian Newsletter*, 86 (Fall 1994): 13–18.

Rosner, Mary. "'A Total Subversion of Character': Dr. Jekyll's Moral Insanity." *The Victorian Newsletter*, 93 (Spring 1998): 27–31.

Sandison, Alan. *Robert Louis Stevenson and the Appearance of Modernism*. Houndsmills, Basingstoke, Hampshire and London: Macmillan Press Ltd., 1996.

Saposnick, Irving S. "The Anatomy of Dr. *Jekyll and Mr. Hyde*." *Studies in English Literature*, 11:4 (Autumn 1971): 715–31.

Showalter, Elaine. *Sexual Anarchy: Gender and Culture at the Fin de Siècle*. New York: Viking, 1990.

Thomas, Ronald. *Dreams of Authority: Freud and the Fictions of the Unconscious*. Ithaca: Cornell University Press, 1990.

Towheed, Shafquat. "R. L. Stevenson's Sense of the Uncanny: 'The Face in the Cheval-Glass.'" *English Literature in Transition*, 42:1 (1999): 23–38.

Tropp, Martin. *Images of Fear: How Horror Stories Helped Shape Modern Culture, 1818–1918*. Jefferson, N.C.: McFarland & Company, 1990.

Veeder, William. "Children of the Night: Stevenson and Patriarchy." In *Dr Jekyll and Mr Hyde after One Hundred Years*, ed. William Veeder and Gordon Hirsch. Chicago: University of Chicago Press, 1988, pp. 107–60.

———. "Collated Fractions of the Manuscript Drafts of *Strange Case of Dr Jekyll and Mr Hyde*." In *Dr Jekyll and Mr Hyde after One Hundred Years*, pp. 14–15.

———. "The Texts in Question." In *Dr Jekyll and Mr Hyde after One Hundred Years*, pp. 3–13.

FILM AND DRAMA CRITICISM

Anobile, Richard J., ed. *Rouben Mamoulian's "Dr. Jekyll and Mr. Hyde."* New York: Universe Books, 1975.

Atkins, Thomas R. "An Interview with Rouben Mamoulian." *The Film Journal*, 2:2 (Jan–Mar 1973): 36–44.

Jenson, Paul M. "Dr. Jekylls and Mr. Hydes: The Silent Years." *Video Watchdog*, 17 (May–June 1993): 42–59.

• King, Charles. "Dr. Jekyll and Mr. Hyde: A Filmography." *The Journal of Popular Film and Television*, 25:1 (Spring 1997): 9–20.

Luhr, William and Peter Lehman. *Authorship and Narrative in the Cinema*. New York: G. P. Putnam's Sons, 1977.

• Nollen, Scott Allen. *Robert Louis Stevenson: Life, Literature and the Silver Screen*. Jefferson, N.C.: McFarland & Company, 1984.

• Pinkston, C. Alex, Jr. "The Stage Premiere of Dr. Jekyll and Mr. Hyde." *Nineteenth Century Theatre Research*, 14 (1986): 21–43.

Rose, Brian. *"Jekyll and Hyde" Adapted: Dramatizations of Cultural Anxiety*. Westport, Conn.: Greenwood Press, 1996.

Wexman, Virginia Wright. "Horrors of the Body: Hollywood's Discourse on Beauty and Rouben Mamoulian's *Dr. Jekyll and Mr. Hyde*." In *Dr Jekyll and Mr Hyde after One Hundred Years*, ed. Veeder and Hirsch, pp. 283–307.